MODULE D

RESPONDING TO MISBEHAVIOR

An Instructional Approach

Module 4 of 6 in *Foundations: A Proactive and Positive Behavior Support System* (3rd ed.)

Randy Sprick
Susan J. Isaacs
Jessica Sprick
Paula Rich

RANDY SPRICK'S
safe & civil
SCHOOLS
Practical Solutions, Positive Results!

Published in the United States by
Pacific Northwest Publishing
21 West 6th Ave.
Eugene, Oregon 97401
www.pacificnwpublish.com

ISBN: 978-1-59909-072-6

Part of *Foundations: A Proactive and Positive Behavior Support System* (3rd ed.)
ISBN: 978-1-59909-068-9

Cover by Aaron Graham
Book design and layout by Natalie Conaway

TRENDS is a registered trademark of Pacific Northwest Publishing
in the United States.

Eugene, Oregon | www.pacificnwpublish.com

CONTENTS

CONTENTS

ABOUT THE AUTHORS

Randy Sprick, Ph.D.

Randy Sprick, Ph.D., has worked as a paraprofessional, teacher, and teacher trainer at the elementary and secondary levels. Author of a number of widely read books on behavior and classroom management, Dr. Sprick is director of *Safe & Civil Schools*, a consulting company that provides inservice programs throughout the country. He and his trainers work with numerous large and small school districts on longitudinal projects to improve student behavior and motivation. Efficacy of that work is documented in peer-reviewed research, and *Safe & Civil Schools* materials are listed on the National Registry of Evidence-Based Programs and Practices (NREPP). Dr. Sprick was the recipient of the 2007 Council for Exceptional Children (CEC) Wallin Lifetime Achievement Award.

Susan J. Isaacs, M.S.

Susan J. Isaacs, M.S., was a teacher for more than 20 years in the Fayette County Public School District in Lexington, Kentucky. She also served as a behavior consultant for the Kentucky Department of Education and as a statewide trainer for the Kentucky Model Schools and Kentucky Instructional Discipline and Supports initiatives. She now works as a consultant for *Safe & Civil Schools*, providing training and technical assistance to schools in the implementation of Positive Behavior and Intervention Supports (PBIS) and classroom management.

ABOUT THE AUTHORS

Jessica Sprick, M.S.

Jessica Sprick, M.S., is a consultant and presenter for *Safe & Civil Schools* and writer for Pacific Northwest Publishing. Ms. Sprick has been a special education teacher for students with behavioral needs and Dean of Students. She is a coauthor of *Functional Behavior Assessment of Absenteeism & Truancy, Absenteeism and Truancy: Interventions & Universal Procedures, Functional Behavior Assessment of Bullying,* and *Bullying: Interventions & Universal Procedures* with William Jenson, Randy Sprick, and others. Ms. Sprick's practical experience in schools with positive behavior support techniques drives her passion to help school personnel develop and implement effective management plans.

Paula Rich, B.Mus.Ed., M.Mus.

Paula Rich, B.Mus.Ed., M.Mus., has been a substitute teacher in public schools and was a freelance musician and taught private music lessons for many years in the Boston, Massachusetts, area. Since joining Pacific Northwest Publishing in 2006, she has contributed original stories and poems to the *Read Well* curriculum for second-grade readers and has edited several of Randy Sprick's staff development and behavior management books and papers. She was instrumental in developing TRENDS, Pacific Northwest Publishing's online behavioral data management system, as well as Connections, an online check-and-connect program.

SAFE & CIVIL SCHOOLS

THE SAFE & CIVIL SCHOOLS SERIES is a comprehensive, integrated set of resources designed to help educators improve student behavior and school climate at every level—districtwide, schoolwide, within the classroom, and at the individual intervention level. The findings of decades of research literature have been refined into step-by-step actions that teachers and staff can take to help all students behave responsibly and respectfully.

The hallmark of the *Safe & Civil Schools* model is its emphasis on proactive, positive, and instructional behavior management—addressing behavior before it necessitates correction, collecting data before embarking on interventions, implementing simple corrections before moving to progressively more intensive and time-intrusive ones, and setting a climate of respect for all. As a practical matter, tending to schoolwide and classwide policies, procedures, and interventions is far easier than resorting to more costly, time-intrusive, and individualized approaches.

Foundations and PBIS

Positive Behavioral Interventions and Supports (PBIS) is not a program. According to the U.S. Department of Education, PBIS is simply a framework to help provide "assistance to schools, districts, and states to establish a preventative, positive, multi-tiered continuum of evidence-based behavioral interventions that support the behavioral competence of students" (A. Posny, personal communication, September 7, 2010). That framework perfectly describes *Foundations*. *Foundations* provides instructions for implementing such an approach—with detailed processes and hundreds of examples of specific applications from successful schools. Furthermore, *Foundations* provides step-by-step guidance for involving and unifying an entire district staff to develop behavior support procedures that will prevent misbehavior and increase student connectedness and motivation. *Foundations* moves well beyond a simple matrix into how to guide and inspire staff to take ownership of managing and motivating all students, all the time, every day.

SAFE & CIVIL SCHOOLS

Resources in the series do not take a punitive approach to discipline. Instead, *Safe & Civil Schools* addresses the sources of teachers' greatest power to motivate: through structuring for student success, teaching expectations, observing and monitoring student behavior, and, above all, interacting positively. Because experience directly affects behavior, it makes little sense to pursue only the undesired behavior (by relying on reprimands, for example) and not the conditions (in behavioral theory, the antecedent) that precipitate experience and subsequent behavior.

The *Safe & Civil Schools* Positive Behavioral Interventions and Supports (PBIS) Model is listed in the National Registry of Evidence-based Programs and Practices (NREPP) after review by the Substance Abuse and Mental Health Services Administration (SAMHSA).

Inclusion in NREPP means that independent reviewers found that the philosophy and procedures behind *Foundations, CHAMPS, Discipline in the Secondary Classroom, Interventions*, and other *Safe & Civil Schools* books and DVDs have been thoroughly researched, that the research is of high quality, and that the outcomes achieved include:

- Higher levels of academic achievement
- Reductions in school suspensions
- Fewer classroom disruptions
- Increases in teacher professional self-efficacy
- Improvement in school discipline procedures

For more information, visit www.nrepp.samhsa.gov.

The most recent evidence of the efficacy of the *Safe & Civil Schools* PBIS Model appeared in the October 2013 issue of *School Psychology Review*. "A Randomized Evaluation of the *Safe and Civil Schools* Model for Positive Behavioral Interventions and Supports at Elementary Schools in a Large Urban School District," by Bryce Ward and Russell Gersten, shows how the *Safe & Civil Schools* PBIS Model improves student behavior and school climate. Thirty-two elementary schools in a large urban school district were randomly assigned to an initial training cohort or a wait-list control group. Results show reduced suspension rates, decreases in problem behavior, and evidence of positive academic gains for the schools in the training cohort.

Observed improvements persisted through the second year of trainings, and once the wait-list control schools commenced *Safe & Civil Schools* training, they experienced similar improvements in school policies and student behavior.

Download and read the full article at:
www.nasponline.org/publications/spr/index.aspx?vol=42&issue=3

Safe & Civil Schools acknowledges the real power educators have—not in controlling students but in shaping their behavior through affecting every aspect of their experience while they are in school: the physical layout, the way time is structured, arrivals and departures, teaching expected behavior, meaningful relationships with adults, and more. These changes in what adults do can create dramatic and lifelong changes in the behavior and motivation of students.

ACKNOWLEDGMENTS

As lead author, I owe a huge debt to many people who have guided the development and revision of *Foundations* over the past three decades. Betsy Norton, Mickey Garrison, and Marilyn Sprick were instrumental in the development and implementation of *Foundations* long before the publication of the first edition in 1992. Dr. Jan Reinhardtsen received the very first federal grant on the topic of positive behavior support and, with Mickey, implemented the first edition of *Foundations* as the basis for Project CREST in the early and mid-1990s. Jan also came up with *Safe & Civil Schools*, which became the name of our staff development services. Dr. Laura McCullough implemented a brilliant state-level Model School project in Kentucky, followed by the Kentucky Instructional Discipline System (KIDS) project that taught me so much about the importance of training and coaching to assist schools with implementation of both schoolwide and classroom behavior support.

I want to thank my coauthors of the different modules within this edition. Susan Isaacs, Mike Booher, and Jessica Sprick are outstanding trainers of *Foundations*, and their respective expertise has added depth to the content that makes this edition more practical, rich, and fun than previous editions. Paula Rich has provided both organizational skill and writing expertise to weave together a vast amount of content with many school- and district-level examples to create a highly accessible and user-friendly resource.

Thanks to the awesome staff of Pacific Northwest Publishing: Aaron Graham and Natalie Conaway with design, Sara Ferris and K Daniels with editing, Matt Sprick for directing both video and print development, Sam Gehrke for video editing, Robert Consentino and Jake Clifton for camera and sound, and the rest of the Pacific Northwest Publishing and *Safe & Civil Schools* staff—Jackie Hefner, Karen Schell, Sarah Romero, Kimberly Irving, Brandt Schram, Caroline DeVorss, and Marilyn Sprick—for their great work.

Implementation of *Foundations*, *CHAMPS*, and *Interventions* would not have thrived without the skill and dedication of great staff developers and trainers: Tricia Berg, Mike Booher, Phyllis Gamas, Laura Hamilton, Andrea Hanford, Jane Harris, Susan Isaacs, Debbie Jackson, Kim Marcum, Bob McLaughlin, Donna Meers, Carolyn Novelly, Robbie Rowan, Susan Schilt, Tricia Skyles, Pat Somers, Karl Schleich, Jessica Sprick, and Elizabeth Winford as Director of Professional Development.

ACKNOWLEDGMENTS

Fresno Unified School District and Long Beach Unified School District in California allowed us to visit with the Pacific Northwest Publishing video crew to capture the excitement, professionalism, and commitment of school and district personnel. These districts have taught us so much about the importance of common language and district support in creating a sustainable implementation.

Lastly, I want to the thank the schools and districts that have implemented *Foundations* over the years and graciously shared their lessons, posters, staff development activities, forms, and policies that you will find as examples throughout the print and video presentations. These real-world examples will help your implementation process by illustrating how other schools and districts have successfully implemented and sustained *Foundations*.

—R.S.

HOW TO USE FOUNDATIONS

This third edition of *Foundations* is constructed as six modules to accommodate schools that are just beginning their implementation of multi-tiered systems of behavior support (MTSS) as well as schools that already have some, but not all, pieces of behavior support firmly in place. For example, a school may have done great work on improving behavior in the common areas of the school but very little work on intentionally constructing a positive, inviting climate or addressing conflict and bullying in a comprehensive way. This school could go directly to Module C: *Conscious Construction of an Inviting Climate*, and after implementing those strategies, move to Module E: *Improving Safety, Managing Conflict, and Preventing Bullying*.

Each module incorporates multiple resources to assist you: video presentations on DVD, the book you are reading now, and a CD with forms and samples. The videos can guide a building-based leadership team through implementing *Foundations*. The same content is available in print format; we provide eight copies of this book for each module, one for each member of the leadership team. Teams can decide which content delivery form works best for them—video or print.

Each book comes with a CD that contains reproducible forms, examples of policies and procedures from real schools that have implemented *Foundations*, and other implementation resources. The CD also includes PowerPoint presentations that correspond directly to the video and print content. Your leadership team can use these presentations to deliver the most relevant *Foundations* information to the entire staff.

Beginning Behavior Support

For schools and districts that are just beginning with behavior support or are unsure where to begin, we suggest starting with Module A: *Foundations of Behavior Support—A Continuous Improvement Process*. This module is the foundation of *Foundations*. It describes the importance of a well-designed leadership team, a formalized continuous improvement cycle, how to use multiple data sources to drive that cycle, and how to involve and unify the staff in implementation. Without laying this groundwork, any specific work on procedures, such as improving the cafeteria, is unlikely to be effective or sustainable.

Once your team is collecting and analyzing data, you will probably move through Modules B–F (described below) in order. You'll work on the common areas of the school, then positive climate, and so on. Once a module has been implemented, you are not done with that module. For example, after implementing the procedures in Module B for a couple of common areas and a couple of schoolwide policies, such as dress code, you may move on to Module C to work on improving school climate. However, you will concurrently continue to implement Module B procedures for additional common areas and schoolwide policies. Working through all six modules will take about two to five years of development and implementation.

MTSS in Progress

Schools and districts that have been effectively implementing other approaches to PBIS should follow these guidelines when implementing *Foundations*.

You may be able to use the modules in a nonlinear fashion if your school has a highly functional team, uses multiple data sources to involve the entire staff in continuous improvement of behavior support, and has worked to improve several common areas or schoolwide policies. To self-assess where to begin, a resource for each module called the Foundations Implementation Rubric and Summary is included in Appendix A of the book and on the CD. The rubric can help your leadership team assess which modules have information useful to your school at this time and help you make judgments about where to begin. Print the rubric, work through it as a team, and summarize your findings, and you will see patterns emerge. (Instructions are included with the rubric.)

For example, if all the conditions described at the beginning of this paragraph are in place, you will probably find that you are already implementing many of the procedures delineated in Modules A and B. One school may have an urgent need to go directly to Module E because the school has no programs or policies to address conflict and bullying, whereas another school may go directly to Module D because staff are very inconsistent about when and how to use disciplinary referral to the office. Another school may go directly to Module F because their schoolwide structures are relatively well established, but they have yet to address classroom management or the integration of universal, targeted, and intensive interventions.

HOW TO USE FOUNDATIONS

Appendix B of each module presents an Implementation Checklist for that module. The Implementation Checklist details the summarized items on the rubric. You will use this tool as you near completion on any module to ensure that you have fully implemented it, and it's also useful for reviewing the implementation every three years or so. The checklist can identify strengths to celebrate and catch gaps in your implementation that you may be able to fill before a major problem emerges.

OVERVIEW OF MODULES

The modules in *Foundations* are designed to be used sequentially by a school or district that is just getting started with behavior support. However, if a school or district is already implementing a team-based, data-driven approach to continuous improvement of climate, safety, discipline, and motivation, the modules can be used in any order.

This module, **Module D: *Responding to Misbehavior—An Instructional Approach,*** focuses on the vital importance of an instructional approach to correction in reducing future occurrences of the misbehavior. It provides information on training and inspiring all staff to correct all misbehavior by giving students information about how to behave successfully and by using the mildest consequences that reasonably fit the infractions. Module D describes how to get consensus among staff about when (and when not) to use office discipline referral. It provides menus of corrective techniques for mild and moderate misbehavior, from gentle verbal correction to time owed after class to restorative justice strategies. All staff learn strategies for de-escalating emotional situations, and administrators are introduced to a comprehensive game plan for dealing with office referrals and for implementing alternatives to out-of-school suspension. This module includes sample lessons for students on how to interact with people in authority.

- Presentation 1: The Relationship Between Proactive Procedures, Corrective Procedures, and Individual Student Behavior Improvement Plans
- Presentation 2: Developing Three Levels of Misbehavior
- Presentation 3: Staff Responsibilities for Responding to Misbehavior
- Presentation 4: Administrator Responsibilities for Responding to Misbehavior
- Presentation 5: Preventing the Misbehavior That Leads to Referrals and Suspensions
- Appendix A: Foundations Implementation Rubric and Summary
- Appendix B: Module D Implementation Checklist
- Appendix C: Guide to Module D Reproducible Forms and Samples

Other modules in *Foundations: A Proactive and Positive Behavior Support System* are:

Module A: *Foundations of Behavior Support—A Continuous Improvement Process* covers the essential processes for involving the entire staff in developing, implementing, and sustaining positive behavior support. It includes detailed information about establishing a building-based leadership team (Foundations Team) to represent the entire staff. This module advises the team on how to collect and analyze data, identify and rank a manageable number of priorities for improvement, and guide the staff in revising, adopting, and implementing new policies and procedures for each priority. This process creates a cycle of continuous improvement that empowers and unifies the entire staff.

- Presentation 1: Foundations: A Multi-Tiered System of Behavior Support
- Presentation 2: Team Processes
- Presentation 3: The Improvement Cycle
- Presentation 4: Data-Driven Processes
- Presentation 5: Developing Staff Engagement and Unity
- Appendix A: Foundations Implementation Rubric and Summary
- Appendix B: Module A Implementation Checklist
- Appendix C: Guide to Module A Reproducible Forms and Samples

Module B: *Managing Behavior in Common Areas and With Schoolwide Policies* delineates processes for ensuring that common areas (arrival, cafeteria, hallways, and so on) and schoolwide policies (dress code, electronics use, public displays of affection, and so on) are structured for success and that expectations for behavior are directly taught with clarity and repetition to students. In addition, this module includes detailed information for all staff about how to provide positive and systematic supervision and how to correct misbehavior calmly, consistently, and respectfully.

- Presentation 1: Laying the Groundwork for Consistency in All School Settings
- Presentation 2: Structuring Common Areas and Schoolwide Policies for Success
- Presentation 3: Teaching Expectations to Students
- Presentation 4: Effective Supervision, Part 1—Protect, Expect, and Connect
- Presentation 5: Effective Supervision, Part 2—Correct and Reflect
- Presentation 6: Supervising Common Areas and Schoolwide Policies—for All Staff
- Presentation 7: Adopting, Implementing, and Monitoring Improvements to Common Areas and Schoolwide Policies
- Appendix A: Foundations Implementation Rubric and Summary
- Appendix B: Module B Implementation Checklist
- Appendix C: Guide to Module B Reproducible Forms and Samples

Module C: *Conscious Construction of an Inviting School Climate* guides the entire staff in creating and sustaining a school environment that makes all students feel welcomed and valued. This process includes developing Guidelines for Success, a set of behaviors and traits that provides a common language and common values among staff, students, and parents. This module explains how and why to maintain at least 3:1 ratios of positive interactions and covers the importance of regular attendance and strategies for improving attendance. Strategies for meeting the basic human needs of all students are also discussed. Finally, the module outlines how to welcome and orient staff, students, and families who are new to the school in a way that connects them to the school community.

- Presentation 1: Constructing and Maintaining a Positive Climate
- Presentation 2: Guidelines for Success
- Presentation 3: Ratios of Positive Interactions
- Presentation 4: Improving Attendance
- Presentation 5: School Connectedness: Meeting Basic Human Needs
- Presentation 6: Programs and Strategies for Meeting Needs
- Presentation 7: Making a Good First Impression—Welcoming New Staff, Students, and Families
- Appendix A: Foundations Implementation Rubric and Summary
- Appendix B: Module C Implementation Checklist
- Appendix C: Guide to Module C Reproducible Forms and Samples

Module E: *Improving Safety, Managing Conflict, and Reducing Bullying* guides the Foundations Team in assessing school strengths and weaknesses related to safety, conflict, and bullying. The module begins by examining the attributes of safe and unsafe schools and offers suggestions for moving your school toward the evidence-based attributes that contribute to safety. One potential risk to safety is poor conflict management, so this module includes a simple conflict resolution strategy students can use to manage conflict in peaceful and mutually beneficial ways. Bullying is another serious risk to safety. Module E provides a step-by-step process for analyzing strengths and gaps in your school's bullying policies and procedures as well as suggestions and examples for turning gaps into strengths. This module provides lessons for students on safety, conflict, and bullying prevention and intervention.

- Presentation 1: Ensuring a Safe Environment
- Presentation 2: Attributes of Safe and Unsafe Schools
- Presentation 3: Teaching Conflict Resolution
- Presentation 4: Analyzing Bullying Behavior, Policies, and School Needs
- Presentation 5: Schoolwide Bullying Prevention and Intervention
- Appendix A: Foundations Implementation Rubric and Summary
- Appendix B: Module E Implementation Checklist
- Appendix C: Guide to Module E Reproducible Forms and Samples

Module F: *Establishing and Sustaining a Continuum of Behavior Support* outlines how the Foundations Team can analyze and guide an integration of universal prevention, targeted support, and intensive support for students. This process includes adopting and supporting a schoolwide or district approach to classroom management that creates a common language and ensures that teachers, administrators, and support staff are on the same page about classroom organization and management. For students who need individual support, this module provides staff training in early-stage interventions and a variety of problem-solving structures that match the intensity of student need to the intensity of school- and district-based resources. Finally, Module F provides guidance in sustaining *Foundations* at the building and district level so that effective procedures are maintained and improvement continues, even when school administration changes.

- Presentation 1: The Vision of a Continuum of Behavior Support
- Presentation 2: Supporting Classroom Behavior—The Three-Legged Stool
- Presentation 3: Articulating Staff Beliefs and Solidifying Universal Procedures
- Presentation 4: Early-Stage Interventions for General Education Classrooms
- Presentation 5: Matching the Intensity of Your Resources to the Intensity of Your Needs
- Presentation 6: Problem-Solving Processes and Intervention Design
- Presentation 7: Sustainability and District Support
- Appendix A: Foundations Implementation Rubric and Summary
- Appendix B: Module F Implementation Checklist
- Appendix C: Guide to Module F Reproducible Forms and Samples

The Relationship Between Proactive Procedures, Corrective Procedures, and Individual Student Behavior Improvement Plans

CONTENTS

INTRODUCTION
Module D Overview

Misbehavior can drive you crazy. As teachers and parents, we care deeply about children; however, their misbehavior can be very frustrating. If poorly implemented, efforts to correct misbehavior can be ineffective, and ineffective correction can result in the same students exhibiting the same misbehaviors over and over. Poorly implemented corrections can even worsen a situation—for example, a student who misbehaves to gain power is rewarded by adult anger and may even earn a 3-day vacation (out-of-school suspension). If the correction is what the student wants, staff are clearly reinforcing—not correcting—the student for his misbehavior. Because managing misbehavior is stressful, aggravating, and even guilt inducing, all staff members need to work together and support each other.

Three broad goals of this module are:

1. Staff understand that their responses to misbehavior can be effective only when accompanied by ongoing work on universal prevention and, as needed, proactive individual intervention plans for students with the greatest needs.

2. All staff respond to misbehavior in ways that have the greatest chance of improving students' behavior, not in ways that risk worsening the situation.

3. Staff develop a schoolwide game plan that outlines "who does what, when" in responding to misbehavior. Every staff member knows his or her role and the role of other staff members, creating a sense of staff unity and consistency.

The author and humorist Mark Twain (1835–1910) said, "For every complex problem, there is a simple answer—and it is wrong." The following simple solutions to correcting misbehavior are wrong. They do not work.

Ineffective Approach 1: Punish harshly—and if that doesn't work, punish more harshly. Research supports our contention that this approach is misguided and ineffective, and drives students out of the system. In today's educational system, the goal is to keep all children in school through the 12th grade. You can't punish a child into wanting to stay in school.

Ineffective Approach 2: Wish that the problem would go away. It won't. Children are living in a complex world, and many of them face extreme life challenges. Just wishing that a student will move away or a problem will disappear buys us nothing.

Ineffective Approach 3: Point fingers. Some people say, "If the principal [or teachers, bus drivers, playground supervisors, counselors, and so on] would just do something, we wouldn't have these problems." This attitude accomplishes nothing. All staff members have roles to play, and if the roles mesh to create a coordinated whole, there will be no reason to point fingers. No single group or individual can be responsible for all the behavior problems.

Ineffective Approach 4: Believe that a student's needs are beyond what this school can provide, so the student needs to go somewhere else. There is nowhere else. Staff need to coordinate with special education (SPED), but just getting a student qualified for SPED is not enough. We must be coordinated in the service delivery that we provide.

So what is an effective approach to correcting misbehavior?

If the above solutions to correcting misbehavior are wrong, what works? Multi-Tiered System of Support (MTSS) for behavior is not a simple solution, but it is a powerful framework for working on all aspects of behavior management, and *Foundations* follows this basic structure. MTSS entails creating a continuum of behavior support. This module, *Responding to Misbehavior: An Instructional Approach,* rests on the base of continuous improvement processes and clear expectations for behavior in common areas and with schoolwide policies such as dress code and electronics use. The relationship between these elements of the continuum is illustrated in Figure 1a on the next page, the *Foundations* continuum graphic. As you can see, the topic Responding to Misbehavior is at the same level as Creating an Inviting Climate and Addressing Safety, Conflict, and Bullying. These three aspects of a safe and civil school go hand in hand, and when implemented well, they can create the next layer in your continuum of behavior support and provide the base for Positive Classroom Management and individual student intervention efforts.

The methodology we just described works. In a district of 20,000 students that implemented *Foundations* and classroom management, the district achieved an 86% reduction in severe behavior incidents and out-of-school suspension after 2 years of work. During the same period, teachers' satisfaction with their sense of efficacy and unity increased dramatically. In one building in the district, teachers responded with 100% agreement to the following confidential survey questions:

- The school has a consistent approach to behavior management and discipline.

- I receive sufficient support when I have to deal with difficult students and/or with discipline problems.

- The school has adequate systems for identifying and helping students who are at risk of falling through the cracks (academically and/or behaviorally).

After only 2 years of work to create a continuum of behavior support, powerful positive changes were evident in this district.

      ဆာ   FOUNDATIONS RECOMMENDATION   ෆ

Adopt an instructional approach to discipline for the best chance of reducing the recurrence of misbehavior.

Figure 1a   *The Foundations continuum of behavior support*

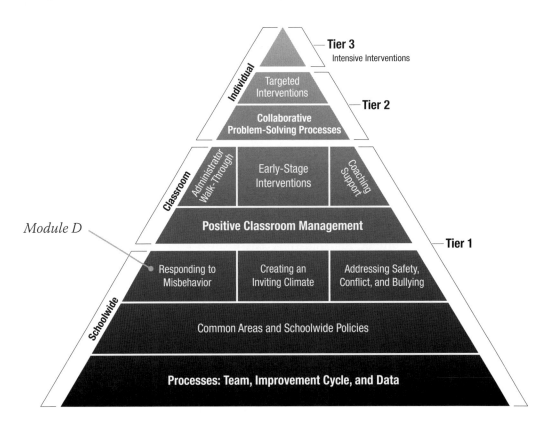

Adopt an instructional approach to discipline.

This entire module is about correcting misbehavior. The goal in correcting any misbehavior is to reduce the future occurrence of that misbehavior. To accomplish that goal, we recommend that you adopt an *instructional* approach to discipline.

This instructional approach uses three strategies (see Figure 1b):

- Proactive universal prevention
- Corrective procedures at the time of the infraction (this module provides information about this process)
- Proactive individual behavior improvement plans (that is, interventions) for students whose behavior does not improve with corrective procedures

Figure 1b *Instructional approach to discipline sandwich*

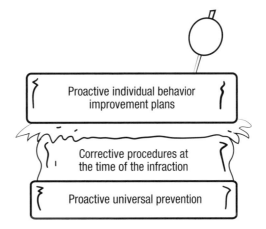

Notice that the corrective procedure strategy is sandwiched between universal prevention and individual behavior improvement plans. Most schools do not have the time and resources to jump directly from universal prevention to individual intervention for students who do not respond to the universal prevention. You must try corrective procedures first. The information you learn from correcting a tough student—what *doesn't* change the behavior, and possibly the function of the misbehavior—informs the process of developing an effective intervention.

How do these three strategies relate? Let's begin with this concept: A consequence for a rule violation is *not* an intervention. When *Safe & Civil School* trainers are asked to help with a difficult behavioral situation, the first question they usually ask is, "What interventions have you tried so far?" Often the answer is timeout, time owed, or sending the student to the office—but those are consequences for rule violations. Assigning a consequence for a rule violation is one of several approaches you can choose to react to misbehavior at the time of the infraction, but it is *not* an intervention. It is a reactive procedure.

For your toughest students, consequences *by themselves* are almost certainly doomed to failure. The German philosopher Friedrich Nietzsche (1844–1900) said, "Speaking generally, punishment hardens and numbs, it produces concentration, it sharpens the consciousness of alienation, it strengthens the power of resistance."

Kids express this sentiment more simply: "You can't make me."

We can't give you a simple, magical corrective consequence that will result in your most-at-risk kids suddenly saying, "I've learned my lesson. From now on, I'll behave." There is no such thing. But we do encourage all staff members to adopt an *instructional approach to discipline.*

Implement proactive universal prevention.

As stated earlier, the first strategy essential to an instructional approach to discipline is proactive universal prevention. Proactive universal prevention encompasses clear expectations and effective procedures for common areas and schoolwide policies, active supervision, adults who build relationships with students, high ratios of positive to corrective adult attention, and other concepts that are spread throughout the *Foundations* program.

Here's an example of proactive universal prevention. A middle school had been working through *Foundations* and *CHAMPS* for about four years and reduced out-of-school suspension by 75%—a wonderful outcome. But data showed that for each of those years, the month of March had the most office discipline referrals, in-school suspensions, and out-of-school suspension. The staff wanted to address this problem.

In January, we met with the school Foundations Team to brainstorm contributing factors and possible solutions for the consistent spike in misbehavior during March. Here's what we came up with:

- March is sandwiched between midwinter break in January and spring break in early April and has no holidays or other breaks.
- Student and staff absenteeism are problematic.
- The third quarter ends.
- Daylight savings time begins.
- Staff become increasingly tense about spring testing that occurs after spring break.

Then we came up with the following possible proactive strategies to counteract the contributing factors.

- **Re-teach expectations** for common areas, schoolwide policies, and classroom procedures before major school breaks, after breaks, and during that 6-week stretch of time between winter and spring breaks.

- **Teach schoolwide expectations** for how students are to treat guest teachers. These expectations can be modeled on common area and schoolwide policy expectations and should be considered just as important. In addition, all teachers should be expected to have consistent teaching plans that guest teachers can use.

- **Work with the district to train the pool of guest teachers in behavior management techniques.** This school uses CHAMPS, so the guest teachers should receive CHAMPS training.

- **Improve staff morale.** The Foundations Team can organize events such as a staff breakfast or a PTA appreciation lunch.

- **Work on student absenteeism with universal procedures** (Module C, Presentation 4 addresses this process).

- **Institute a temporary reward system** such as CARE. In CARE, students are rewarded with lottery tickets for demonstrating qualities that are highlighted each week for 4 weeks: Careful Commuting, Awesome Attitude, Responsible Leadership, and Exceptional Empathy. (CARE is described in Module C, Presentation 6.)

- **Hold a mini-inservice for staff** on de-escalating student emotion and misbehavior and avoiding power struggles. (Module D, Presentation 5 discusses this issue.)

So we identified at least seven proactive strategies that were successful in other schools we've worked with and that the school could implementing before March, when they anticipated problems with student misbehavior. The school doesn't need to use all the ideas (that's probably unrealistic), but even one, two, or three of them can make a real difference in the school climate and reduce student misbehavior.

Proactive universal prevention, the first component of an instructional approach to discipline, needs to be continually refined so you can home in on your school's unique needs and reduce the misbehaviors that lead to serious consequences such as suspension. Even with the best universal prevention, however, misbehavior will occur. It's inevitable. So you still need effective correction procedures in place. If the corrections don't result in reduced misbehavior, you need to be able to implement proactive individualized behavior improvement plans—that is, interventions.

Develop menus of effective corrective procedures.

The second component of an instructional approach to discipline is corrective procedures at the time of the infraction. Keep in mind that corrective procedures must be sandwiched between proactive universal prevention and intervention.

The focus of this entire module is corrective procedures. You will develop menus of corrective actions for the classroom, in common areas, and with schoolwide policies. Administrators will develop a game plan for dealing with students with severe and chronic problems. We encourage you to avoid out-of-school suspension (which amounts to rewarding the toughest kids with vacation) and emotional responses to misbehavior. We recommend stopping misbehavior in its earliest stages as the best way to reduce it. Your goal should be to provide corrections that *change* behavior by giving students instructions for how they should behave.

Restorative justice is one of the responses to misbehavior we discuss in this module. It's a wonderful concept, and we encourage you to include it in your menu of consequences. However, you can't rely on just one option—you need a full range of corrective responses. For example, many communities are beginning to use restorative justice practices for criminal offenses such as drugs, robbery, and assault, but they still need parking tickets for parking infractions. They can't conduct learning circles for everyone with a parking ticket. Similarly, school personnel need a range of corrective techniques, from simple, quickly implemented corrections for minor misbehavior to responses such as restorative justice for serious misbehavior.

Despite the best universal prevention and the best, most consistent responses to misbehavior, some students will continue to push the limits. They need proactive individual behavior improvement plans.

Be prepared to develop proactive individual behavior improvement plans.

The third required component of an instructional approach to discipline is a staff of educators prepared to implement proactive individual behavior improvement plans. In the continuum of behavior support, this attention to individuals defines the Tier 2 and Tier 3 portions. Proactive plans are built for students who need the additional support, and plans might include Connections, Meaningful Work, structured reward systems, and self-monitoring interventions, for example. These programs are presented in Module C, *Conscious Construction of an Inviting School Climate*, and in Module F, *Establishing and Sustaining a Continuum of Behavior Support*.

This entire module is about developing a schoolwide instructional approach to discipline that all staff members will be able to use with fidelity.

- Presentation 1 is geared toward the entire staff. Task 1 focuses on understanding the importance of staff unity and consistency. Task 2 is about ensuring that every staff member understands why out-of-school suspension is an ineffective consequence.

- Presentation 2 guides your Foundations Team and the entire staff through defining three levels of misbehavior for your school so that everyone knows when and how to respond to misbehavior and when and when not to involve counselors and administrators in discipline.

- Presentation 3 offers sample menus of corrective responses for mild and moderate misbehavior and suggestions for implementing them in classrooms and common areas and with schoolwide policies. We also discuss writing effective referrals for severe misbehavior. The entire staff may find this presentation useful.

- Presentation 4 presents ideas for the Foundations Team on coordinating the staff and administration and the teaching staff and counselors to ensure seamless support for staff and students. We also offer tips to administrators on the range of alternatives to out-of-school suspension that may be more effective in correcting severe misbehavior, suggest office procedures for dealing with referrals, and recommend ways to use in-school suspension productively.

- Presentation 5 returns to content that may be useful to the entire staff. We explore teaching students how to interact with adults and teaching staff to avoid power struggles and de-escalate student emotion. This presentation includes a set of sample lessons you can review and use to teach students how to accept corrections and compliments and interact appropriately with adults.

- Appendix A contains the Foundations Implementation Rubric for use in assessing implementation of each *Foundations* module.

- Appendix B provides a detailed Implementation Checklist for tasks in this module.

- Appendix C presents the contents of the Module D CD for easy reference.

- The *Foundations* Module D CD provides electronic copies of the forms discussed in this module, the sample lessons from Task 3, and other resources.

We hope that by using the information in this module, you will reduce the degree to which misbehavior interferes with instruction in your school and increase staff confidence in implementing an instructional approach to responding to student misbehavior.

Presentation 1 Overview

This presentation sets the groundwork for developing an effective and instructional schoolwide approach to student misbehavior.

Task 1: Create Staff Unity on Corrective Procedures ensures that staff understand the importance of responding to student misbehavior in a consistent and unified manner. Staff members should follow through with a correction for every misbehavior they witness (and students should be held equally accountable for their actions). Staff should also agree on the schoolwide expectations for student behavior—what constitutes a dress code violation, for example, or the appropriate voice level for the cafeteria.

Task 2: Know the Weaknesses of and Drawbacks to Out-of-School Suspension covers issues such as disproportionality and negative outcomes linked to out-of-school suspension. Though a common response to office referrals, out-of-school suspension has several drawbacks that make it ineffective at best and harmful at worst.

The rest of Module D guides administrators and staff through setting up a structured schoolwide response to student misbehavior along with strategies for preventing misbehavior in the first place.

TASK 1

Create staff unity on corrective procedures

One of the most common concerns and complaints from school staff about school-wide behavior management is inconsistent responses to student misbehavior. And they are right to be concerned—consistency is important. Here are three compelling reasons for staff to be unified in their approach as they respond to student misbehavior:

- Principals do not have time to deal with discipline problems that might be more effectively corrected by the staff member who viewed the infraction.
- Students are under the authority of many different adults during a school day.
- More and more students have challenging behavior problems.

Why is staff unity important for schoolwide behavior management?

In the past 25 years, the role of the principal has changed significantly. Historically, principals were the managers of their buildings. They ensured that supplies were ordered and they hired the teachers, but they trusted the teachers to deal with most classroom misbehavior. They had time to deal with serious student misbehavior almost singlehandedly, and they often relied on out-of-school suspension. Just 10 years ago, some principals would tell staff to send all serious discipline problems to the office.

Now, principals no longer have the time to handle all discipline. Administrators are the instructional leaders in the building and are expected to be skilled in all areas of teaching, from lesson design to lesson delivery. They are also under pressure to avoid using out-of-school suspension because it is ineffective, so they must use alternative consequences that require more time and effort to develop and implement. With a greater emphasis on teacher development, administrators are expected to conduct frequent classroom walk-throughs and spend time coaching teachers in the art of teaching. This new role for the principal requires all staff members to be competent in responding to student misbehavior so that the principal is not inundated with unnecessary referrals and therefore cannot do anything else.

Another reason that staff unity on corrective procedures is important is that students may interact with many different adults during a school day. At the middle and high school levels, students encounter as many as six different teachers in a day. As early as second grade, some schools split classes between two or more teachers (one for language arts and reading and another for science and math, for example), and students spend time with specialists for PE, computers, art, music, library, and so on.

Consider also the common area supervisors and even the bus drivers, and you find that most students interact with at least ten different adults each week. When some staff members do not correct misbehavior in common areas or with schoolwide policies, students get inconsistent information about expectations.

Perhaps the most important reason that staff unity is important is that schools have more and more students who present behavioral challenges. Years ago, teachers might say as they reviewed their class roster at the beginning of the year, "I have a tough student this year." No one has just one tough student anymore—now there are five tough ones in most classes. In addition, today's focus on academic accountability forces teachers to see those students not as a challenge but as interference to the learning process.

As the number of students with challenging behavior increases, the level of consistency must also increase so that staff members can support each other. If everybody does a little, then nobody has to do a lot. If every staff member who hears an obscenity or observes one student intimidating another steps in and corrects the misbehavior, that misbehavior is far more likely to stop than if only some of the staff correct and others ignore the misbehavior.

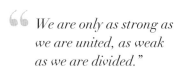
We are only as strong as we are united, as weak as we are divided."

J. K. ROWLING (1965–),
Harry Potter and the Goblet of Fire

Define consistency as it relates to student behavior.

So what does it mean to be consistent? First let's look at what it *doesn't* mean. Consistency does not mean that all misbehavior gets the same consequence, as enticing as that might seem! That idea assumes that all students are equipped with the same social competencies and are at the same developmental level—an unrealistic assumption when students' ages might differ by 4 years in a high school or 7 years in a pre-K to fifth-grade elementary school!

Consistency should also not be confused with fairness. Fairness does not mean that everyone is treated the same; it means that everyone gets what they *need*. Consider an academic analogy: If all students were able to achieve at the same level, there would be no reason for after-school tutoring. But schools *do* offer extra help for academics. Similarly, some students need extra support to learn additional social behaviors. Like academics, behavior is learned.

Consistency means that every staff member who observes student behavior that violates schoolwide expectations for common areas and schoolwide policies corrects that behavior. The staff members do not have to use identical corrective consequences, but it is essential that *every* staff member follow through with a correction for every misbehavior he or she witnesses. One adult might correct an obscenity with a quick one-liner, another might pull the student aside and remind her why business-like language is the expectation in school, and yet another might require the student to apologize, but in each case the behavior is being addressed.

Consistency is essential from adult to adult, from student to student, and from day to day.

- **Adult-to-adult consistency** means that staff are unified in their expectations for student behavior—everything from the definition of appropriate school language to the interpretation of the school dress code to the voice levels that should be used in the hallways—and students know that staff will consistently correct them on these expectations.

- **Student-to-student consistency** means that every student is equally accountable for his or her actions. Whether the student is a star athlete or a challenging student, he should be corrected when he chooses to not follow the school expectations.

- **Day-to-day consistency** means that no matter your mood, the day of the week, or the time of year, you correct misbehavior.

Consistency of classroom expectations is also important, but it is up to each teacher to set expectations that meet the students' needs and fit the teacher's style, to teach the expectations clearly, and to enforce them consistently. Each teacher establishes his or her own internal classroom consistency; collectively, the staff needs to establish unity in relation to expectations for common areas and schoolwide policies.

You also need to develop staff unity in regard to misbehavior that is severe enough for the student to be removed from instruction and sent to the office. We discuss how to define levels of misbehavior and coordinate office referrals in Module D, Presentation 2. Staff members need to know that when they send students to the office, they'll get support. Administrators need to know that staff members will send students to the office only for offenses that are truly serious.

Be aware of the inconsistencies with progressive consequences.

A unified staff consistently responds to misbehavior and supports one another with challenging students. In some schools, a classroom management procedure called *progressive consequences* is used in an effort to achieve consistency. We find that this system actually makes it more difficult for staff to be consistent, especially in relation to the definition of severe misbehavior that can result in office referral. Here's why.

Many teachers use a classroom management plan in which each student has a set of colored cards contained in a pocket chart. The pocket chart is located in a prominent place in the classroom. When a student misbehaves, the teacher (or the student) pulls a card from the student's pocket. Each card is a different color, and the colors represent a progression of consequences. When the green card is pulled, it serves as a warning. When the yellow card is pulled, the student loses recess. When the orange card is pulled, the parents are contacted. When the red card is pulled, the student is sent to the office. (See Figure 1c below for an illustration of a pocket chart.)

Figure 1c   *Pocket chart (D-26)*

In a less colorful but similar system, teachers simply write students' names on the board and place checkmarks next to the names for each infraction. At checkmark four, the student goes to the office.

It can be difficult for a teacher to be consistent, day after day, in handing out progressive penalties, especially if that teacher is with the same children for the entire day. It's probably easier for a middle or high school teacher to implement a system of progressive consequences. For an elementary teacher, it can be almost impossible.

Consider the following scenario:

8:10   Teddy is tapping his pencil, which annoys the teacher. She has him pull the green card from his pocket.

8:30   Teddy calls a classmate a name, so he has to pull the yellow card.

8:40   Teddy is out of his seat. He's now at orange.

8:45   Teddy is tapping his pencil again. To be consistent, the red card must be pulled and Teddy must be sent to the office—for pencil tapping.

Most administrators, however, are not happy to see students in their offices for pencil tapping, and they let their staff know that office referrals are for serious misbehavior—assault, threats, and so on—not pencil tapping.

So what happens? The teacher, in an effort to avoid pulling cards for minor misbehavior, begins to issue warnings instead of consequences. "Teddy, I don't want to have to pull the next card. You don't want to miss recess, do you?" The teacher begs and cajoles Teddy to behave or ignores the misbehavior to delay the next consequence.

By the middle of the afternoon, Teddy has misbehaved 17 times but has received only three consequences—the teacher has been inconsistent 14 times. Finally, the teacher has had it and sends Teddy to the office, writing on the referral form, "Teddy has been disruptive, disrespectful, and defiant all day long!" Well, at least the office referral wasn't for pencil tapping.

When every misbehavior needs to be corrected by pulling a card, teachers cannot be consistent with children who display many minor misbehaviors. Misbehaviors are not equivalent. Tapping a pencil is not the same as angrily pushing someone. If the government used such a system, we could easily end up in jail for parking tickets! Fortunately, the local government doesn't consider parking tickets as serious as speeding tickets and DUIs, so it issues consequences on different levels for the different infractions.

We do not recommend progressive discipline. Later in this module, we offer information about constructing a system of consequences that we call the *3-level system* for responding to misbehavior. We find that the 3-level system is more likely to elicit consistent responses from staff and reduce student misbehavior. Every misbehavior is corrected, but not with progressively serious consequences. Rather, minor misbehavior is corrected every time it occurs with consequences of parking-ticket magnitude—that is, consequences that annoy the student enough that she will likely change her behavior to avoid the consequence, just as parking tickets encourage drivers to park legally and feed the meters.

❧ FOUNDATIONS RECOMMENDATION ☙

Use a 3-level system instead of progressive consequences to respond to misbehavior. We find that the 3-level system is more likely to elicit consistent responses from staff and reduce student misbehavior.

Modify progressive consequences for better consistency.

We do not recommend progressive consequences, but if you are using them, you can improve their effectiveness by following the government's example—recognize that misbehavior can be minor or serious and respond appropriately. Set up a parallel system for misbehaviors. One category includes the speeding-ticket misbehaviors.

Those misbehaviors receive progressive consequences, and you might use the pocket chart of colored cards for these. The second category includes the parking-ticket misbehaviors. These are treated with consequences (separate from the pocket chart) that you hold on the same level for each infraction, such as time owed.

For example, tapping a pencil is a minor misbehavior—a parking ticket. A teacher might simply choose to take time from the student. Every time Teddy taps his pencil (or exhibits a similar minor disruption), he loses 15 seconds from time on the computer. If Teddy misbehaves 12 times, he is corrected 12 times and has lost 3 minutes of computer time. If you get 12 parking tickets, it does not bankrupt you, but it is annoying enough that you are more likely to put money in the meter next time you park. If the consequence is a small amount of time owed for each infraction, you are not escalating the punishment over some trivial offense and so you can be calm and consistent in correcting the misbehavior every time it occurs.

In addition, if you plan to use a progressive system, consider implementing it so students can move back and forth—from green to red *and* from red to green. For example, if the green card is pulled but then the student begins behaving appropriately, you can put the green card back into the pocket. A system like this can teach students how to recover from their mistakes and provides an additional way for you to acknowledge appropriate behaviors in addition to correcting rule violations.

Before you implement any system of consequences, it is important to clearly and explicitly teach students what to expect—which misbehaviors merit progressive consequences (for example, pulling the next card), which merit nonprogressive consequences (for example, 15 seconds owed off recess or 15 seconds owed from a passing period), and what those consequences will be.

In Module D, Presentation 3, we present menus of appropriate and effective corrections for mild and moderate misbehavior.

If staff use progressive consequences in your school, ensure that they are used consistently and fairly for all students. Although we don't recommend this system—we recommend a 3-level system instead—if you do use it, follow the suggestions above. When staff members are consistent within their classrooms and are unified with a consistent approach to correcting behavior in common areas and with schoolwide policies, they support one another and can make it easier to deal with challenging students.

Task 1 Action Steps & Evidence of Implementation

Action Steps	Evidence of Implementation
Plan to have a staff discussion to address the following questions: • Are all staff members correcting misbehavior consistently, especially in common areas and with schoolwide policies such as dress code? • Are staff members concerned about who does what in relation to discipline? (What is the teacher's role? What is the principal's role?) • How are we using progressive discipline? Are students allowed to move back and forth between the levels? You don't need to get closure now, but if any of these discussion topics are concerns, consider working through the rest of the module to address them.	Foundations Process: Meeting Minutes

TASK 2

Know the weaknesses of and drawbacks to out-of-school suspension

All staff should know and understand the drawbacks to out-of-school suspension (OSS). We think it's important to address this topic because OSS is used frequently in many districts. Often, teachers think they are not being supported when administrators don't assign OSS for office referrals, yet at the same time administrators feel tremendous pressure to reduce their use of OSS. Sounds like a recipe for inconsistent discipline!

In this task, we first give some historical context and then describe why OSS is a problematic behavior support practice, the relationship between zero-tolerance policies and increasing suspension rates, the deleterious effects of OSS, and the disparate impact OSS has on minorities and students with disabilities.

Consider a historical perspective on exclusionary discipline practices.

In 2010, approximately 76% of public high school students graduated on time with a regular diploma (U.S. Department of Education). Depending on the source, graduation rates range from about 74% to 80%. In 2014, Balfanz et al. reported an historic high of 80% for 2012.

From a glass-half-empty viewpoint, the educational system is still not reaching roughly 25% of our students. Some say schools could do better if they were just tougher on kids, but before we start bemoaning how today's students don't take school seriously, let's consider some historical graduation rates (U.S. Department of Education):

- In 1940, 50.8% of 17-year-olds graduated.
- In 1870, just 2% of 17-year-olds graduated. That's right—2%.

What do those statistics tell us? Historically, schools were not expected to educate 100% of the population. When there were plenty of jobs on farms and in factories, everybody didn't need an education. In today's society, however, having an education is essential for economic success. The continued use of exclusionary discipline is a holdover from the time when schools weren't expected—and didn't even try—to keep everyone in school through the 12th grade.

What conditions must be met for OSS to be successful?

OSS as a behavior support practice is not bad or wrong; it's not inhumane or intentionally demeaning. But if it is going to help a child, the following conditions need to be in place:

- The student's parents must be able to take 3 or more days off work with as little as 12 hours' notice. Only high-level professionals usually have the leeway to take 3 days off without notice.

- The parents must supervise the student throughout the entire suspension period (not just school hours).

- The parents must *interact skillfully* with the student during the suspension period. They must:
  - Restrict the student's privileges and communication with friends.
  - Treat the student with respect.
  - Counsel the student about the importance of success in school.

How many of your students' parents are able to meet all these conditions?

If parents can't meet these conditions and the student is unsupervised during school hours, the student may learn that being out of school is much less stressful than being in school, and the student is potentially lost.

How do zero-tolerance policies relate to increased suspension rates?

Zero-tolerance policies are relatively recent additions to school discipline practices. With the increase in disastrous events such as school shootings and the corresponding increased focus on safety, zero-tolerance policies were seen as a strong, decisive, and necessary step toward preventing violence and ensuring the safety of students. Zero-tolerance policies typically mandate predetermined harsh consequences such as suspension and expulsion, and they were implemented initially for serious offenses such as weapons, drugs, and violence. Over time, however, zero tolerance has been creeping into misbehavior that has little effect on school safety—misbehavior such as disruptions, dress code violations, public displays of affection, electronics policy violations, and disrespect.

According to the National Center for Education Statistics, millions of children are suspended out of school—3,328,750 in 2006, for example. Of those 3,328,750 suspensions, only 5% were for weapon- and drug-related offenses—offenses that truly warrant zero-tolerance policies. The remaining 95% of suspensions were categorized as *Disruptive Behavior* and *Other.*

Suspension rates have dramatically increased because of zero-tolerance creep—zero-tolerance policies have been instituted for misbehavior that is not typically considered severe or threatening to others. As a result, more and more students have been suspended for misbehavior that does not truly fit into the category of zero tolerance.

Since the early 1970s, out-of-school suspensions for misbehavior not covered by zero-tolerance policies (that is, misbehavior that does not involve violence, weapons, or drugs) have (Losen, 2011):

- Nearly doubled for Whites, from 3% to 5%.
- More than doubled for Hispanic/Latinos, from 3% to 7%.
- More than doubled for Black/African Americans, from 6% to 15%.
- Almost tripled for Native Americans, from 3% to 8%.

What are the deleterious effects of suspension?

Because OSS is so frequently used, you might assume it is an effective consequence for misbehavior and successfully teaches the student a lesson. However, many data have been collected on the deleterious outcomes associated with OSS. The following outcomes are all directly related to the use of OSS:

- Involvement with the judicial system
- Lower academic achievement
- Dropping out of school
- Chronic school attendance problems
- Retention

Paradoxically, more youth crime occurs on school days than on nonschool days. Although the highest rate of youth crime occurs immediately after school at around 3 p.m., more youth crime occurs on school days during school hours than after 9 p.m. Why is this crime happening during school hours? Because the toughest kids, with possibly the most behavioral and home problems, aren't in school—they are suspended or not attending (see Figure 1d on the next page).

Understand the disparate impact of OSS on minorities and students with disabilities.

Disproportionality—the over- or underrepresentation of a particular population or demographic group—is a concern with OSS. The following information comes from the research literature. We also suggest some resources for further reading.

Losen (2011) published a chart about suspension rates for first-time offenders in North Carolina (see Figure 1e on the next page) that reveals great disparity between Black/

African American and White students. Black/African American first-time offenders were suspended at higher rates than White first-time offenders for the same minor offenses.

- Cell phone offenses: 13% if White, 31% if Black/African American
- Dress code offenses: 15% if White, 36% if Black/African American
- Disruptive behavior: 22% if White, 38% if Black/African American
- Display of affection 13% if White, 41% if Black/African American

Figure 1d   *Occurrence of violent crimes by juveniles*

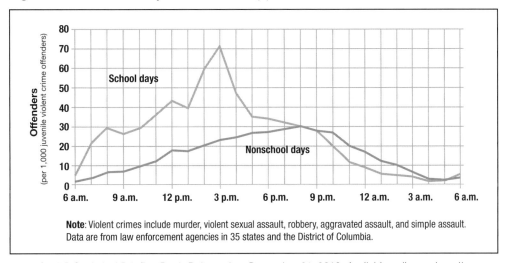

From *OJJDP Statistical Briefing Book*. Released on December 21, 2010. Available online at: http://www.ojjdp.gov/ojstatbb/offenders/qa03301.asp. Adapted from Snyder, H., & Sickmund, M. (2006). *Juvenile Offenders and Victims: 2006 National Report*. Washington, DC: Office of Juvenile Justice and Delinquency Prevention. Used with permission.

Figure 1e   *North Carolina suspension rates for Black/African American and White students (first offense)*

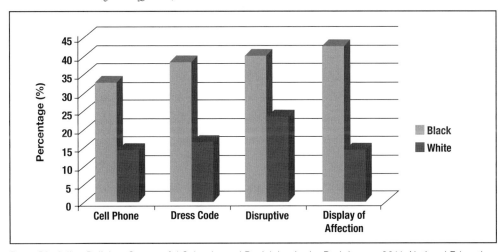

From *Discipline Policies, Successful Schools, and Racial Justice* by D. J. Losen, 2011, National Education Policy Center, Boulder, CO, p. 7. Retrieved from http://nepc.colorado.edu/publication/discipline-policies. Used with permission.

Kim, Losen, and Hewitt (2010) provide the following definition of *disparate impact*:

> *Under the "disparate impact" theory, a method of discipline that is racially neutral on its face but has a discriminatory effect may be found to be unlawful absent sufficient justification, such as educational necessity. Even if a school's action is found to be justified, it still may be unlawful if equally effective, less discriminatory alternatives are available. (p. 39)*

In other words, administrators are under increasing pressure to avoid using OSS because they might encounter legal problems with civil rights issues.

Some staff members in some schools think that if students they've referred are not suspended, the administrators are too soft on the students. We contend that OSS risks being a reward for students rather than a corrective consequence. For many reasons, we encourage your staff to collectively recognize that the best way for administrators to support teachers who have referred students for severe misbehavior is to avoid rewarding those students with a 3-day vacation. The teaching and supervisory staff should support the administrative staff as they explore alternatives to OSS.

 Disproportionality: The over- or underrepresentation of a particular population or demographic group in a program or targeted group. For example, disciplinary disproportionality means that one group of students—one racial group, one gender, or one socioeconomic group, for example—receives many more referrals, suspensions, expulsions, or other disciplinary actions than other groups."

Disproportionality Resources

These resources provide more detailed information about the problems of disproportionality and disparate impact.

- Skiba, R. J., Michael, R. S., Nardo, A. C., & Peterson, R. L. (2002). The color of discipline: Sources of racial and gender disproportionality in school punishment. *The Urban Review, 34*(4), 317–342.

  The authors found that students of color were suspended at rates two to three times higher than those for White students.

- Wald, J., & Losen, D. J. (2003). Defining and redirecting a school-to-prison pipeline. *New Directions for Youth Development, 99.*

  According to Wald and Losen, Black/African American students' risk for suspension is almost three times as great as for White students.

- Donovan, M. S., & Cross, C. T. (Eds.) (2002). *Minority students in special education and gifted education.* Washington, DC: National Academy Press.

  Donovan and Cross report that students with disabilities, particularly emotional-behavioral disabilities, are suspended at much higher rates than other students.

- Skiba, R. J., Horner, R. H., Chung, C.-G., Rausch, M. K., May, S. L., & Tobin, T. (2011). Race is not neutral: A national investigation of African American and Latino disproportionality in school discipline. *School Psychology Review, 40*(1), pp. 85–107.

  Skiba et al. examined patterns of disproportionality in office referral rates and disciplinary decisions across different racial/ethnic groups at the elementary (K–6) and middle school (6–9) levels. Across the sample, significant disparities exist for Black/African American and Hispanic/Latino students. Results indicate that both office referrals and administrative decisions significantly contribute to racial and ethnic disparities in school discipline. Compared with White students, Black/African American students are twice as likely to receive office referrals at the elementary level and four times as likely to receive office referrals at the middle school level. Latino students were over-represented in disciplinary actions at the middle school level but under-represented at the elementary level.

- Council of State Governments Justice Center & The Public Policy Research Institute, Texas A & M University (2011). *Breaking schools' rules: A statewide study of how school discipline relates to students' success and juvenile justice involvement.* Retrieved from http://csgjusticecenter.org/wp-content/uploads/2012/08/Breaking_Schools_Rules_Report_Final.pdf.

  Breaking Schools' Rules is an analysis of school and juvenile justice records in Texas intended to improve policymakers' understanding of who is suspended and expelled from public secondary schools. It examines the impact of those exclusionary policies on students' academic performance and juvenile justice involvement.

  This 6-year statewide longitudinal study examined records for all seventh-grade students in Texas public schools and tracked progress across multiple years. Key findings of the study include:

- Nearly six in ten students were suspended or expelled at least once between 7th and 12th grade.

- Black/African American students and those with particular educational disabilities were disproportionately more likely to be removed from instruction for disciplinary reasons. Most Black/African American male students (83%) had at least one discretionary referral, compared with 74% for Hispanic/Latino male students and 59% for White male students (see Figure 1f). A discretionary referral is one that is not required by policy.

- When a student was suspended or expelled, the likelihood of that student's being involved in the juvenile justice system in the subsequent year increased significantly.

- Students suspended or expelled for discretionary violations were twice as likely to repeat grades compared with students who had the same characteristics, attended a similar school, and had not been suspended or expelled.

- Suspension and expulsion rates among schools—even those with similar student composition and campus characteristics—varied significantly. Some schools used suspension a lot, some used it very judiciously.

Figure 1f   *Percentage of male students with at least one discretionary referral*

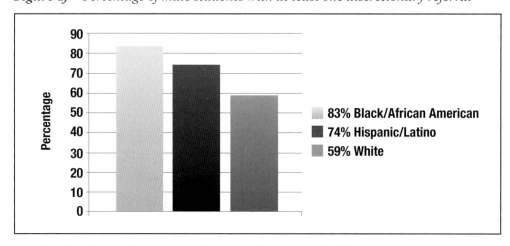

From *Breaking Schools' Rules: A statewide study of how school discipline relates to students' success and juvenile justice involvement,* by the Council of State Governments Justice Center & The Public Policy Research Institute, 2011, Texas A & M University. Retrieved from http://csgjusticecenter.org/wp-content/uploads/2012/08/Breaking_Schools_Rules_Report_Final.pdf.

The use of suspension can become a part of school culture. We advocate that you—the entire staff—work together to reduce the degree to which your school depends on the culture of OSS."

The use of suspension can become part of school culture. We advocate that you—the entire staff—work together to reduce the degree to which your school depends on the culture of OSS.

You can find current information about suspension rates on the U.S. Department of Education website. One interesting example is at http://www2.ed.gov/about/offices/list/ocr/docs/crdc-discipline-snapshot.pdf.

What can we conclude about the use of exclusionary discipline?

- Suspension is a good practice for only a small percentage of students—likely those with parental support (and with those students, almost any other consequence is likely to work as well!).

- In the name of zero tolerance, all students are two to three times more likely to receive OSS than they were in the early 1970s. And students of color or those who have disabilities have an even higher likelihood of being suspended.

In many ways, OSS is comparable to the archaic medical practice of leeching. From about 200 A.D. through the 19th century, physicians used leeches to bleed patients, and the practice was considered a viable treatment for almost any sickness. In the modern era, science has demonstrated that leeching is useful only in very specific circumstances. In most medical situations, leeches are not effective and could be harmful. It would be unconscionable for a hospital to leech patients just because it is what physicians have always done.

Similarly, in the modern era, the science of education has demonstrated that OSS is not effective and is probably harmful. Therefore, we recommend that you use alternative consequences whenever possible for non-zero-tolerance offenses.

> ❧ FOUNDATIONS RECOMMENDATION ☙
>
> *Whenever possible, use alternative consequences to out-of-school suspension for non-zero-tolerance offenses.*

Task 2 Action Steps & Evidence of Implementation

Action Steps	Evidence of Implementation
Have a staff discussion on the following topics: • Do staff members understand and agree that OSS has limited benefits and grave potential drawbacks? What actions would help increase this awareness? • Do staff members know and understand the national data on disparate impact of OSS for minorities and students with disabilities? • Do staff members pressure administrators into using OSS? Do they think that administrators are not supportive of teachers if OSS is not assigned? Do not try to achieve closure on these topics now, but encourage staff to learn more about these issues. We recommend several sources in this task.	Foundations Process: Meeting Minutes

Developing Three Levels of Misbehavior

CONTENTS

DOCUMENTS*

- Example of 3-level system for responding to misbehavior (D-11)
- Example of three levels of behavior definitions (D-12)
- Behavior Incident Notification Form (D-03)
- Behavior Incident Referral Form (D-04)
- TRENDS referral forms (D-05)

* All documents listed are available on the CD.

INTRODUCTION

This presentation will help the Foundations Team guide the staff in developing a structured system for responding to misbehavior that will work in your school. Remember that the goal of this work is to ensure that all staff can respond to misbehavior calmly, consistently, and confidently. The team and staff will develop agreement and clarity about:

- What misbehaviors staff should handle independently, with no written record, at the time of the incident.

- When and how the administrator should be involved in responding to misbehavior—that is, when and how are students sent to the office.

- When and how staff will handle misbehavior on their own, but also create paperwork that goes to the office.

- When staff should collaborate on individual behavior improvement plans for students.

The entire staff should view this introduction and Task 1. The Foundations Team should view Tasks 2 and 3 on guiding the development process and using data to analyze the effectiveness of your procedures.

Everyone should understand the advantages of having a plan for responding to misbehavior that everyone agrees to follow. With a plan, staff members can be on automatic pilot when they respond to misbehavior. They don't have to stop and think about what to do or second-guess their responses. Staff responses to misbehavior will be more consistent (day to day, setting to setting, staff member to staff member, and student to student) and thus more effective. Finally, staff members can put more time and energy into teaching, connecting with students, and recognizing student successes.

When a schoolwide plan for responding to misbehavior is *not* defined and in place, the following problems can occur:

- Staff members might be unsure about how they are supposed to correct misbehavior.

- Staff members might feel frustrated, helpless, and angry with students when the students misbehave.

- Staff responses to misbehavior are likely to be inconsistent. For example, when office referral is based on emotion (how the referring staff member feels at the moment) more than on the behavior the student exhibited, inconsistency from staff member to staff member is likely.

- Some staff members might expect someone else to handle their students' behavior problems and feel frustrated when the other person doesn't cure the problem.

- Some staff members might have unrealistic expectations about what administrators can or should do with students who have been referred to the office. For example, a teacher might think a problem is serious, but the administrator thinks it's minor and doesn't assign the consequences the teacher expects.

- The effectiveness of office referral as a correction might be weakened.

  - If referral is used too often for mild and moderate as well as severe misbehavior, it becomes a joke to students.

  - Administrators who are deluged with office referrals might simply process referred students rather than try to solve the problems that led to the misbehaviors. Imagine you are an administrator and you have to deal with 10 to 15 students every class period. No matter how well-meaning you are, your goal will probably become just to get the students in and out of your office as quickly as possible. To each student, you have time to say only, "What did you do? Why did you do it? Don't do it anymore. Go back to class. Next!"

  - Staff members might feel that they are simply handing off referred students instead of feeling like they are part of a coordinated effort.

  - Staff members might feel that the administrator is inconsistent or too lenient.

- Patterns of misbehavior (for individual students or across many students) might go unnoticed.

- Staff will continue to respond reactively to misbehavior rather than deal with problems proactively.

So your goal is to establish policies and procedures that create consistency. Every member of the team needs to understand the proposed 3-level approach so you can guide the staff in tailoring this concept to your school, and all staff members should be prepared to work together to develop a plan for responding to misbehavior.

All the tasks in this presentation are geared toward the team. We suggest that the entire staff also view Task 1 so they can gain a better understanding of the 3-level system they will develop.

Task 1: Establish a 3-Level System for Responding to Misbehavior explains why and how to categorize student misbehavior into three levels and suggests criteria for misbehavior that will consistently result in office referral.

Task 2: Reach Staff Consensus on the Three Levels of Misbehavior gives an example of how to work through the process of categorizing misbehavior with the staff.

Task 3: Document and Monitor Level 2 and Level 3 Misbehaviors discusses referral forms and database systems for effectively tracking misbehavior.

The next presentation in this module, Presentation 3, provides more information about developing menus of corrective consequences that correspond to the 3-level system.

Note: You may need to modify the language that we suggest for the levels based on your school's current system and any state- or district-level definitions. Of course, use the labels and language you are required to use. Some schools use a 4-level system in which the fourth level is used only by administrators for offenses that must be reported to the state or federal government. From a staff perspective, however, the school uses three levels.

TASK 1

Establish a 3-level system for responding to misbehavior

In this task, we explain why and how to categorize student misbehavior into three levels—mild, moderate, and severe—and suggest criteria for misbehavior that will consistently result in office referral. Task 2 provides detailed suggestions for working through the process of defining the categories.

The 3-level system that we advocate is not complicated. You won't create long menus of misbehaviors and consequences that staff have to consult before they address the misbehavior. Rather, the staff will develop a clear definition of the misbehaviors that *must* result in office referral and the misbehaviors that *may* result in office referral so that the administrator and all staff members are on the same page. For all other misbehaviors (mild and moderate), staff have great discretion in choosing how to respond, and *Foundations* offers guidance for staff on how to respond effectively.

In many schools, a range of misbehaviors can result in office referral. You might find a student who started a fire in the bathroom sitting next to a student who tapped his pencil during study time—and both are waiting to see the principal. What does this discrepancy say about the seriousness of starting a fire or getting sent to the office? If some teachers assign office referral for pencil tapping and others assign it only for fighting and gross disrespect, what message does that send to students? Some students are going to think that gross disrespect is no more serious than pencil tapping and that office referral is not a serious consequence. And of course the administrator has to spend valuable time determining how serious every office referral really is.

What are the advantages of a 3-level system for responding to misbehavior?

The 3-level system has many advantages:

- It helps staff members recognize the need for a team approach to dealing with students who exhibit severe or chronic misbehavior. All staff must understand that simply sending students to the office is unlikely to be effective.

- It allows administrators to deal effectively with severe and chronic misbehavior because they don't have to spend time on mild and moderate misbehavior.

- Administrators have more time to provide support for staff members who deal with students who exhibit severe or chronic misbehavior.

- It enhances cooperation between administrators and staff regarding student misbehavior.

- It provides useful information for guiding staff development. Knowing the patterns of mild, moderate, and severe misbehavior can help staff understand what needs work—classroom management or individual behavior improvement plans, for example.

- It allows for the delineation of consequences without getting into progressive consequences, the system we discussed in Presentation 1. Categorizing the infractions is less problematic than mandatory escalation (first offense, second offense, and so on).

Define the three levels of misbehavior.

Consider both the student behavior *and* the required adult response when you define the three categories of infractions. Avoid long menus and complicated definitions. You don't want staff to have to stop in the middle of correcting a student to look up the misbehavior and determine what to do. Following are recommended definitions for mild, severe, and moderate misbehavior. Notice that the misbehaviors are categorized more by how the staff member chooses to respond than by what the student did.

Level 1 (mild) infractions

Definition: Level 1 infractions are minor misbehaviors that staff can correct adequately at the time and in the environment in which they occur. They do not require documentation.

Adult response: A staff member who observes a Level 1 infraction corrects the student at the time and in the setting where it occurred. The adult is confident that he or she can handle the problem without involving another adult or removing the student from the setting.

We skip Level 2 and discuss Level 3 next, because it's easier to understand Level 2 when you understand Levels 1 and 3.

Level 3 (severe) infractions

Definition: Level 3 infractions are serious misbehaviors that require immediate administrative involvement (office referral) and written documentation. Level 3 includes behaviors that are illegal or so severe that the misbehaving student's continued presence in a setting poses a threat to physical safety or to adult authority (that is, the adult could lose control of the situation if the student stays in the setting). We explain more about defining Level 3 behaviors later in this task.

Adult response: A staff member who observes a Level 3 infraction sends the student to the office or calls for help to remove the student, then completes an incident referral form that goes to the administration (either on paper or through a data management system such as TRENDS).

Staff should understand that when they remove a student from the setting, they are indicating that the misbehavior was severe: It involved illegal activity, there was real danger of someone getting hurt, or the staff member was at risk of losing control of the situation.

Note that Level 3 behaviors should be both limited in number and agreed to in advance by the entire staff. If you define this category too broadly, so many students will be removed from settings for relatively trivial infractions that when a student is removed for overt insubordination, that student might not get appropriate attention from the administrator who is overburdened with office referrals.

Be sure to clarify which misbehaviors *must* be considered Level 3 and which behaviors *may* be considered Level 3 at the discretion of the staff member. Administrators must ensure that district, state, and federal regulations are followed. Certain behaviors, such as illegal activity, must be dealt with by the administrator, not staff.

So Level 1 infractions are corrected in the setting and no paperwork is required. Level 3 infractions require the student to be removed from the setting and sent to the office and the incident to be documented. Level 2 falls between these two scenarios: The student stays in the setting, but paperwork goes to the office.

Level 2 (moderate) infractions

Definition: Level 2 infractions don't require immediate administrative involvement, but they do require documentation. In other words, the student stays in the setting, but paperwork goes to the office. We refer to this Level 2 documentation as *notifications*, not referrals.

Notification to the office is particularly important when the reporting staff member has assigned a schoolwide correction that involves other staff members (detention or time in another teacher's room, for example). We recommend that a notification be written and entered into a database any time a student is removed from a setting so that the behavior and the lost instructional time (if any) are tracked over time.

A reporting staff member who wants or needs administrative input on the incident should also notify the office. For example, let's say you heard a boy teasing a girl and you are not sure whether the incident should be considered harassment. You can say to the student, "I'm going to write down what you said and submit it to the office as a notification. I want the principal to help me decide whether I need to call your parents or take some other action." The behavior is not so severe that you are in danger of losing control of the situation, but you think that the administrator should be aware and involved at a lower level of priority than Level 3.

Finally, a staff member might notify the office if he or she thinks the administrator should be aware and have a record of the situation. For example, a student's Level 1 disruptive misbehavior is becoming chronic and neither your proactive efforts nor your corrective consequences have been effective. Even though you don't need help immediately, notifying the principal about the student's behavior and your intervention efforts can help increase the principal's knowledge of what's going on in the school. If an intervention plan becomes necessary, a comprehensive written record of the student's moderate misbehavior can help in the functional analysis of the behavior.

Adult response: A staff member who observes a Level 2 infraction corrects the student at the time or assigns a schoolwide correction (or both) and completes an incident notification form that goes to the administrator (either on paper or through a data management system such as TRENDS).

Coordination between all staff—teachers, paraprofessionals, counselors, deans, and administrators—is essential. Whenever a teacher writes a notification about moderate misbehavior (The students did _____. I handled it by _____. Please advise.), someone must respond quickly (most schools specify by the end of the day).

In Presentation 4 of this module, we provide detailed information for Foundations Teams and administrators on responding to Level 2 notifications and Level 3 incident referrals. For Level 2, we recommend that you identify a dedicated person who will receive the notifications and decide on further actions—provide feedback to the referring staff, contact other staff members, involve parents or outside agencies, and so on.

One of the goals of a Level 2 notification framework is for all staff to know that they should try to handle problems independently in the settings in which they occur, but also that support is available if they think they need it. Notifications are how staff can indicate they need support. It's also important that all staff know that when they take the time to write a Level 2 notification, a professional-level person will review it and provide timely feedback. The notification does not just fall into a black hole.

Define Level 3 infractions.

The 3-level system for responding to misbehavior empowers all staff members to confidently and quickly decide in any situation:

- For this behavior, I must send the student to the office. (Level 3)
- For this behavior, I may send the student to the office and I know I'll get support, or I can handle it on my own if I know I can maintain control of the situation. (Level 2)
- For this behavior, I simply handle it on my own. (Level 1)

We recommend that the following misbehaviors be considered Level 3 (severe) infractions:

Illegal acts involve breaking state or federal laws. Staff members not only may report illegal behavior, they *must* do so.

Physically dangerous acts pose a threat to physical safety. Any physically dangerous act may be considered a Level 3 infraction. However, not all potentially dangerous acts have to be reported as Level 3 infractions—observing staff members should use their discretion. For example, very young children may not understand how much they can hurt others by, say, pulling a chair out from under them. If this happens, but no one is hurt, the teacher can rightfully correct the young student in the classroom and use the incident to teach proper respect for others.

Refusal to follow reasonable adult direction (also known as defiance or insubordination). The student engages in overt and immediate refusal to comply with a reasonable adult direction. Staff might have difficulty defining where to draw the lines between Level 1, Level 2, and Level 3 defiance—sometimes it's a judgment call. In fact, we suggest you do not use the terms *defiance* or *insubordination* as part of Level 3 referrals because those concepts are so broad and open to interpretation. Some staff members might consider it insubordination when a student rolls her eyes in response to a request; however, as frustrating as the student's reaction might be, it should not be treated as a Level 3 misbehavior. We encourage you to call the category of Level 3 severe misbehavior *refusal to follow reasonable adult direction*. Then you can further define the misbehavior by stipulating that staff members need to implement specific steps before the misbehavior rises to a Level 3 referral to the office. For example, refusal to follow reasonable adult direction will be considered a Level 3 infraction only when the direction meets the following conditions:

- *Reasonable.* The direction is clear and observable. Examples of directions that are not clear and observable are "Change your attitude" and "Shape up." Even a phrase like "Take your seat" can be turned into a joke by some students—they'll reply, "Take it where?" Clear directions are "Sit down at your desk" and "Raise your hand if you want to say something."

- *Immediate.* You want the direction carried out in the next minute or so. If you instruct a student to bring her homework the next day and she doesn't, that incident should not be viewed as refusal to follow a reasonable direction. Students can easily forget or get confused about long-term directions.

- *Given three times.* The second time you give the direction, emphasize the seriousness of the student's choice. The third time you give the direction, literally write the direction and the student's inappropriate response on paper (do *not* write on the referral form). This action slows the momentum toward more serious conflict between you and the student, and it usually forces two things to occur that can de-escalate the incident: The time it takes to write gives the student time to think and respond appropriately, and your eye contact with the student is broken. In direct confrontational power struggles, defiant students will not blink first. The act of writing allows you to blink first without backing down. (See the Jot It Down Strategy below.)

Jot It Down Strategy

Here's a scenario that illustrates giving a direction three times and writing the direction and student response the third time. We call this the Jot It Down strategy.

Teacher: Alan, take your seat. (The direction is not clear.)

Alan: Take it where?"

Teacher: Alan, I'm not joking. You need to sit down. You're disturbing people in the lab area.

Alan: I don't have to do anything you say. (One clear direction has been given and the student has refused.)

Teacher: Alan, you need to sit down. If you choose not to, I have to write it up an as act of defiance, which is very serious in this school. Think carefully. Please sit down.

Alan: I don't have to do anything you tell me to do. (Two clear directions have been given and the student has refused both.)

Teacher: I want to be real clear about what's happening here. I said, "Sit down," and you said you won't. I just want to be sure that the vice principal knows what's going on and that I'm interpreting your response correctly." (Begins writing.) "I said, 'You . . . need . . . to . . . sit . . . down,' and you said, 'I . . . don't . . . have . . . to.' Do I understand what's going on here, Alan?

Alan: I was just joking. (Sits down)

In most cases, the student will comply while the teacher is writing. When the student begins to follow directions, the teacher has regained instructional control and should resume teaching immediately. She can address the misbehavior at the end of class.

Teacher: Wow, class, you did a great job in your groups today. Everyone used their time wisely and completed the entire lab assignment. Look around your area and make sure you have all your belongings. Alan, I need to see you for a few minutes after class. (The bell rings.) OK, you are dismissed. See you tomorrow!

The teacher has communicated to everyone that she will address the issue without using instructional time and without humiliating Alan by discussing his potential consequence in front of the class. She might decide to write a Level 2 notification.

Teacher (after class leaves): Alan, because of your actions today, I will be calling your parents and notifying the principal . . .

If Alan had not complied and the incident became a Level 3 office referral, the teacher has written evidence of the reasonable, observable direction that she gave, along with the student's response.

Staff members do not have to follow these steps *every* time a student refuses to follow a direction. But when there's a good possibility that the student will escalate the misbehavior, staff will know what to do to have a good chance of de-escalating the situation. They will also gather evidence of the level of misbehavior if they do need to send the student to the office.

The Jot It Down strategy is very powerful. We've taught it in many schools and have found that in about 90% of incidents, students comply while the teacher is writing.

Along with illegal acts, physically dangerous acts, and refusal to follow reasonable adult direction, you may choose to categorize the following as Level 3 misbehaviors:

- Code of Conduct violations
- Misbehaviors related to district, state, and federal mandates
- Other misbehaviors the administrator believes should be included, such as:
  - Flagrant disrespect
  - Obscene language about or directed toward someone
  - Racial and gender-based teasing
  - Bullying and harassment (note that in most states, bullying and harassment are illegal behaviors)

The above misbehaviors will require some discussion about the definition of a Level 3 offense. In some schools, for example, obscene language is rampant, and if staff sent every student who swore to the office, there would be 300 students in the office every day for obscene language. Some of those incidents need to be handled as Level 1 or 2 offenses, and only the most egregious violations, such as verbally assaultive statements, should rise to Level 3. Staff need to collectively decide where to draw the line.

Does a misguided but light-hearted "Girls can't play soccer" comment constitute harassment? What is bullying, and what is misguided youthful banter? Staff need to know in advance how to make these kinds of judgments so they can properly apply the 3-level system of responding to misbehavior.

Many schools and districts have done great work incorporating the 3-level concept into their disciplinary system. Figure 2a on the next two pages shows a planning document and flowcharts from Fresno Unified School District in California (provided courtesy of Lissa Vasquez, who led the effort to establish a 3-level system in the district). Figure 2b on pp. 45–46 shows an example of three levels of behavior as defined by Wichita High School North in Wichita, Kansas.

Conclusion

If you can handle a situation on your own in the setting in which it occurs, you communicate to the student (and all other students) that you are the authority figure. When you remove a student from the setting and assign a Level 3 office referral, you are saying to the administrator that the misbehavior was severe—it was illegal, it posed a threat to physical safety, or you could have lost control of the situation. You want to use Level 3s reasonably.

The next task, Task 2, explains the process of developing staff agreement for the levels. We walk you through a process for getting recommendations and opinions from staff and then reaching consensus about the definitions of the three levels for your school. A well-designed system can improve your school's climate and culture. Staff will feel empowered, supported, and collegial. Students will miss less instructional time because of fewer referrals to the office. Students who need proactive behavior improvement plans will get the support they need to thrive and reduce future misbehavior.

Figure 2a *Example of 3-level system for responding to misbehavior (D-11); thanks to Alissa Vasquez of Fresno Unified School District (California), Department of Prevention and Intervention*

SCHOOL SAMPLE

Process for defining Levels of Misbehavior at the School Site
(Resource-Foundations Module III Presentations 3 & 4)

1. **First staff meeting**-Safe & Civil Team facilitates whole staff discussion on definitions of mild, moderate and severe levels (use definitions provided in Foundations).

   a. Purpose is to help staff members recognize the need for a team approach to address students with severe/chronic behavior problems.
   b. Present different scenarios about student misbehavior that allow staff members to distinguish between the three levels of behavior.
   c. Ask staff members to spend time before next meeting thinking about specific misbehaviors that should be categorized as a level three.

2. **Second staff meeting**-reaching staff consensus on level three behaviors***

   a. Staff as a whole should define in advance the specific behaviors that will be considered level three infractions-i.e., infractions requiring immediate administrative involvement and written documentation.
      • Misbehaviors that should be considered level three are *illegal acts, physically dangerous acts, acts of defiance.*
      • *Acts of defiance* become level three when the following conditions are met:
         o Direction is clear and observable
         o Direction is immediate
         o Direction is given three times
            ✓ With the second repetition, staff member emphasizes the seriousness of the student's choice
            ✓ Third repetition, staff member writes direction

3. **Third staff meeting**-reaching staff consensus on level one behaviors*** (staff lists what behaviors they feel should be handled in the classroom) Once a list of level one behaviors is developed, staff can also assist in generating a list of level one responses/strategies, which includes the universal base of *a comprehensive classroom management plan, weekly class meetings and weekly social emotional skill lessons.*

   a. Safe & Civil team compiles staff input into levels, behaviors not designated level one or three become level two behaviors. Proposal is developed to take forward to staff.

4. **Fourth staff meeting**-a Safe & Civil team presents a revised proposal for staff to adopt. If proposal is rejected, Safe & Civil team continues process until a proposal is adopted (recommend using consensus building framework for adoption).

   a. Professional learning is provided on the use of Atlas and documenting misbehaviors.

***Meeting structures to gather feedback and reach staff consensus on proposal for levels of misbehavior:
   ❖ Whole staff develops draft proposal -Safe & Civil team facilitating discussion
   ❖ Safe & Civil team develops draft and brings forward to whole staff for feedback
   ❖ Safe & Civil team develops draft and provides to each accountable community to provide feedback

This sample can be printed from the Module D CD.

Figure 2a (continued)

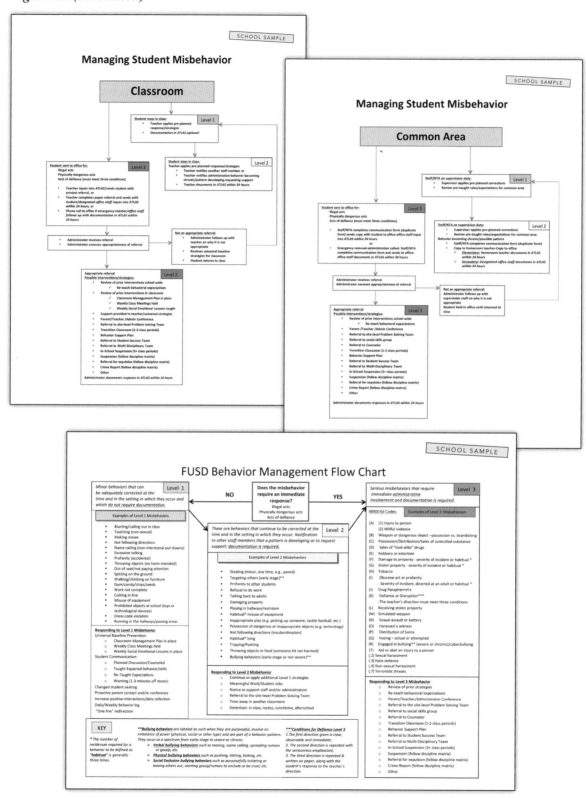

Figure 2b *Example of three levels of behavior definitions (D-12; 4 pages); thanks to Wichita High School North in Wichita, Kansas*

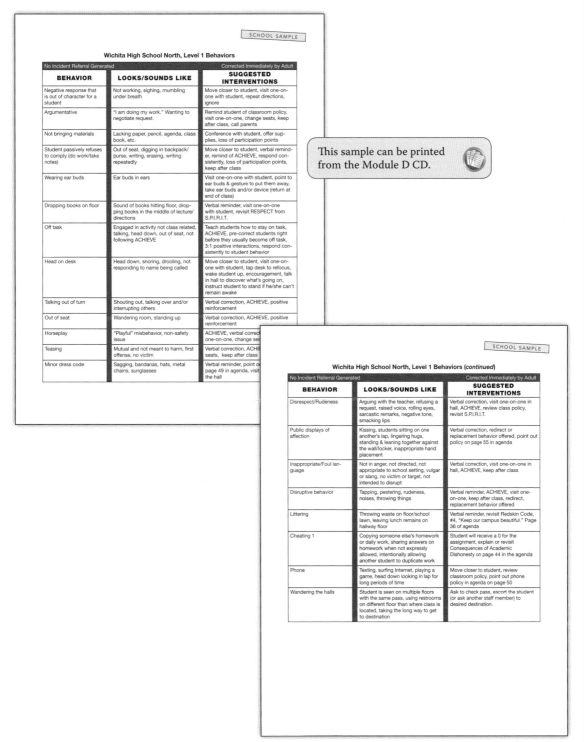

This sample can be printed from the Module D CD.

Figure 2b (continued)

SCHOOL SAMPLE

Wichita High School North, Level 2 Behaviors

No Incident Referral Generated, Parent Contact Is Needed.		Corrected Immediately by Adult
BEHAVIOR	**LOOKS/SOUNDS LIKE**	**SUGGESTED INTERVENTIONS**
Repeated Level 1 behavior	Ignoring a teacher request while continuing to display unwanted behavior.	Give student a choice of two acceptable corrections, call parent with notice of problem and next step when problem persists.
Student stands up and says, "I'm not doing this work."	Student stands during class. Student speaks out of turn, raises voice, perhaps throws a tantrum by dropping objects on the floor.	Remain calm. Restate request with a calm voice. If student still refuses, ask student to step into hall; visit with student to find out what is going on. If this is a frequent occurrence, set up a behavior contract with the student. If the student doesn't change his/her tone in the hall, give him/her the option of returning to class or going to administrator.
Throws material at someone or across room	Items are seen flying through the air. Thrown with intent to harm or in an aggressive manner to distract class. You hear someone ask for a student to stop throwing items. A student approaches a teacher about items being thrown while class is going on.	Teacher picks up items to ensure the safety of students and conferences with student. Restate classroom policy, revisit RESPECT from S.P.I.R.I.T. Contact parent about incident and discuss setting up a behavior contract.
Student routinely uses inappropriate language during class time. Though not directed toward staff or students, student disrupts the learning process.	Use racial, stereotypical, or culturally insensitive words. Talk about inappropriate things and/or make sexual comments. Use sensitive words in an insulting or joking manner, "gay," "fag," etc.	Verbal warning. Hallway discussion. Remove/isolate student. Call or email parent. Contact counselor or administrator.
Physical contact/Safety: arising from horseplay	Aggressive behavior, student safety a concern, student-to-student physical contact made, property damage, "neck," "tap"	Verbal reminder, remind students of Redskin Code of Conduct, change seats if needed, call or email parent about behaviors.
Walks out of classroom	Student leaves academic area without permission.	Ask student to please have a seat, conference in hall, make call to administrator about AWOL student, refer to BIP if applicable, call or email parent about situation.
Cheating 2	Cheating on daily work/homework—second offense. Cheating on test or major assignment	Student will receive 0 on the assignment. Parent will be contacted, and administration will be notified. Student's name will be entered on Tier 2 Honor Code database.
Wandering halls	Repeatedly seen in the halls during instruction time, repeatedly seen on wrong floor to use restroom	Ask to check student's pass[...] back to class (or get anoth[er] member to) ,gather student['s...] so that you can make paren[t...] either by phone or email, dis[...] consequences for repeated [...]

SCHOOL SAMPLE

Wichita High School North, Level 3 Behaviors

Incident Referral Generated	Requires Administrative Action
BEHAVIOR	**LOOKS/SOUNDS LIKE**
General fighting	Aggressive, obvious victim/suspect(s), student-to-student physical contact made, injury occurs
Profanity/Vulgar language	Directed at another student, spoken in anger or derogatory tone, causes a disruption, cursing at a staff member
Threatening speech	Obvious victim/suspect(s), spoken in anger or derogatory tone, causes a disruption, directed at a staff member
Physical contact/Safety: arising from horseplay	Aggressive misbehavior that has been taken to another level (mood changes), student safety a concern, obvious victim/suspect(s), physical contact made, property damage
Bullying	Purposeful behavior that intends to cause harm or distress; is repeated over time; occurs in a relationship where there is an imbalance of power; includes cyberbullying, which is sending or posting harmful text or images using the Internet or other digital media sources
Harassment	Verbal or physical behavior that puts another person down or shows hostility toward another person and group of persons based on their race, color, religion, gender, national origin, age, sexual orientation, or disability
Sexual harassment	Unwanted and unwelcome sexual behavior that interferes with your right to get an education or to participate in school activities; may result from words or conduct of a sexual nature that offend, stigmatize, demean, frighten, or threaten because of gender; may cause the target to feel uncomfortable, embarrassed, or threatened; can happen once or many times
Acting to incite/Verbal escalation to fight	Any language whose intent is to instigate a conflict with an individual or group. Can also be participating in a group whose purpose is to instigate or continue a conflict.
Major disruption to room	Intentional behavior that hinders students' learning and teacher's ability to maintain classroom control.
Gang-like behavior	Graffiti, complex hand gestures or signs and multistep handshakes, bandanas, tagging, referring to sets, folks, etc., any activity deemed by administration as gang related.
Refusing to leave the classroom	Student remains in area and refuses to comply with request to go to academy.
Cheating 3	Repeat offense of any type listed on Level 1 & 2
Cheating 4	Further repeat of any type listed on Level 1 & 2
Gross misbehavior	Extortion, gambling, exploding of fireworks, causing a false fire alarm, carrying or using weapons, drugs, or alcoholic beverages

Task 1 Action Steps & Evidence of Implementation

Action Steps	Evidence of Implementation
1. Arrange for the entire staff to view or read all of Module D, Presentation 2, especially Task 1 about the concept of three levels of misbehavior.	Foundations Process: Presentations/ Communications With Staff
2. Have a team discussion about categorizing student misbehavior into mild, moderate, and severe levels. This discussion (and the activities and questions below) is a preview of the discussion process for the entire staff covered in the next task. Don't try to reach closure on the activities and questions below—you'll do that with the staff. • Present different scenarios about student misbehavior to help team members distinguish between Level 1 and Level 2 infractions. • Discuss team member's thoughts about the specific misbehaviors that should be categorized as Level 3 infractions. • What misbehaviors are *must refer*? (Administrators should relate information about district, state, and federal regulations that affect this decision.) • What misbehaviors are *may refer* (but do not have to be referred)? *Note:* Remind the staff that the more behaviors designated as Level 3 infractions, the less time the administrator will have to deal with each incident. 3. Get input from the administrator on your team about the types of misbehaviors that currently result in office referrals. (Do not mention names, grade levels, or departments.) 4. Anticipate concerns and objections that staff might express. For example, some staff might think that out-of-school suspension is the best way to handle most misbehavior.	Foundations Process: Meeting Minutes

TASK 2

Reach staff consensus on the three levels of misbehavior

It's important that all staff participate in the process of defining the three levels of misbehavior. Staff experience, opinions, and recommendations will be valuable, and they will feel more ownership and allegiance to a system that they helped design. Following are suggested steps for working through the process of categorizing misbehavior into three levels—mild, moderate, and severe. We thank Pat Jernigan of Long Beach Unified School District in California for developing this streamlined process and sharing it with us.

Step 1 (Administrator). During a staff meeting, provide information about the advantages of a 3-level system for responding to misbehavior and the definitions and adult responses for each level. Present different scenarios about student misbehavior to help staff members distinguish between Level 1 and Level 2 infractions. Ask staff members to spend time before the next meeting thinking about specific misbehaviors they believe should be categorized as Level 3 infractions. You might ask staff to review referrals they have written in the previous few months and perhaps even bring the referrals to the next meeting.

Note: Remind the staff that the more behaviors they categorize as Level 3 infractions, the less time the administrator will have to deal with each incident.

Step 2 (Administrator). Gather all available incident referrals to date (or from the previous year) and make a list of all the misbehaviors indicated on the referrals. Do not include student and staff names.

Step 3 (Administrator). Create a handout for staff that lists all the misbehaviors you identified. Alternatively, type the list in a large font, then cut it so that each misbehavior is on a separate strip of paper. Each staff member has a set of these strips. (The strips might be used in Step 5.)

Step 4 (Administrator). Schedule a staff meeting to define three levels of misbehavior. Prepare chart paper or poster board with three columns labeled Mild, Moderate, and Severe. Staff will work in groups of five or six, so prepare one chart or poster for each group.

Step 5 (Administrator). Begin the meeting by reviewing the advantages of a 3-level system for responding to misbehavior and the definitions and adult responses for each level (review Module D, Presentation 1, Task 3). Have staff work in groups for at least 30 minutes. Keep these tips in mind:

- Mix the composition of the groups to prevent groupthink. For example, form vertically aligned groups in elementary schools (representative teachers from each grade in each group) or interdepartmental groups in middle and high schools. The goal is to expand the thinking and encourage discussion among the teachers.

- Include a Foundations Team member in each group, if possible.

- Assign a leader for each group. This might be an administrator or Foundations Team member.

- Provide handouts or a set of strips (see Step 3) and one chart or poster to each group.

Step 6 (Group Leader). Direct your group to think about and discuss in turn each listed misbehavior. Write each misbehavior on the prepared chart or poster in the column (Mild, Moderate, or Severe) where group members think it belongs. If you use paper strips, glue each misbehavior in the column where the group thinks it belongs.

Step 7 (Foundations Team). At the conclusion of the meeting, collect the charts or posters. Thank the teachers for their time and their recommendations.

Step 8 (Foundations Team). Meet to compile the information. Determine which misbehaviors the staff reached consensus on and which need more discussion.

Step 9 (Foundations Team). Report the results to the staff. During a brief (10–15 minutes) staff meeting, discuss the behaviors that the groups did not agree on and attempt to reach consensus.

Step 10 (Foundations Team). Meet again to develop a proposal for three levels of misbehavior.

Step 11 (Foundations Team). Present the proposal to the staff, who will vote to adopt or reject it. If the staff reject the proposal, develop a revised proposal that incorporates staff recommendations. Present the revised proposal for staff adoption or rejection. Continue this process until a proposal is adopted. If consensus is not reached after two additional revision attempts (a total of three voting cycles), the issue should go to the principal, who will develop the final policy. Limiting the number of revisions keeps the Foundations Team from getting stuck endlessly on an issue—neither the team nor the staff has time to waste. Divisive issues are often best resolved by a principal who has the courage to just say, "This is what we are going to do, and here's why."

Step 12. Develop menus of consequences for each level. *This process is discussed in Presentations 3 and 4 of this module.*

Step 13 (Foundations Team). Implement the new system. Document the final decision on the misbehaviors your school considers mild, moderate, and severe. Include this document in the Foundations Archive and the Staff Handbook, along with a menu of consequences for each level.

Communicate the system to students and parents. For example, explain it at a parent-teacher association meeting, during parent conferences, through postings on the school website, and in emails and letters sent home.

Task 2 Action Steps & Evidence of Implementation

Action Steps	Evidence of Implementation
1. At a staff meeting, introduce the 3-level system for responding to misbehavior and review examples to illustrate the differences between the levels.	Foundations Process: Meeting Minutes
2. Gather data on misbehaviors referred to the office in the past and provide to staff.	
3. At a staff meeting, split staff into groups to define the three levels of misbehavior by categorizing the past misbehaviors as Mild, Moderate, or Severe.	
4. Compile the results. Determine which misbehaviors the staff reached consensus on and which need more discussion.	
5. At a staff meeting, briefly discuss the behaviors that staff disagreed on and attempt to reach consensus.	
6. Meet to develop a proposal for a 3-level system of misbehavior.	
7. Present the proposal to the entire staff.	
8. Have the staff adopt or reject the proposal. • If the proposal is rejected, develop a revised proposal that incorporates staff recommendations. • Present the revised proposal for staff adoption or rejection. • Continue the process until a proposal is adopted. After two additional attempts to revise the proposal (a total of three voting cycles), the principal will develop the final policy.	Foundations Archive: 3-Level System for Responding to Misbehavior Staff Handbook: 3-Level System for Responding to Misbehavior

TASK 3

Document and monitor Level 2 and Level 3 misbehaviors

To collect useful data, you need to link data collection processes to your 3-level system for responding to misbehavior. One important data source is simply the number of student misbehavior incidents. For example, compare year-to-date consequences that required students to miss instructional time. Figure 2c shows data from a real middle school that is implementing *Foundations*. Because this school staff designed their 3-level system and their reporting system to coordinate well, the data show great progress in keeping students in class. This school uses four consequences that may result in students missing class. The year-to-date data show that:

- In-school (class period) suspensions decreased from 9 to 4.
- Out-of-school suspensions decreased from 17 to 8.
- In-school suspensions decreased from 24 to 9.
- Office disciplinary referrals decreased from 63 to 39.

Some schools successfully reduce out-of-school suspension only to see dramatic increases in in-school suspension—at least students are not vacationing at home, but they are not in class either. Your school should work to reduce all incidents and consequences that result in loss of instructional time.

Figure 2c *Data from a* Foundations *middle school shows reductions in suspensions and office referrals*

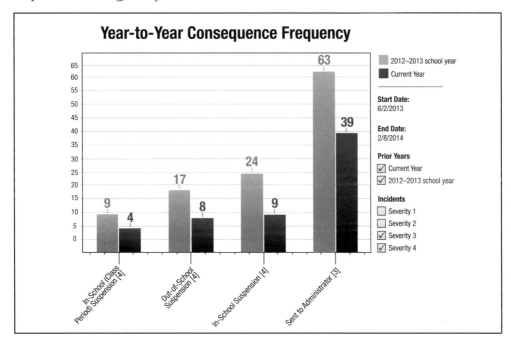

Also plan to analyze your referrals (Level 3) and notifications (Level 2) separately. If the Level 3 numbers are decreasing while Level 2 notifications are increasing, you can interpret this positively—teachers, administrators, counselors, and school psychologists are coordinating and communicating about student misbehavior *before* it reaches Level 3, and students are missing less instructional time as a result.

Develop forms for documenting Level 2 and Level 3 infractions.

An important data collection tool is the form a teacher completes to document student misbehavior. We provide two examples on the CD. The form for Level 2 infractions is called Behavior Incident Notification Form (Form D-03 shown in Figure 2d), and the form for Level 3 is called Behavior Incident Referral Form (Form D-04). A completed sample is shown in Figure 2e on pp. 54–55). Some schools combine the two levels onto one form and include a place to indicate the level of the misbehavior. Also note that some schools must use forms mandated by the district or state for misbehaviors that correspond to Level 3. If this is the case in your school, plan to design a parallel form to use for your Level 2 notifications.

You have probably heard the saying about data—"garbage in, garbage out." In other words, the quality of the charts and reports you will analyze later in the year depends on the quality of the data that you enter into the database now. Consequently, carefully design the forms that teachers will complete (either online or on paper). Ask, What information do we need to enable meaningful analyses later?

With input and approval from staff, the team must decide whether to use a data management system (such as TRENDS or SWIS) or a spreadsheet program (such as Excel). Also determine whether staff will use paper forms, online forms, or both. Another consideration mentioned earlier is whether to use separate forms for Level 3 incident referrals and Level 2 notifications or to combine the levels on one form.

If you create your own forms, carefully consider what data to collect, keeping in mind their relation to the analyses you will want to conduct. At the least, include this information:

- Location (classroom, hallway, restroom, and so on)
- Type of offense (the behavior the student exhibited)
- Time of day or period
- Day of week
- Corrective action taken (both immediately and previously for similar problems)
- Hypothesis about the function of the misbehavior (attention seeking, avoidance, and so on)

Figure 2d   *Sample Behavior Incident Notification Form (D-03)*

Behavior Incident Notification Form
(Level 2 only)

Student Name: _____   Gender: F / M   Period/Time of Day: _____

Referring Adult: _____   Grade: _____   Date: _____

Location (if classroom, indicate subject): _____

MODERATE (Level 2, paper goes to office)

❑ Chronic misbehavior (e.g., late to class, late or no homework or classwork, disruption)
❑ Not following direction (but eventually complies)
❑ Disrespect to an adult (low-level)
❑ Name calling, put-downs, or mild behavior that might be gender- or race-based
❑ Other _____

Description of problem/situation: _____
_____
_____

Functional hypothesis/contributing factors:

- Lack of: awareness ___   ability ___
- Gain attention from: adults ___   peers ___
- Get desired: items ___   activities ___   power/control ___
- Avoid or escape: activities ___   tasks ___   attention ___
- Avoid or escape: adults ___   peers ___
- Relieve: anxiety ___   stress ___
- Other or function unknown ___

Immediate actions taken by referring adult:

❑ Used a one-liner (e.g., "That is not OK. Keep your hands to yourself.")
❑ Instructional/verbal correction (e.g., for minor disrespect)
❑ Stated that you will follow up ("We'll talk later.")
❑ Off-limits or otherwise restricted activity
❑ Had student stay with supervisor

❑ Problem-solving room
❑ Detention (When: ___
❑ Parental contact
❑ Had student demonstra
   (positive practice)
❑ Restitution
❑ Other _____

Previous actions taken by referring adult for similar behavior (include dat
_____
_____
_____

Action taken by administrator: _____
_____
_____
_____

How did the student disregard the Guidelines for Success? (Check at least one and briefly describe.)

❑ Always try.
_____
_____

❑ Do your best.
_____
_____

❑ Cooperate with others.
_____
_____

❑ Treat everyone with respect.
_____
_____

I understand how my behavior did not comply with [*Kennedy Middle School*]'s Guidelines for Success.

Student signature _____

    This form can be printed from the Module D CD.

Figure 2e   *Sample Behavior Incident Referral Form (D-04)*

Behavior Incident Referral Form
(Level 3 only)

Student Name: __Susan Jones__   Gender: (F) M   Period/Time of Day: __3rd__

Referring Adult: _____   Grade: _7_   Date: __11/14__

Location (if classroom, indicate subject): __Science lab__

SEVERE (Level 3, student goes to office)	
☐ Illegal (e.g., threats, weapons, drugs, assault)	☐ Code of Conduct violation
☐ Physically dangerous	☐ Violation of district, state, or federal mandate
☐ Not following direction (even when direction is written)	☐ Gender- or race-based teasing
☐ Flagrant disrespect	☐ Bullying or harassment
☒ Obscene language directed toward staff	☒ Other: __threatening, property destruction__

Description of problem/situation: __Susan was poking the ends of scissors into the desk and__ __digging holes in the desktop. I told her to stop, and she refused. I repeated the direction and she__ __pointed the scissors at me, saying, "Just try and make me," with an angry expression and tone.__

Functional hypothesis/contributing factors:

- Lack of: awareness ___   ability ___
- Gain attention from: adults _X_   peers _X_
- Get desired: items ___   activities ___   power/control _X_
- Avoid or escape: activities ___   tasks ___   attention ___
- Avoid or escape: adults ___   peers ___
- Relieve: anxiety ___   stress ___
- Other or function unknown ___

Immediate actions taken by referring adult:

☐ Used a one-liner (e.g., "That is not OK. Keep your hands to yourself.")	☐ Problem-solving room
	☐ Detention (When: _____)
☐ Instructional/verbal correction (e.g., for minor disrespect)	☐ Parental contact
☐ Stated that you will follow up ("We'll talk later.")	☐ Had student demonstrate or practice the rule (positive practice)
☐ Off-limits or otherwise restricted activity	☐ Restitution
☐ Had student stay with supervisor	☒ Other __Called for administrative removal__

Previous actions taken by referring adult for similar behavior (include dates when possible): _____

__Resitution, parental contact, discussion__

_____

_____

 This form can be printed from the Module D CD.

Figure 2e (continued)

Action taken by administrator: _____

_____

_____

_____

How did the student disregard the Guidelines for Success? (Check at least one and briefly describe.)

❑ Always try.

_____

_____

❑ Do your best.

_____

_____

❑ Cooperate with others.

_____

_____

☒ Treat everyone with respect.

   Susan's behavior caused destruction of property that is shared by others. Her words
   and actions toward me were threatening.

I understand how my behavior did not comply with [*Kennedy Middle School*]'s Guidelines for Success.

Student signature _____

The forms should reflect staff agreements about the categories of misbehaviors and corrective consequences. Following are some important fields to include:

- A place to indicate the type of incident and, if you use just one form, whether it is a Level 2 or Level 3 infraction

- A list of the agreed-upon Level 3 infractions

- A place to indicate the reporting staff member's action taken in response to a Level 2 infraction, both immediately and previously for similar behavior

- A place to indicate administrative action taken in response to a Level 3 infraction (so staff and others can see on the completed form what the administrator did)

- (*Optional*) The school's Guidelines for Success (so the reporting staff member can indicate which guideline should be emphasized during discussions with the student)

Some online behavior data management systems allow staff to enter incidents directly into the database. When the student is referred to the office, the administrator can add a record of his or her actions and comments to the online incident record. A paper form is not necessary when using this kind of system, although some staff might find it easier to fill out paper forms. In these cases, data entry personnel can enter the staff member's report later. Like the paper form, the electronic form should match your definitions of Level 2 and 3 incidents.

Figure 2f on the next page shows examples of referral forms available in the TRENDS online data management system. Notice that you can include information about functional hypothesis and location on these forms. Because TRENDS offers users the ability to write positive reports (Commendations) and report behaviors that are not infractions but are nonetheless worrisome (Concerns), those categories are also included on the form. The forms align with the database, so it is easy for data entry personnel to enter the information for staff members who do not wish to enter it themselves.

Also consider who, in addition to the administrator and the reporting staff member, should receive copies of the form or have access to the record in your database. You might decide that the student's homeroom teacher, parents, or another staff member who works with the student should have a copy.

When you have a draft form ready, have a few staff members field-test it for a couple of weeks before you submit it to the entire staff for adoption. Use the testers' suggestions to modify the form, as necessary. Once it's adopted, ensure that all staff members receive training in when and how to use the form.

Figure 2f *Example of TRENDS referral forms (D-05)*

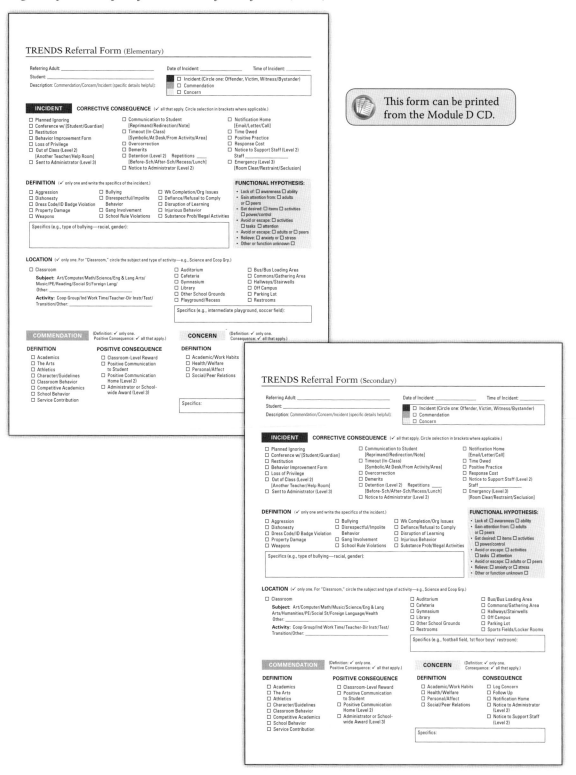

Staff should understand the importance of using correct spelling and grammar and objective language on the referral forms. We discuss in detail how to write effective and appropriate referrals in Module D, Presentation 3, Task 3.

Emphasize staff communication through incident referral and notification forms.

Much of the frustration that school staff experience is a result of breakdowns in communication. Using your incident referral and notification forms consistently and properly will help keep the lines of communication open between the office and staff. Consider the following guidelines for the use of incident referral and notification forms:

- The administrator should deal with Level 3 incidents as soon as possible. In some schools we've worked with, administrators were so deluged with referrals that there was a 2-week delay between the time a student was sent to the office and the time the administrator spoke with the student and assigned a consequence. That's not an effective way to handle Level 3 incidents!

- The administrator should advise reporting staff members of the actions he or she took in response to Level 3 incidents. It's important for staff to know that the administrator took action—this emphasizes the idea that all staff, including administrators, are working collaboratively to improve student behavior in the school.

- The notification reviewer (a staff role we discuss in Module D, Presentation 4), who might be the school counselor, should review Level 2 incident notification forms as soon as reasonable (the same day) and follow through with the reporting staff members and with further actions, as needed.

- Staff members should feel comfortable suggesting to administration that repeated Level 2 incidents that involve the same student represent a chronic problem that requires staff to collaborate on a behavior improvement plan for the student. For example, let's say a teacher has written a Level 2 notification for the same student and the same behavior every day for 2 weeks. Even though she dealt with the behavior adequately in the classroom, she and the administrator should recognize that the student needs a proactive plan to reduce the behavior. (Find more information about dealing with chronic behavior problems in Module F, Presentations 4, 5, and 6.)

- Decide in advance whether the notification reviewer will, as standard procedure, give a copy of Level 2 notifications to students' homeroom teachers (when the notifications were written by other staff, such as a paraprofessional or the math teacher). Most elementary schools will probably choose to follow this procedure. The question is slightly more complex for secondary schools. You may wish to have copies go to advisory teachers, but there is no right or wrong answer. Just ensure that you consider the pros and cons of doing so, decide on a standard procedure, and follow through.

Use a computer-based data management system efficiently.

Enter the information from Level 2 and Level 3 forms into a database such as TRENDS, or have staff members enter the information directly into the database instead of on the paper form. Ensure that the two categories of incidents can be analyzed separately. A dedicated data entry person who works in the front office can transfer the information from the paper forms into the database. See "TRENDS Online Data Management System" below for more information. TRENDS is also covered in Module A, Presentation 4, or you can visit pacificnwpublish.com/products/TRENDS.

TRENDS Online Data Management System

TRENDS—Tracking Referrals, Encouragements, Notifications, Discipline, and Safety—is a behavioral data management system that allows all staff members access to the system. Staff can also create feedback loops through the system. For example, a teacher can write a Level 2 behavior incident record and include a "Notice to Administrator" with the record. As soon as she submits the record, it appears on the administrator's TRENDS home page (optionally, the administrator also receives an email alert). The administrator can then add comments to the record, send a message back to the teacher, or simply read and close the record. It is added to the student's history and securely archived. The teacher can access the record at any time.

TRENDS is configurable, so you can create menus of misbehaviors and Level 1, 2, 3, and 4 consequences that match what your school uses. (Level 4 consequences in TRENDS typically include expulsion, alternative placement, and police liaison referral, for example.) You can also associate staff members with particular students so that staff can access all Level 2 and 3 records for students they work with.

The Foundations Team should review summaries of incident referrals and notifications quarterly. Examine the data for trends and patterns, and identify and evaluate your improvement priorities. (Module A, Presentation 3, Task 1 provides information about quarterly reviews and Module A, Presentation 4 provides information about analyzing data.)

Note to administrators: It's important to present data about referrals and notifications to the team and staff so they can see broad trends and patterns, but don't include summary data on individual teachers or students in these presentations.

Task 3 Action Steps & Evidence of Implementation

Action Steps	Evidence of Implementation
1. Develop a behavior incident referral form (or two forms—one for Level 2, one for Level 3) that reflects staff agreement on the levels of student misbehavior—in particular, the misbehaviors considered Level 3 infractions. Have a few staff members field-test the form. If needed, modify the form based on field-test feedback. 2. Present the new incident referral form to the entire staff for adoption or rejection.	Foundations Process: 3-Level System for Responding to Misbehavior
3. When staff have adopted the incident form, print and distribute copies. Provide training to staff on how to complete the form appropriately.	Foundations Archive: 3-Level System for Responding to Misbehavior Staff Handbook: 3-Level System for Responding to Misbehavior
4. Consider purchasing a computer-based data management system where information from the forms can be entered and archived. As an alternative to paper forms, train staff to enter incident information into the database. See Module A, Presentation 4 for more information on establishing and maintaining a database of incident referral and notification information.	Foundations Process: Meeting Minutes

Staff Responsibilities for Responding to Misbehavior

CONTENTS

Introduction

Task 1: Define Corrective Techniques for Mild Misbehavior

For the Foundations Team or task force working on this task, and possibly the entire staff

---

Task 2: Define Corrective Techniques for Moderate Misbehavior

For the Foundations Team or task force working on this task, and possibly the entire staff

---

Task 3: Write Effective and Appropriate Referrals for Severe Misbehavior

For the Foundations Team or task force working on this task, and possibly the entire staff

DOCUMENTS*

- Behavior Counting Form (D-06)
- Family Contact for Early-Stage Problems (D-08)
- Behavior Improvement Form (D-10a)
- Corrective Procedures for Mild and Moderate Classroom Misbehavior (D-07)
- Sample Foundations Archive Entry [on Correcting Misbehavior] (D-14)
- Sample Staff Handbook Entry [on Correcting Misbehavior] (D-13)

* All documents listed are available on the CD. Other documents that are not shown in this presentation are also available on the CD (see Appendix C for a complete list).

INTRODUCTION

This presentation continues the discussion we began in Presentation 2 about creating a plan for dealing with student misbehavior. An agreed-upon schoolwide plan improves the consistency and effectiveness of staff disciplinary practices and increases staff cooperation and communication about discipline issues.

In the previous presentation, we discussed how to create the basic 3-level structure for dealing with student misbehavior. In this presentation, we discuss the roles and responsibilities of staff members (who does what, when) when responding to mild, moderate, and severe misbehavior. In the next presentation, we discuss ways to ensure that schoolwide systems are in place to support students with moderate and severe misbehavior and the staff who deal with them. We also discuss the role of administrators in the office referral process.

The Foundations Team or a special task force should lead the effort to define the options for responding to student misbehavior. As with other aspects of the *Foundations* improvement process, the team or task force should try to save time for the entire staff by representing them—giving them a voice in the decision-making process. You might have the staff view or read this entire presentation so they understand the rationale for our suggested corrective techniques and procedures.

At this point, the staff should have agreed on the misbehaviors that *must* be considered severe and result in office referral and the misbehaviors that *can* be sent to the office based on the staff member's judgment. The Foundations Team (or special task force) will use recommendations from the next two tasks, data on consequences (What works to reduce misbehavior? What doesn't work?), and existing corrective procedures to develop a proposal for Level 1 and Level 2 menus of corrective consequences. The team will then guide the proposal through the adoption process and revise it as needed based on staff suggestions. They will then follow through with all aspects of implementing the adopted procedures.

Task 1: Define Corrective Techniques for Mild Misbehavior explains why and how to create menus of corrections and responses for Level 1 student misbehavior and provides examples of appropriate Level 1 corrections.

Task 2: Define Corrective Techniques for Moderate Misbehavior discusses procedures for dealing with Level 2 student misbehavior and provides examples of appropriate Level 2 corrections.

Task 3: Write Effective and Appropriate Referrals for Severe Misbehavior offers suggestions for writing office referral and notification forms and explains why well-written forms are important.

TASK 1

Define corrective techniques for mild misbehavior

After a brief review of Level 1 infractions, this task guides you through the creation of menus of appropriate corrections for and responses to Level 1 misbehavior. Sample menus of corrections for classrooms and common areas are provided to assist you. Once completed, your menus must be documented so that staff has easy access to them.

What are Level 1 infractions?

As we stated in the previous presentation, Level 1 infractions are misbehaviors that observing staff members can adequately correct in the setting in which they occur. The observing staff member should not expect any other staff member to take additional action.

A misbehavior should be treated as Level 2 any time one or more of the following actions occur:

- The staff member assigns a schoolwide correction that involves other staff members (after-school detention or problem-solving room, for example).

- The staff member wants or needs administrative suggestions or clarification about the situation.

- The staff member believes the administrator should be aware of the situation.

Create menus of appropriate corrections and responses to Level 1 misbehavior.

We suggest that you develop two Level 1 menus, one for classroom corrections and one for common area corrections. The menus should include a range of reasonable consequences that all staff agree are appropriate for mild misbehavior. The purpose of a menu is *not* to tell staff "you must use this consequence for this behavior." Rather, it gives staff flexibility to respond as they see fit within the parameters of an administrator-backed policy.

Administrative backing for the corrections and responses is important to assure staff members of support if parents or students object to a consequence. Let's say a teacher thinks that assigning a student to write lines (write "I will not throw spitballs" 300 times, for example) is an appropriate consequence. If the administrator disagrees (and possibly is unaware that the teacher uses the consequence), she will have difficulty supporting that teacher if the student's family complains, and she will have to correct the teacher and possibly review the teacher's other corrective techniques. Neither the teacher nor administrator wants to go through that scenario.

The discussions you'll have as you plan the menu of Level 1 corrections will also serve to reveal and weed out the consequences the school and the administrator cannot support. Because all staff members are part of the process of defining the corrections, they will know that they should not implement any corrections that are not on the approved menus.

So, to ensure administrative support for actions taken by staff, follow these guidelines for Level 1 menu items.

- Include only corrections and responses that are supported by the administrative staff.

- Do not include corrections and responses that can be assigned *only* by administrative staff (suspension, for example).

- Do not include corrections and responses that involve academic behavior (writing lines uses handwriting as a punishment, for example).

- Do not include corrections and responses that are intentionally humiliating.

View a sample menu of Level 1 classroom corrections.

The following corrections are time tested and effective for responding to mild misbehavior in the classroom. Note that in the early stages of misbehavior, corrections should include information—that is, provide instruction about the rule the student is breaking and how to follow it. If the misbehavior continues, move on to using corrective consequences. More detailed information about classroom corrections is available in the following references:

- Sprick, R. (2009). *CHAMPS: A proactive & positive approach to classroom management* (2nd ed.). Eugene, OR: Pacific Northwest.

- Sprick, R. (2012). *Teacher's encyclopedia of behavior management: 100+ problems/500+ plans* (2nd ed.). Eugene, OR: Pacific Northwest.

- Sprick, R. (2014). *Discipline in the secondary classroom: A positive approach to behavior management* (3rd ed.). San Francisco: Jossey-Bass.

Nonverbal correction. You might place a finger to your lips to indicate quiet (but don't say "Shhh"), give a hand signal to indicate sit down, or subtly shake your head to indicate no. These are simple gestures that address the misbehavior without requiring a verbal response from the student. (Nonverbal correction is sometimes called *paraverbal response*.)

Gentle verbal reprimand. Stand close to the student, but don't invade her personal space or stand directly in front of her in a confrontational stance. In a calm, quiet voice, state the positive expectation and tell the student what she should start doing. Avoid telling the student what to *stop* doing, and avoid asking questions such as, "What are you supposed to be doing?" Do not call attention to the student and the misbehavior. Keep the reprimand brief and don't invite debate.

Avoid approaching the student from behind; students who have been victims of abuse may become anxious or react negatively.

Research shows that gentle verbal reprimands, when used consistently, are effective in correcting a wide range of misbehavior.

Proximity correction. Move slowly toward the student who is misbehaving. This prompts the student to stop the misbehavior and act appropriately. Avoid making eye contact with the student. As you approach, you might interact positively with other students—"Your handwriting is really improving, Robert. Kayaba, let me know if you need any help." Stand near the student until he realizes he has to change his behavior, then move away. A few seconds later, you can return and praise the student for resuming work.

If the student asks why you are standing nearby, explain proximity correction—your presence should prompt him to think about whether he is following the expectations for the current activity.

Humor. Humor can be a powerful and effective way to respond to misbehavior, especially with older students. A quick-witted teacher might be able to respond to a student's smart-aleck comment in a way that makes the student laugh and diffuses a tense moment. But please note that you should not use sarcasm or ridicule. The sensitive use of humor brings people closer together. Sarcasm or ridicule makes a student feel hostile and angry that you made a joke at his expense.

The word *sarcasm* derives from the French word *sarkazein*, which means "to tear flesh." *Merriam-Webster's Collegiate Dictionary* (11th ed.) defines sarcasm as "a sharp and often satirical or ironic utterance designed to cut or give pain." Sarcasm can hurt, so we recommend you avoid using it with your students.

❧ FOUNDATIONS RECOMMENDATION ☙

Do not use sarcasm or ridicule as a response to misbehavior. Sarcasm and ridicule can make a student feel hostile and angry that you made a joke at his expense. However, the sensitive use of humor can bring people closer together.

If you do use humor in response to misbehavior, plan on talking to the student later to make sure that he understands his behavior was not acceptable and that he knows you expect him to behave more responsibly in the future. Check to see that you did not embarrass the student with your humorous comment.

*E*xample From the Field

A high school English teacher told me this story, a wonderful example of how humor can disarm a hostile student. This teacher is, by his own admission, generously proportioned as well as vertically challenged. A student who had just been released from juvenile detention joined his class. This student had been arrested numerous times for assault, including one instance when he broke a teacher's arm. The six-foot-four, all-muscle student was well behaved the first couple of days. On day three, however, the student came to class in a mood. The pent-up rage was obvious. The student began pacing the back of the classroom. The teacher tried a verbal reprimand: "Al, please sit down so you don't disturb the other students." With clenched fists, Al began to walk up the aisle toward the teacher, saying, "You fat f---! I don't have to do anything you tell me to do!" In this potentially dangerous situation, the teacher had the presence of mind to say mildly, "Do you really think I'm fat?" The student stopped his march toward the teacher, looked at the other students, and said, "Look at him. He *is* fat." The teacher also looked at the class and said, "My goodness, why have none of you told me this before? I'll think about dieting. Al, you think about sitting." And the student sat down.

This teacher neutralized a situation that was by all rights a Level 3 immediate removal to the office by using self-deprecating humor, and he managed to turn the class's attention from Al to himself, giving the student a chance to save face. The teacher talked with Al after class and explained that he wouldn't report the incident this time, but he also wouldn't tolerate that kind of behavior again. He expressed confidence that the student could do well in his class.

When this teacher related the story to me, about 6 weeks had gone by since the incident. He said that Al was doing well in his class and had even begun to stop by the teacher's classroom after school to talk. The teacher has become a mentor to this student who was once so threatening.   —R.S.

Frequency count. If you've already discussed the problem behavior with the student but have seen no improvement, explain to the student that you are going to conduct a frequency count to help her understand just how often she is misbehaving. Record the number of times the misbehavior occurs by writing tally marks on a recording sheet. Give the student a signal every time you record an instance, or have the student do the recording when you signal. Tell the student you will use the data to determine her progress and whether you need to talk with her parents or involve an administrator.

You can also use this technique in a class situation, when many students exhibit the same minor misbehavior, such as sarcasm toward other students. Each time a student displays the misbehavior you would like to reduce—name calling, for example—write a tally mark on the recording sheet. (Don't record individual names.) Graph the results each day so students can see whether their behavior is improving.

You can use a form like the Behavior Counting Form (Form D-06) to record frequency. See Figure 3a on the next page for an example.

Family contact. Communication between a student's family and school may increase the effectiveness of behavioral supports provided at school and promote the maintenance of positive behavior over time. Parents often have additional insight into their child's behavior and can support the child's success at school.

Provide an objective description of the problem behavior and offer suggestions for what the parents can do to help the student, such as talk with him. Do not say anything that suggests the parents should punish the child. Be sure to call the parents again when the student is doing better to report his success.

A family contact worksheet like the one illustrated in Figure 3b on p. 69 (Form D-08) can help ensure that you give and receive all the necessary information efficiently, and it prompts you to take notes about the conversation for the student's records. Prepare the worksheet before you make the telephone call so the call can be focused and as brief as possible. Some teachers contact families during dinnertime: "I'm so sorry to bother you during the dinner hour. I'm sure your dinner is about ready—so is mine—so I don't want to take too much of your time. I'm calling about Karen . . ." This preface clarifies that you are not initiating a family conference, just a brief family contact.

Discussion. Sometimes a reprimand isn't enough—you need to discuss the misbehavior in more detail with the student. For example, if the student is disrespectful, you might want to discuss the importance of treating others with respect. Provide a gentle reprimand immediately and tell the student that the behavior is serious enough that you need to discuss it later, after class.

Figure 3a   Behavior Counting Form (D-06)

Behavior Counting Form

Student: _____   Grade/Class: _____
Teacher: _____   Week of: _____

Monday	① ② ③ ④ ⑤ ⑥ ⑦ ⑧ ⑨ ⑩ ⑪ ⑫ ⑬ ⑭ ⑮ ⑯ ⑰ ⑱ ⑲ ⑳ ㉑ ㉒ ㉓ ㉔ ㉕
Tuesday	① ② ③ ④ ⑤ ⑥ ⑦ ⑧ ⑨ ⑩ ⑪ ⑫ ⑬ ⑭ ⑮ ⑯ ⑰ ⑱ ⑲ ⑳ ㉑ ㉒ ㉓ ㉔ ㉕
Wednesday	① ② ③ ④ ⑤ ⑥ ⑦ ⑧ ⑨ ⑩ ⑪ ⑫ ⑬ ⑭ ⑮ ⑯ ⑰ ⑱ ⑲ ⑳ ㉑ ㉒ ㉓ ㉔ ㉕
Thursday	① ② ③ ④ ⑤ ⑥ ⑦ ⑧ ⑨ ⑩ ⑪ ⑫ ⑬ ⑭ ⑮ ⑯ ⑰ ⑱ ⑲ ⑳ ㉑ ㉒ ㉓ ㉔ ㉕
Friday	① ② ③ ④ ⑤ ⑥ ⑦ ⑧ ⑨ ⑩ ⑪ ⑫ ⑬ ⑭ ⑮ ⑯ ⑰ ⑱ ⑲ ⑳ ㉑ ㉒ ㉓ ㉔ ㉕

Monday	① ② ③ ④ ⑤ ⑥ ⑦ ⑧ ⑨ ⑩ ⑪ ⑫ ⑬ ⑭ ⑮ ⑯ ⑰ ⑱ ⑲ ⑳ ㉑ ㉒ ㉓ ㉔ ㉕
Tuesday	① ② ③ ④ ⑤ ⑥ ⑦ ⑧ ⑨ ⑩ ⑪ ⑫ ⑬ ⑭ ⑮ ⑯ ⑰ ⑱ ⑲ ⑳ ㉑ ㉒ ㉓ ㉔ ㉕
Wednesday	① ② ③ ④ ⑤ ⑥ ⑦ ⑧ ⑨ ⑩ ⑪ ⑫ ⑬ ⑭ ⑮ ⑯ ⑰ ⑱ ⑲ ⑳ ㉑ ㉒ ㉓ ㉔ ㉕
Thursday	① ② ③ ④ ⑤ ⑥ ⑦ ⑧ ⑨ ⑩ ⑪ ⑫ ⑬ ⑭ ⑮ ⑯ ⑰ ⑱ ⑲ ⑳ ㉑ ㉒ ㉓ ㉔ ㉕
Friday	① ② ③ ④ ⑤ ⑥ ⑦ ⑧ ⑨ ⑩ ⑪ ⑫ ⑬ ⑭ ⑮ ⑯ ⑰ ⑱ ⑲ ⑳ ㉑ ㉒ ㉓ ㉔ ㉕

Monday	① ② ③ ④ ⑤ ⑥ ⑦ ⑧ ⑨ ⑩ ⑪ ⑫ ⑬ ⑭ ⑮ ⑯ ⑰ ⑱ ⑲ ⑳ ㉑ ㉒ ㉓ ㉔ ㉕
Tuesday	① ② ③ ④ ⑤ ⑥ ⑦ ⑧ ⑨ ⑩ ⑪ ⑫ ⑬ ⑭ ⑮ ⑯ ⑰ ⑱ ⑲ ⑳ ㉑ ㉒ ㉓ ㉔ ㉕
Wednesday	① ② ③ ④ ⑤ ⑥ ⑦ ⑧ ⑨ ⑩ ⑪ ⑫ ⑬ ⑭ ⑮ ⑯ ⑰ ⑱ ⑲ ⑳ ㉑ ㉒ ㉓ ㉔ ㉕
Thursday	① ② ③ ④ ⑤ ⑥ ⑦ ⑧ ⑨ ⑩ ⑪ ⑫ ⑬ ⑭ ⑮ ⑯ ⑰ ⑱ ⑲ ⑳ ㉑ ㉒ ㉓ ㉔ ㉕
Friday	① ② ③ ④ ⑤ ⑥ ⑦ ⑧ ⑨ ⑩ ⑪ ⑫ ⑬ ⑭ ⑮ ⑯ ⑰ ⑱ ⑲ ⑳ ㉑ ㉒ ㉓ ㉔ ㉕

 This form can be printed from the Module D CD.

Family Contact for Early-Stage Problems

1. Introduce yourself and provide an appropriate greeting:

2. Inform the family that you are calling about a problem:

3. Describe the problem (avoid labeling or passing judgment on the child):

4. Describe why the behavior is a problem (keep the focus on the student, not on yourself or the other students). Emphasize that you know the student can be successful:

5. If appropriate, ask whether the family has any insight into why the behavior may be occurring. If they share with you, adjust the remainder of this call based on what you learn:

6. Make suggestions about how the family might help the child:

Date of this contact:

Notes on the contact:

This form can be printed from the Module D CD.

Talk with the student at a neutral time, such as after class or during an independent work period. A discussion right after the misbehavior occurs tends to give the student too much attention and power, and you are likely to be frustrated or angry. Make sure the discussion is respectful, and talk about better ways the student can handle similar situations in the future.

Bumpy bunny timeout (pre-K to second grade). This timeout is for prekindergarten and kindergarten students. Invite students to bring toys from home (or choose toys from the classroom) and display the toys on a bookshelf. Each student should have one toy. Create a timeout area on the bookshelf with colored tape. If a student misbehaves, place his toy in the timeout area for 3–5 minutes during recess or the next play break. While the toy is in timeout, the student must sit at his desk instead of participating in recess or play break. For multiple infractions, the time can accumulate toward a longer timeout period during the next recess or play break (from *The Tough Kid Book* by Ginger Rhode, Bill Jenson, and Ken Reavis, 2010, Pacific Northwest Publishing, Eugene, OR).

Here's a variation on the bumpy bunny timeout: Have the student bring a stuffed animal to class. The toy can sit on the student's desk as long as the student is behaving appropriately. If the student misbehaves, remove the animal from the desk and set it on a nearby shelf or table with its back toward the student. Tell the student that the animal is learning to behave, so it can't watch the student misbehave. When the student's behavior improves, return the animal to the student.

Timeout at the student's desk (elementary). Ask the student to put her head down on her desk and close her eyes for a short period—1 or 2 minutes, for example. The student should have no access to reinforcing events (participation or conversation) or objects (games or books, for example).

Timeout at a designated timeout area. Establish a timeout area in a low-traffic (but visible to you) area of the classroom. The timeout area should not be used for other purposes and should not provide the student with access to reinforcing stimuli. Do not have the student work on academic tasks while in timeout. Send the student to the timeout area each time the student misbehaves. For primary students, a 2- or 3-minute timeout is best. For intermediate, middle, and high school students, 5 minutes is optimal. (At the secondary level, you might call the timeout area the "attitude adjustment area.")

Timeout in another teacher's room. (This procedure requires Level 2 notification.) Work in partnership with another teacher to provide a location and supervision for misbehaving students. Send the misbehaving student to your partner teacher's room, where the student sits at a prearranged location in a low-traffic area. The class needs to be taught to ignore the student in timeout. This strategy is most effective when the other class is at a different grade level. The classroom must be nearby so you can stand at your doorway and monitor the student until the student has entered the partner teacher's room. During the timeout, the student may complete a Behavior Improvement Form (see Figure 3c). The partner teacher sends the student back to your classroom when the predetermined timeout period—usually 5 to 15 minutes—is over. The partner teacher monitors the student's travel back to your classroom.

Timeout partners should agree on their use of this consequence—for example:

- How long should students stay in the partner teacher's room?
- How often can teachers send students?
- How many students can be sent at one time or during a day's time?
- Should certain times be avoided?

Keep data on your use of this consequence so you can assess its effectiveness. Track assigned students, frequency, length of time in setting, and so on. Remember that the student is missing instruction while he is in the other classroom. Be sure to think about how many times a student can go to another teacher's room before a different consequence or intervention should be implemented. This procedure requires Level 2 notification, so if it is used frequently for an individual student, additional support and problem solving should be triggered.

Each quarter or semester, discuss with your partner whether this consequence is effective and whether any modifications to your timeout plan are needed.

Time owed. For each incident of misbehavior, the student loses a short amount of time from an activity the student values—recess or lunch, for example. Thirty seconds per incident should be effective for elementary students. Secondary students might owe 15 seconds immediately after class for each incident; if the student accumulates three 15-second consequences, the next incident during that class results in detention and a Level 2 notification.

These brief interruptions to a student's schedule are surprisingly effective. A 15-second delay won't make the student late to the next class but is enough to interrupt between-class social activities. Highly social middle or high school students perceive 15 seconds of lost free time as quite a hardship.

Planned ignoring. Ignore all instances of a specific misbehavior. Do not acknowledge the behavior verbally or physically (including facial expressions and gestures). You may choose to inform the student of the planned strategy or just initiate it. Planned ignoring can teach the student that misbehaving to get attention is ineffective. However, keep in mind that ignoring a behavior does not mean that you should ignore the student. Plan to keep the ratio of interactions high for behavior other than the targeted misbehavior.

When verbal reprimands and other mild corrections haven't been effective, the student (or class) might just want attention, and you've been providing that attention with your corrections. In this case, planned ignoring can be a very effective next step. A classic example of a behavior that responds well to planned ignoring is blurting out. If students continue to blurt out without raising their hands, the reason is because you interact with them (at least occasionally) when they do so. Ignore students consistently when they blurt out, and the behavior will be extinguished in a few days or weeks.

Restitution. Students make amends or compensate for any damage that results from their actions. The students try to restore their relationships with individuals they hurt physically or verbally by apologizing, or they restore the environment they damaged by cleaning up or repairing the damage. You may have to model and rehearse a sincere apology with some students.

Positive practice. If a student breaks a rule about a behavior that can easily be practiced correctly, have her rehearse the behavior and pay attention to learning the task. For example, ask a student who runs in the hallways to go back and walk. A student who runs in the hallways repeatedly might be required to spend time during recess or after school practicing walking in the halls.

Behavior Improvement Form. The purpose of a Behavior Improvement Form is to make students think about their misbehavior as well as more appropriate ways to behave. The form includes items such as: Describe your behavior during the incident. How could you have behaved differently? If this happens again, how do you plan to behave or respond? The student fills out the form and then discusses his responses with you. Figure 3c shows a Behavior Improvement Form (Form D-10a). Another version of the form (Form D-10b) is also available on the Module D CD.

Demerits. Demerits are points given to a student for misbehavior. Specify in advance the behaviors that may result in demerits and develop a system to record the demerits. Also determine the consequence assigned for an accumulation of demerits within a prescribed time (for example, 3 demerits = after-school detention). Because a demerit is a mild but accumulative consequence, you are more likely to consistently intervene with disruptive behavior.

Demerits can also be used as a positive policy. For example, students who earn fewer than 5 demerits are allowed to participate in a free-time activity, but those with 5 or more demerits do not get to participate.

Response cost/Loss of points. If you are already using a reward system, have the student lose points or tickets every time she misbehaves. Ensure that the student is also receiving tickets for positive behaviors with even greater frequency. Another

Figure 3c   *Behavior Improvement Form (D-10a)*

Behavior Improvement Form (Version 1)

Name: _____   Date: _____

Teacher: _____   Period: _____   Class: _____

1. Describe the incident.

2. Describe your behavior during the incident.

3. How would the teacher describe your behavior during the incident?

4. How could you have behaved in a different way?

5. If this happens again, how do you plan to behave or respond?

6. Are you willing to commit to making this effort?

7. How can we help you be successful?

 This form can be printed from the Module D CD.

option is to have the student start with a certain number of points or tickets, and take one away for each infraction. For example, the student can start each day with 20 points. Every time you have to correct her, she loses a point. At the end of the day, write the remaining number of points on a note that she takes home. Each point is worth 5 minutes of television or video game time (or some other privilege) at home.

Response cost lottery. Form teams, and make sure that the students with troublesome behavior are distributed more or less evenly among the teams. (Don't use this system if one student's behavior stands out as dramatically worse than other students' behavior.) Each team begins each day (or each week for secondary classes) with a certain number of tickets. The teams lose a ticket for every misbehavior by a team member. Collect each team's remaining tickets at the end of the day (or week) and place them in a bowl. Draw a ticket and give the winning team a small reward, such as no homework for a day.

Loss of privilege. If a student engages in a specific misbehavior, the student will not have access to a predetermined privilege. Or, if the student does not meet an expectation for behavior, the student does not earn the privilege. Tell the student in advance of the consequence for misbehavior. The privilege should be mild and fairly immediate. Appropriate examples are loss of computer game time or loss of recess that day. Don't have the student lose, for example, a field trip scheduled 2 weeks later or recess every day for the next month.

Each classroom can define the range of what are considered privileges. For example, eating lunch with peers may be considered a privilege in some classrooms but not in others.

Emotional reaction. Exhibiting an emotional reaction (such as anger) is a strategy that should be used very sparingly, no more than twice a year with any group of students (so you don't lose the shock value) and not at all during the first 5 or 6 weeks with a new class—you don't want to reveal any buttons they can push to upset you. It is appropriate to use with a group, but not with individuals. For example, say that a class acts silly with a guest speaker. Usually the class is respectful. It might help to let the class know that you are angry and disappointed in them. If the class has never seen you angry before, it may have a bit of a shock effect and help improve the class's behavior in the future. This strategy will be effective only if you are calm and unemotional at all other times.

Detention (classroom). Level 1 classroom-based detention might consist of the teacher keeping the student in the classroom during lunch or after school for a few minutes. During this time, the student should not have access to any reinforcements, such as toys and games, and should get limited attention. The student may work on academic tasks.

Jot It Down. The Jot It Down strategy is particularly powerful when the student is overtly refusing to follow directions. If the student refuses to follow a direction, restate the direction, making sure it is clear, observable, and immediate. (Say "Sit down at your desk" instead of "Shape up.") If the student refuses a second time, literally write the direction and the student's inappropriate response on paper. This action slows the momentum toward more serious conflict between you and the student, and the student will probably sit down while you write. If the student complies, you might write a Level 2 notification about the incident. If the student doesn't comply, you should probably write a Level 3 office referral and include the written evidence of your direction and the student's refusal. We describe the Jot It Down strategy in more detail in Module D, Presentation 2, Task 1.

Figure 3d on pp. 76–79 presents all the consequences described above in a concise, bulleted format for quick reference (Form D-07). You can print this document from the Module D CD.

Figure 3e shows a handbook made as a staff development activity by the school district of Clay County in Florida. The correction procedures are taught to staff members, and they leave the inservice with this handy reference guide.

Figure 3e *Quick Reference Guide: Corrective Techniques for Misbehavior; thanks to Fleming Island Elementary School and the School District of Clay County in Florida*

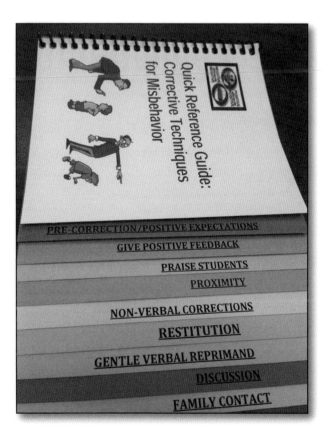

Corrective Procedures for Mild and Moderate Classroom Misbehavior (1 of 4)

1. Nonverbal correction

Give a respectful gesture or use body language to indicate that the behavior should stop.

- Finger to lips (without the accompanying "Shhh")
- Hand signal to indicate "sit down"
- Subtle head shake to indicate no

2. Gentle verbal reprimand

- Use short sentences: *The expectation now is that you work quietly.*
- Give in close proximity.
- State the expected behavior.
- Create the illusion of privacy.
- Think of it as a hit-and-run reprimand.

3. Proximity correction

- Move near students who exhibit misbehavior.
- Continue to walk the room.
- Make no eye contact with students who engage in mild misbehavior.

4. Humor

- Do not use sarcasm or ridicule.
- Talk to the target student after class to ensure that he knows you weren't trying to embarrass him.
- Don't attempt humor if you aren't naturally funny.

5. Frequency count

- Give the student a signal every time you record a misbehavior, or have the student do the recording.
- Use a form like the Behavior Counting Form (Form D-06).

6. Family contact

- Provide an objective description of the behavior.
- Ask the family to discuss the behavior with the student.
- Do not suggest that the family punish the child.
- Try to establish a family-school working relationship.

7. Discussion

- Talk with the student at a neutral time—after class or during independent work time.
- Discussion right after the misbehavior gives the student too much attention and power.
- Make sure the conversation is respectful.

 This form can be printed from the Module D CD.

Figure 3d (continued)

Corrective Procedures for Mild and Moderate Classroom Misbehavior (2 of 4)

8. Bumpy bunny timeout (pre-K to second grade)
- This correction is appropriate for primary grades.
- Invite students to bring toys from home (or choose toys from the classroom) and display the toys on a bookshelf. Each student should have one toy.
- Create a timeout area on the bookshelf with colored tape.
- If a student misbehaves, place his toy in the timeout area for 3–5 minutes during recess or the next play break.
- While the toy is in timeout, the student must sit at his desk instead of participating in recess or play break.
- For multiple infractions, the time can accumulate toward a longer timeout period during the next recess or play break.

Variation:
- Have the student bring a stuffed animal to class.
- The toy can sit on the student's desk as long as the student is behaving appropriately.
- If the student misbehaves, remove the animal from the desk and set it on a nearby shelf or table with its back toward the student.
- Tell the student that the animal is learning to behave, so it can't watch the student misbehave.
- When the student's behavior improves, return the animal to the student.

9. Timeout at the student's desk (elementary)
- Have the student put her head down on desk and close her eyes.
- Length should be just 1 or 2 minutes.
- Do not allow access to reinforcement, such as conversation, games, or books.

10. Timeout at a designated timeout area
- Use an isolated area in the classroom that is visible to you.
- For primary students, assign 2- or 3-minute timeouts; for intermediate, middle, and high school students, assign 5 minutes.
- The timeout begins when the student is seated and calm in the timeout area.
- Do not have the student work on academic tasks.
- Use it consistently; send the student to timeout each time he misbehaves.

11. Timeout in another teacher's room
- Write a Level 2 notification each time this consequence is used.
- Establish a timeout partner—a nearby teacher of a different grade.
- Use a designated area in the classroom.
- Agree with your partner on how long and how often you can send students to each other's classroom and on any times to avoid sending students.
- Do not have the student work on academic tasks.
- The host class ignores the student in timeout.
- Length of timeout is usually 5 to 15 minutes.

Corrective Procedures for Mild and Moderate Classroom Misbehavior (3 of 4)

12. Time owed
- This consequence is useful for frequent misbehavior.
- Time owed can equal time the student wasted during class.
- Have student lose the time from an activity she values—e.g., recess or lunch.
- Time assigned should be short; the consequence works best in 30-second increments for elementary and 15-second increments for secondary.
- Time owed assignments can accumulate.
- Do not have students pay the time for more than 1 minute during passing periods.

13. Planned ignoring
- Ignore all instances of a specific misbehavior.
- Keep ratio of interactions high for appropriate behavior.

14. Restitution
- Students repair damages they caused.
- The time or effort involved in the consequence should increase if the student repeats the misbehavior.
- If a student must clean up a mess, use only soap and water (no chemicals).

15. Positive practice
- This is a good on-the-spot correction and is effective for simple misbehavior such as running.
- Say, "Go back and show me the right way to . . ."
- The correction should match the misbehavior.

16. Behavior Improvement Form
- Student may complete the form during timeout in another teacher's room.
- Use simple forms for younger students and more sophisticated forms for older students.

17. Demerits
- Give students points (demerits) for misbehavior and predetermined consequences for an accumulation of demerits.
- The mild, accumulative consequence allows you to set up a more consistent policy.
- Demerits function as warnings.
- Demerits can be used as a positive policy (students who earn less than x demerits get earned free time).

18. Response cost/Loss of points
- Students start with x number of points each day.
- Subtract points for misbehavior.
- Remaining points are sent home each day.
- Students receive privileges at home based on points.

 This form can be printed from the Module D CD.

Corrective Procedures for Mild and
Moderate Classroom Misbehavior (4 of 4)

19. Response cost lottery
- Form teams of students, with students with troublesome behavior distributed among the teams.
- Give *x* number of tickets to teams at the beginning of each day (or week). Use a different color for each team.
- When individual students misbehave, take tickets away from the student's team.
- Collect remaining tickets at the end of the day (or week) and place them in a bowl.
- Draw a ticket and give the winning team a small reward, such as a homework pass or extra free time.

20. Loss of privilege
- Determine a privilege, such as eating lunch with peers.
- Inform the student that she will lose the privilege if she engages in specific misbehavior or fails to meet an expectation for behavior.
- This consequence pairs well with demerits and time owed.

21. Emotional reaction
- Use emotion (anger, disappointment) with the class, not with individual students.
- Act angry—don't display real anger or lose control.
- Use emotion no more than twice per year with the same group of students.
- Don't use an emotional reaction during the first 6 weeks of school.

22. Detention (classroom)
- Students spend a set time in a nonstimulating setting (before school, after school, or during lunch).
- Student may work on academic tasks.
- Student should not have access to reinforcement.
- Collect data to determine whether the consequence is working to reduce misbehavior.
- Modify with a correction plan, if necessary.

23. Jot It Down
- When a student refuses to follow a reasonable direction, restate the direction.
- If the student refuses a second time, write the direction and the student's response on paper. (This action gives the student time to think.)
- If the student doesn't comply a third time, you have written evidence of the refusal for a Level 3 office referral.

View a sample menu of Level 1 common area corrections.

Common area supervisors might find the following corrections effective. Details about implementing each one are in Module B, Presentation 5, Task 2.

- Proximity management
- Gentle verbal reminders and reprimands
- Brief delay
- Positive practice
- Restitution
- Change in location
- Notify the student's teacher
- Stay with supervisor
- Demerits
- Assign a timeout at the place the infraction occurred
- Assign a timeout at a set location
- Have student fill out a Behavior Improvement Form
- Referral to a more intensive consequence

Document the discipline policy information.

Document your adopted discipline policies and procedures in both your Foundations Archive and your Staff Handbook. Figures 3f and 3g on pp. 82–85 show pages from a Foundations Archive and Staff Handbook, respectively.

Task 1 Action Steps & Evidence of Implementation

Action Steps	Evidence of Implementation
1. Arrange a staff brainstorming and discussion session (or sessions) to develop menus of corrections for Level 1 infractions. (We suggest two menus—one for classrooms and one for common areas.)	Foundations Process: Meeting Minutes
2. With the administrator, prepare a proposal that defines two menus of corrections for Level 1 infractions (classroom and common areas). With the administrator, present the proposal to the entire staff.	Foundations Process: 3-Level System for Responding to Misbehavior

Action Steps	Evidence of Implementation

3. Have the staff adopt or reject the proposal.
 	
   • If the proposal is rejected, develop a revised proposal that incorporates staff recommendations.
   • Present the revised proposal for staff adoption or rejection.
   • Continue the process until a proposal is adopted. After two additional attempts to revise the proposal (a total of three voting cycles), the issue should go to the principal, who will develop the final policy.
	Foundations Process: 3-Level System for Responding to Misbehavior

4. Document in writing all adopted procedures and menus for Level 2 infractions.
 	
   • Include summaries of essential information in the Staff Handbook.
   • Include detailed information in the Foundations Archive.
   • Give copies of all relevant information to all staff members who will be implementing the policies and procedures.
	Foundations Archive: 3-Level System for Responding to Misbehavior
	
	Staff Handbook: 3-Level System for Responding to Misbehavior

5. If appropriate, make arrangements for supervisory staff to view (or review) Module B, Presentation 5, "Effective Supervision, Part 2—Correct and Reflect," and provide training in correction techniques, if needed. Faculty can review Module B, Presentation 6, "Supervising Common Areas and Schoolwide Policies—for All Staff. " These presentations include information on effective supervision practices for responding to student misbehavior. Although the focus of the presentation is common area supervision, the principles are applicable to classroom supervision as well.	

Figure 3f *Sample Foundations Archive Entry (D-14)*

Sample Foundations Archive Entry

Discipline Problems: Staff Policy and Procedures

We use a 3-level system for responding to misbehavior. Misbehavior is categorized into three levels—mild, moderate, and severe—and all staff members agree to use predetermined menus of corrections. Staff should review the plan each year and renew their commitment to the system. The plan allows staff to be on automatic pilot when they respond to misbehavior. They don't have to stop and think about what to do or second-guess their responses. Staff responses to misbehavior will be more consistent and thus more effective. In addition, a plan allows staff members to put more time and energy into teaching, connecting with students, and celebrating student successes.

The 3-level system has many advanges:

- It helps staff members recognize the need for a team approach to dealing with students who exhibit severe or chronic misbehavior. All staff have to understand that simply sending students to the office is unlikely to be effective.
- It allows administrators to deal effectively with severe and chronic misbehavior because they don't have to spend time on mild and moderate misbehavior.
- Administrators have more time to provide support for staff members who deal with students who exhibit severe or chronic misbehavior.
- It enhances cooperation between administrators and staff regarding student misbehavior.
- It provides useful information for guiding staff development. Knowing the patterns of mild, moderate, and severe misbehavior can help staff understand what needs work—classroom management or individual behavior improvement plans, for example.

The misbehaviors are categorized more by how the staff member choo[...] student did. Level 1 (mild) infractions are corrected in the setting, and 3 (severe) infractions require the student to be removed from the sett[...] incident is documented. Level 2 (moderate) falls between these two s[...] setting, but paperwork goes to the office.

The next few pages outline our definitions of the levels and the corres[...]

This sample can be printed from the Module D CD.

Sample Foundations Archive Entry (continued)

Level 1 Infractions

More information about the corrections and responses and how to implement them can be found in *Foundations* Module D, Presentation 3. (A full set of *Foundations* books and videos is available in the Staff Resource Room.)

LEVEL AND DEFINITION	TYPES OF BEHAVIOR	CORRECTIONS/RESPONSES
Level 1 (mild) infractions are minor misbehaviors that can be adequately corrected at the time they occur. They do not require documentation. A staff member who observes a Level 1 infraction corrects the student in the setting.	Disruption, not completing assignments or homework, teasing, minor disrespect, running in the hall or other rule infraction in a common area.	**Classroom:** • Nonverbal correction • Gentle verbal reprimand • Proximity correction • Humor • Frequency count • Family contact • Discussion • Bumpy bunny timeout (preK to 2) • Timeout at student's desk • Timeout at a designated timeout area • Timeout in another teacher's room • Time owed • Planed ignoring • Restitution • Positive practice • Behavior Improvement Form • Demerits • Response cost/Loss of points • Response cost lottery • Loss of privilege • Emotional reaction • Detention (classroom) • Jot It Down strategy

Sample Foundations Archiv[...]

Level 1 Infractions *(continued)*

LEVEL AND DEFINITION	TYPES OF BEHAVIOR
Level 1 (mild) infractions are minor misbehaviors that can be adequately corrected at the time they occur. They do not require documentation. A staff member who observes a Level 1 infraction corrects the student in the setting.	Disruption, not completi[...] assignments or homewor[...] teasing, minor disrespect[...] running in the hall or other rule infraction in a common area.

Figure 3f (continued)

FOUNDATIONS SAMPLE

Sample Foundations Archive Entry (continued)

Level 2 Infractions

LEVEL AND DEFINITION	TYPES OF BEHAVIOR	CORRECTIONS/RESPONSES
Level 2 (moderate) infractions are misbehaviors that do not require immediate administrative involvement, but do require documentation for one or more of these reasons: • The correction involves other staff members (e.g., detention, problem-solving room). • The student was removed from the setting and lost instructional time. • The reporting staff member wants or needs administrative input (e.g., a teasing incident might be harassment). • The reporting staff member thinks the administration should be aware of the situation	Severe disruption, chronic noncompletion of assignments or homework, severe teasing, any behavior for which the staff member assigns detention.	• Any Level 1 correction • Lunchtime detention • After-school detention

FOUNDATIONS SAMPLE

...ndations Archive Entry (continued)

...ctions and responses and how to implement them can be found in ...tion 4, Task 4.

TYPES OF BEHAVIOR	CORRECTIONS/RESPONSES
Any illegal behavior **Physically dangerous behavior** (e.g., fighting) **Refusal to follow reasonable adult direction**—An act in which a student engages in overt and immediate refusal to comply with reasonable adult direction. Student refusal to comply should be considered a Level 3 infraction only when the following conditions are met: • The direction is clear and observable. • The direction is immediate. • The direction is given three times. At the second repetition of the direction, the staff member emphasizes the seriousness of the student's choice. At the third repetition, the staff member writes the direction (thus giving the student time to respond).	Corrective consequences will be assigned only by the administrator: • Any item on the menus for Level 1 and Level 2 infractions • Debriefing form • Restorative practices • Co- or extracurricular activity suspension • Mini-courses or skill modules • Short-term skill group • Behavior monitoring • Behavior contracting • Parent supervision at school • In-school suspension • Alternative education program • Out-of-school suspension • Expulsion • Filing criminal charges

FOUNDATIONS SAMPLE

Sample Foundations Archive Entry (continued)

Administrative Responsibilities

Daily

Ensure that the notification reviewer reviews all Level 2 notifications and follows up with additional action, when needed.

Log (or have clerical staff log) all Level 2 and 3 incidents into the database. Review and follow up on flagged referrals that indicate students in need of individual behavior improvement plans.

Process all Level 3 office referrals as quickly as possible.

- Collect any additional information about the incident.
- Meet with the student.
- Assign appropriate consequences and contact the student's parents.
- Rehearse a re-entry plan with the student. If the student is being suspended, do this when the student returns from the suspension.
- Determine whether an individual behavior support plan is needed and, if so, involve the appropriate staff members.
- Provide feedback to the referring staff member on the actions taken.

Quarterly

Provide summary data to the Leadership team on Level 2 and Level 3 incidents.

Assist the Leadership team in preparing a report for the staff on the implications of the quarterly incident data.

Annually

1. Guide the staff in a review of the misbehaviors included in each of the three levels (mild, moderate, and severe). Use actual office referrals and notifications to guide this discussions.

2. Guide the staff in a discussion of approved and supported corrections and responses to misbehavior in each of the three categories. This process ensures that when staff members use these corrections and responses, they will be supported by the administrator.

3. Review the procedures for lunchtime detention and provide staff training, if necessary.

4. Establish a "Who Is Responsible" sequence to specify staff members authorized to deal with Level 3 office referrals and other emergencies. Provide all necessary training and coordination to ensure seamless handling of disciplinary referrals.

FOUNDATIONS SAMPLE

...undations Archive Entry (continued)

...ure that all staff are trained to supervise and deal effectively with stu-
...rrals. For example, staff must inform the office when they have sent a
...e that office staff are trained in the following procedures:

...attention as possible.

...avoid engaging in power struggles or escalating interactions.

...ue or tell what happened, use a one-liner such as "I understand" or

...s in the office (e.g., uses an obscenity), calmly but firmly tell the
...a clear instruction on what the student should do. If the student does
...e instruction or try to make the student stop.

...ontrol, immediately turn the situation over to the administrator or

...l expectations for a student's return to the setting after a referral has
...so receives training on the procedures for accepting a student back
...mple sequence:

...of the completed referral form (after the administrator has filled out
...o the classroom.

...up to the teacher (or staff member who wrote the referral) and waits
...ledges his or her presence.

...n to the teacher.

...her for the incident or at least acknowledges that the behavior

...to do next.

...tudent back into the setting without revisiting the incident.

...Team to establish a menu of resources—people and materials—that
...dual behavior improvement plans for students with chronic and

8. Work with the Foundations Team to establish a set of flagging criteria that identifies students who may be at risk of falling through the cracks. In addition, establish procedures to rally system resources to ensure that effective support plans are designed and implemented.

Figure 3g *Sample Staff Handbook Entry (D-13)*

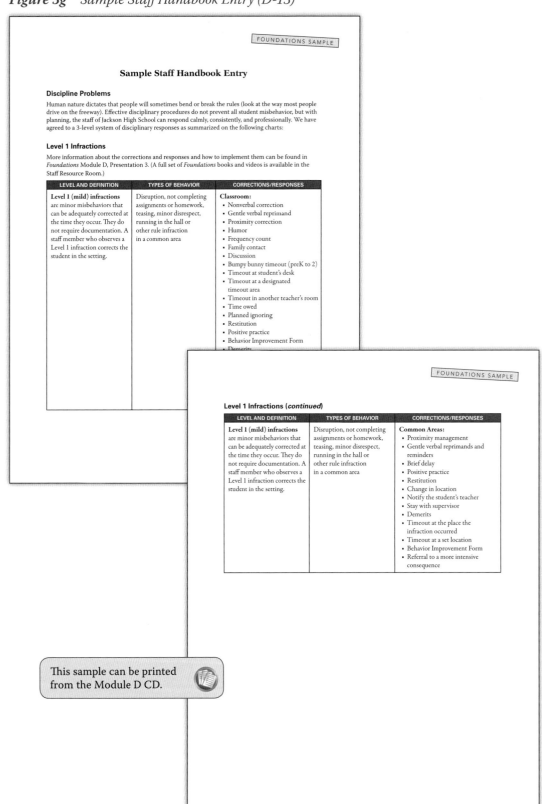

Sample Staff Handbook Entry

Discipline Problems

Human nature dictates that people will sometimes bend or break the rules (look at the way most people drive on the freeway). Effective disciplinary procedures do not prevent all student misbehavior, but with planning, the staff of Jackson High School can respond calmly, consistently, and professionally. We have agreed to a 3-level system of disciplinary responses as summarized on the following charts:

Level 1 Infractions

More information about the corrections and responses and how to implement them can be found in *Foundations* Module D, Presentation 3. (A full set of *Foundations* books and videos is available in the Staff Resource Room.)

LEVEL AND DEFINITION	TYPES OF BEHAVIOR	CORRECTIONS/RESPONSES
Level 1 (mild) infractions are minor misbehaviors that can be adequately corrected at the time they occur. They do not require documentation. A staff member who observes a Level 1 infraction corrects the student in the setting.	Disruption, not completing assignments or homework, teasing, minor disrespect, running in the hall or other rule infraction in a common area	**Classroom:** • Nonverbal correction • Gentle verbal reprimand • Proximity correction • Humor • Frequency count • Family contact • Discussion • Bumpy bunny timeout (preK to 2) • Timeout at student's desk • Timeout at a designated timeout area • Timeout in another teacher's room • Time owed • Planned ignoring • Restitution • Positive practice • Behavior Improvement Form • Demerits

Level 1 Infractions (*continued*)

LEVEL AND DEFINITION	TYPES OF BEHAVIOR	CORRECTIONS/RESPONSES
Level 1 (mild) infractions are minor misbehaviors that can be adequately corrected at the time they occur. They do not require documentation. A staff member who observes a Level 1 infraction corrects the student in the setting.	Disruption, not completing assignments or homework, teasing, minor disrespect, running in the hall or other rule infraction in a common area	**Common Areas:** • Proximity management • Gentle verbal reprimands and reminders • Brief delay • Positive practice • Restitution • Change in location • Notify the student's teacher • Stay with supervisor • Demerits • Timeout at the place the infraction occurred • Timeout at a set location • Behavior Improvement Form • Referral to a more intensive consequence

This sample can be printed from the Module D CD.

Figure 3g (continued)

Level 2 Infractions

LEVEL AND DEFINITION	TYPES OF BEHAVIOR	CORRECTIONS/RESPONSES
Level 2 (moderate) infractions are misbehaviors that do not require immediate administrative involvement, but do require documentation for one or more of these reasons: • The correction involves other staff members (e.g., detention, problem-solving room). • The student was removed from the setting and lost instructional time. • The reporting staff member wants or needs administrative input (e.g., a teasing incident might be harassment). • The reporting staff member thinks the administration should be aware and have a record of the situation (e.g., a Level 1 misbehavior such as rudeness to adults has become chronic). • A staff member who observes a Level 2 infraction corrects the student at the time or assigns the student a schoolwide correction (or both), then completes a Behavior Incident Notification Form that goes to the administrator.	Severe disruption, chronic noncompletion of assignments or homework, severe teasing, any behavior for which the staff member assigns detention	• Any Level 1 correction • Lunchtime detention • After-school detention

Level 3 Infractions

LEVEL AND DEFINITION	TYPES OF BEHAVIOR	CORRECTIONS/RESPONSES
Level 3 (severe) infractions are serious misbehaviors that require immediate administrative involvement and written documentation. They include misbehaviors that are illegal or are so severe that the misbehaving student's continued presence in a setting poses a threat to physical safety or to adult authority (i.e., if the student stays in the setting, the adult could lose control of the situation). A staff member who observes a Level 3 infraction sends the student to the office or calls for help to remove the student, then completes a Behavior Incident Referral Form that goes to the administrator. **NOTE:** Level 3 misbehaviors should be both limited in number and agreed to in advance by the entire staff.	**Any illegal behavior** **Physically dangerous behavior** (e.g., fighting) **Refusal to follow reasonable adult direction**—An act in which a student engages in overt and immediate refusal to comply with reasonable adult direction. Student refusal to comply should be considered a Level 3 infraction only when the following conditions are met: • The direction is clear and observable. • The direction is immediate. • The direction is given three times. At the second repetition of the direction, the staff member emphasizes the seriousness of the student's choice. At the third repetition, the staff member writes the direction (thus giving the student time to respond). **Flagrant disrespect** (e.g., swearing at a staff member) **Racial or gender-based teasing** **Bullying and harassment**	Corrective consequences will be assigned only by the administrator: • Any item on the menus for Level 1 and Level 2 infractions • Debriefing form • Restorative practices • Co- or extracurricular activity suspension • Mini-courses or skill modules • Short-term skill group • Behavior monitoring • Behavior contracting • Parent supervision at school • In-school suspension • Alternative education program • Out-of-school suspension • Expulsion • Filing criminal charges

TASK 2

Define corrective techniques for moderate misbehavior

Task 2 discusses procedures for dealing with Level 2 student misbehavior and provides examples of appropriate Level 2 corrections.

Review the definition of Level 2 infractions.

For Level 2 infractions, the student is corrected (or assigned a schoolwide consequence such as detention) by the observing staff member, who also completes an incident notification form. Level 2 infractions don't require immediate administrative involvement, but they do require documentation. In other words, the student stays in the setting, but paperwork goes to the office. There are several possible reasons why it's important to document moderate misbehavior:

- The reporting staff member has assigned a schoolwide correction that involves other staff members (detention or time in the problem-solving room, for example). Consider requiring written notifications for incidents that involve more than one adult.

- The reporting staff member wants or needs administrative input on the incident—for example, he is not sure whether a teasing incident should be considered harassment. In this case, the staff member is asking, *Did I handle this incident appropriately, or should I do something differently in the future?*

- The reporting staff member thinks the administrator should be aware and have a record of the situation. For example, a Level 1 misbehavior is becoming chronic—the student regularly fails to turn in his homework. A comprehensive written record of a student's moderate misbehavior can help in the functional analysis of the behavior and in determining an intervention plan to help the student, if such steps become necessary.

Define procedures for Level 2 infractions.

The assigned schoolwide correction or the administrator contact, more than the actual misbehavior, defines an incident as Level 2. That is, disrespect is considered a Level 1 infraction when the teacher handles it independently in the classroom. The infraction would be elevated to Level 2 when the teacher:

- Assigns a schoolwide consequence such as detention (thus involving other staff members).

- Asks the administrator for her opinion on whether the student crossed the line into threatening behavior.

- Notifies the administrator that the student's disrespect has been steadily increasing in the previous 3 weeks—it is becoming chronic.

An example of a schoolwide consequence that should be considered a Level 2 infraction is detention. Consider your available resources, both financial and human, before implementing a consequence such as detention or a problem-solving room. We are not advocating that you set up such consequences in your school; each school needs to carefully allocate personnel to essential procedures. Rather, we are simply stating that any schoolwide consequence that teachers can assign but do not need to supervise must be considered Level 2 so that administrators and counselors can monitor the use (and potential overuse) of the procedure. In other words, if one teacher is sending five students to detention every day or one student is assigned detention day after day, regular monitoring can ensure that someone will recognize the problem and step in to address it proactively.

In some schools, anyone can send a student to detention for almost any reason—yet the school keeps no records of student names or how much detention students are assigned. Because there are no data and several different staff members are involved with assigning and supervising detention, no one notices that detention tends to be filled with the same students week after week. If staff wrote a Level 2 incident report whenever they assigned detention, the cumulative data would allow schools to realize that detention is doing nothing to discourage misbehavior by the repeat offenders. If it did, the students wouldn't be in detention 3 or 4 days a week for weeks on end. Those schools need to try other consequences to help those students.

Also consider assigning similar consequences, such as sending a student to another classroom. Although this consequence can be Level 1, attaching Level 2 paperwork to it allows you to track how often it is assigned, what subjects the student is missing while she is in the other classroom (if it's always math, the student might be misbehaving just to get out of math), and whether the consequence is having any effect on the student's behavior

Inappropriate schoolwide consequences for Level 2 infractions are corrections that require administrative involvement, such as in-school and out-of-school suspension. Administrators may choose to assign suspension for an incident that was reported to them as Level 2, but teachers and paraprofessionals should not have the authority to assign a consequence that takes students out of the instructional environment.

About Problem-Solving Rooms

Problem-solving rooms for students can help reduce misbehavior, but only if the rooms are carefully structured to avoid overuse by teachers who simply want troublesome students out of their rooms. The room should be staffed by a highly skilled professional or well-trained paraprofessional under the direct supervision of an administrator, school counselor, or school psychologist. This environment should be designed to teach students behavioral skills. It should be supportive of students without being overly reinforcing.

Data should be continually collected and analyzed regarding which students are sent to the setting, the frequency and length of time they are there, and the recidivism rate. These data will help you determine whether the consequence is affecting the student's behavior. Students who chronically miss classroom instruction because of the frequency or length of time they are in the problem-solving room require immediate intervention with plans that reduce missed class time.

Problem-solving rooms sometimes become dumping grounds for problem students. All staff members need to know that it is unacceptable to use the problem-solving room just to get troublesome students out of the classroom. The goal is for teachers to correct most misbehavior immediately in the classroom and for students to remain in the instructional setting.

Procedural decisions you'll need to make include the following:

- *Should reporting staff members contact students' parents whenever they report Level 2 infractions?*

  Consider that you may have paraprofessionals writing reports—do you want them contacting families? We recommend that teachers contact parents when they write Level 2 notifications so they can avoid situations like this: The administrator notices that many Level 2 incidents have accumulated for a student, so she contacts the parents. She tells the parents that the misbehavior has been going on for weeks, and the parents say they didn't know because no one from the school contacted them.

- *Should students be required to sign the Level 2 notification forms?*

  One advantage of this procedure is that the student acknowledges that he is responsible for the misbehavior. However, if the student refuses to sign, the situation may escalate to Level 3. If it is likely that the student will refuse, do not require this step. Also, some parents might object to the school's asking students to sign what might be considered a legal document.

- *What should the administrator's initial responsibilities be regarding Level 2 notification forms?*

  Review them for potential legal issues and to assess whether you need to get involved or talk with students, staff members, or parents.

  Enter (or have them entered) into a database so you can analyze the long-term trends and patterns of behavior in the building and for individual students.

  Ensure that other staff members have the information they need for the assigned schoolwide correction. For example, the detention supervisors need to know which students are scheduled for detention each day.

- *When should the administrator become actively involved with Level 2 notifications?*

  The notification reviewer can decide whether the administrator should get involved and provide feedback to the author of the Level 2 notification as soon as possible. (Module D, Presentation 4, Task 1 provides more information about who reviews the notifications.)

  The administrator must get involved after a certain number of notifications have been written for the same student. For example, you might decide that four Level 2 notifications in a 6- to 8-week period indicate a chronic problem and require the development of a coordinated behavior improvement plan.

  Whenever a staff member requests it, the administrator should collaborate with the staff member to address the student's problem.

Define a menu of Level 2 corrections.

A Level 2 menu of corrections should include all of your defined corrections for Level 1 infractions as well as all schoolwide corrections that do not require administrative involvement; for example,

- Detention (after school, lunchtime, Friday evening)
- Problem-solving room
- Timeout in another room

Staff should try to approach the administrator (or counselor, or school psychologist) skillfully when notifying or following up about moderate misbehavior.

- Be objective.
- Be calm.
- Ask for guidance rather than for someone else to solve the problem.
- Use data. When you can show data about frequency, duration, trends, and patterns and you can describe the strategies you've tried, administrators and others will be better able to help you.

Task 2 Action Steps & Evidence of Implementation

Action Steps	Evidence of Implementation
1. Have the administrator, with or without the task force, develop a proposal on the administrative role in Level 2 procedures. • Identify the administrator's initial responsibilities regarding Level 2 notification forms. • Identify when the administrator will become actively involved with Level 2 incidents. 2. Develop a proposed menu of corrections for Level 2 infractions. • Include all corrections from the Level 1 menus. • Include all schoolwide corrections that do not require administrative involvement.	Foundations Process: 3-Level System for Responding to Misbehavior

3. Conduct a staff meeting to review and refine procedures for Level 2 infractions.
 	
• Get staff opinions about the proposal for the administrator's initial responsibilities and on the proposed menus of corrections.
• Get staff recommendations for other Level 2 procedural decisions:
   ◦ Should parents be contacted?
   ◦ Should students sign the incident report forms?
	Foundations Process: Meeting Minutes

Action Steps	Evidence of Implementation
4. Incorporate staff suggestions into a final proposal on procedures for Level 2 infractions. Present the final proposal to the entire staff for adoption or rejection. • If the proposal is rejected, develop a revised proposal that incorporates staff recommendations. • Present the revised proposal for staff adoption or rejection. • Continue the process until a proposal is adopted. After two additional attempts to revise the proposal (a total of three voting cycles), the issue should go to the principal, who will develop the final policy.	Foundations Process: 3-Level System for Responding to Misbehavior, Meeting Minutes
5. Document in writing all adopted procedures and menus for Level 2 infractions. • Include summaries of essential information in the Staff Handbook. Sample discipline policy information for a Staff Handbook is available on the CD. • Include detailed information in the Foundations Archive. Samples are available on the CD. • Give copies of all relevant information to all staff members who will be implementing the policies and procedures.	Foundations Archive: 3-Level System for Responding to Misbehavior Staff Handbook: 3-Level System for Responding to Misbehavior
6. Arrange for staff members to get any necessary training for the Level 2 procedures.	Foundations Process: 3-Level System for Responding to Misbehavior

TASK 3

Write effective and appropriate referrals for severe misbehavior

A well-written referral increases the administrator's efficiency and reduces the likelihood that parents will misunderstand the incident. Staff should understand the importance of the following guidelines for writing incident referrals and notifications.

Spelling and syntax count! If you want others to respect your actions and comments, write professionally, with correct spelling, grammar, and punctuation. Parents might read the forms as well; you don't want to give them reason to question the competence of their children's teachers.

Do not prepare forms for problem students ahead of time. To do so sends the message that you *expect* the student to cause trouble and gives the student no reason to believe he can succeed.

Use objective language. The administrator needs an objective description in concrete terms that explains what you saw and heard that prompted you to refer the student. Don't use jargon, labels, or judgments, all of which are conclusions about, rather than observations of, events. Conclusions can be biased by whether you are having a good day, whether you like the student, or even whether you have unconscious prejudices about ethnicity, gender, age level, or other issues. Figure 3h shows the difference between objective and nonobjective descriptions of the same event that resulted in an office referral.

Figure 3h   *Objective vs. nonobjective descriptions*

Objective Description	Jargon/Label/Conclusion (Nonobjective Description)
Kindra was pounding on her desk. When I asked her to stop, she loudly shouted, "You fat, ugly b___."	Kindra was obscene and obnoxious.
During a cooperative group activity, Allen and Alphonso were disagreeing. As I made my way to that part of the room, Allen got out of his seat, grabbed Alphonso by the shirt, and threw him to the floor. I was able to intervene at that point.	Allen attacked Alphonso.
James was out of his seat, pulling students' hair and knocking work off their desks. When I told him to go to his desk and sit down, he kept running around the room, refusing to go to his seat. I repeated the instruction three times.	James's ADHD is out of control, and I can't take it any more!

Nonobjective responses tell very little about what actually took place. In some cases, as in James's example in Figure 3h, they tell more about the teacher than what the student actually did. The goal is to ensure that teachers and administrators are on exactly the same page. In some schools, teachers feel they are not supported by administrators on disciplinary issues, and the administrator feels that teachers should handle more behaviors on their own without involving administration. When teachers and administrators feel this way, there is probably some miscommunication about the details of implementing office referrals.

Be specific. Describe observable and measurable behaviors. Don't write vague descriptions or describe your emotions.

Following are some examples—taken from actual referral forms—of what *not* to write. Imagine you are the administrator who has to process these referrals. How would you know what to say to the students or what consequences to assign? How would you explain the teachers' comments to the parents, who receive copies of the referrals?

- *Straw—camel's back.* (Clearly the teacher is expressing frustration. He gives no information about the specific rules the student violated.)

- *This student needs to see a psychiatrist, or at least be on some kind of medication. He's out of control.* (Unless she has a medical license, this teacher has no business diagnosing the student. Concern for the student has crossed the line of professionalism.)

- *Student does his level best to trash my class's learning every day. Needs SUSPENSION. How can he be allowed to ruin other students' chances to learn? I'm sick of writing him up, only to learn he received a too-lenient pun-ishment that encourages him to play the class clown.* (This teacher describes her reaction to the student's misbehavior rather than the misbehavior.)

- *I'm done with this student.*

- *Sam is laughing and enjoying school entirely too much!*

- *I was yelling at the student, and she yelled back at me!*

- *I told the student he needed to stop acting like a three-year-old, and he told me I was acting like a three-year-old. Incredibly disrespectful.*

Referral forms with descriptions like the above create problems for the administrator. The administrator has to investigate to determine the specifics of the misbehavior, perhaps while the student waits in the office. Referral forms are legal documents and may be used in a due process mediation or hearing for students who are protected under IDEA or Section 504. If the disciplinary action is questioned by the parents or their attorney, office referrals may be reviewed and become evidence in a legal action. The referral forms could be requested through an open records request.

Figure 3i on pp. 95–96 shows an example of a form that is filled out appropriately. Staff need to remember that copies of referrals are sent home to parents, so they shouldn't write anything they wouldn't say to parents directly.

Consider conducting a session on writing effective office referrals during a staff development inservice. You might hold this session at the beginning of every new school year. Include all staff who write office referrals, including paraprofessionals. The information can serve as a reminder for experienced staff and can greatly benefit new staff who may have encountered little severe misbehavior during their student-teaching experience.

The staff development session should emphasize the importance of professionalism in documenting severe misbehavior. Be sure to cover the following topics:

- **Using correct grammar and spelling.** You don't want a parent to fixate on a misspelled word and downplay the misbehavior: "How dare this teacher write up my child when she can't even spell?"

- **What is judgmental language?** Ask the staff to generate examples of judgmental language—words and phrases that should never appear on an office referral form.

- **What is objective language?** Ask staff to turn judgmental language into objective language. Provide written examples of well-written office referrals as well as poorly written ones. Don't use real examples from your school; however, the poor examples may be amalgamations of several referrals.

Task 3 Action Steps & Evidence of Implementation

Action Steps	Evidence of Implementation
1. Conduct a staff development session on writing effective and appropriate office referrals. Include the following topics: • The importance of correct grammar and spelling • The importance of objective language vs. emotional, reactive or judgmental language	Foundations Process: Planning Calendar
2. Document the recommendations for writing appropriate referrals and distribute to staff.	Foundations Archive: 3-Level System for Responding to Misbehavior Staff Handbook: 3-Level System for Responding to Misbehavior

Figure 3i   Behavior Incident Referral Form, completed appropriately (D-04)

Behavior Incident Referral Form
(Level 3 only)

Student Name: __Susan Jones__   Gender: Ⓕ M   Period/Time of Day: __3rd__

Referring Adult: __Mr. Ortiz__   Grade: __7__   Date: __11/14__

Location (if classroom, indicate subject): __Science lab__

SEVERE (Level 3, student goes to office)	
☐ Illegal (e.g., threats, weapons, drugs, assault)	☐ Code of Conduct violation
☐ Physically dangerous	☐ Violation of district, state, or federal mandate
☐ Not following direction (even when direction is written)	☐ Gender- or race-based teasing
☐ Flagrant disrespect	☐ Bullying or harassment
☒ Obscene language directed toward staff	☒ Other: __threatening, property destruction__

Description of problem/situation: _Susan was poking the ends of scissors into the desk and digging holes in the desktop. I told her to stop, and she refused. I repeated the direction and she pointed the scissors at me, saying, "Just try and make me," with an angry expression and tone._

Functional hypothesis/contributing factors:

- Lack of: awareness ___   ability ___
- Gain attention from: adults _X_   peers _X_
- Get desired: items ___   activities ___   power/control _X_
- Avoid or escape: activities ___   tasks ___   attention ___
- Avoid or escape: adults ___   peers ___
- Relieve: anxiety ___   stress ___
- Other or function unknown ___

Immediate actions taken by referring adult:

☐ Used a one-liner (e.g., "That is not OK. Keep your hands to yourself.")

☐ Instructional/verbal correction (e.g., for minor disrespect)

☐ Stated that you will follow up ("We'll talk later.")

☐ Off-limits or otherwise restricted activity

☐ Had student stay with supervisor

☐ Problem-solving room

☐ Detention (When: _____)

☐ Parental contact

☐ Had student demonstrate or practice the rule (positive practice)

☐ Restitution

☒ Other __Called for administrative removal__

Previous actions taken by referring adult for similar behavior (include dates when possible): ____

__Resitution, parental contact, discussion__

_____

_____

 This form can be printed from the Module D CD.

Action taken by administrator: _____

_____

_____

_____

How did the student disregard the Guidelines for Success? (Check at least one and briefly describe.)

❑   Always try.

_____

_____

❑   Do your best.

_____

_____

❑   Cooperate with others.

_____

_____

☒   Treat everyone with respect.

   Susan's behavior caused destruction of property that is shared by others. Her words and
   actions toward me were threatening._____

I understand how my behavior did not comply with [*Kennedy Middle School*]'s Guidelines for Success.

Student signature _____

Administrator Responsibilities for Responding to Misbehavior

CONTENTS

Introduction

Task 1: Identify Staff and Processes for Dealing Wtih Level 2 Notifications

For the Foundations Team and school administrators or counselors not on the Foundations Team who deal with discipline issues

---

Task 2: Identify Staff and Processes for Dealing With Level 3 Referrals

For the Foundations Team and school administrators or counselors not on the Foundations Team who deal with discipline issues

---

Task 3: Develop Alternatives to Out-of-School Suspension

For the Foundations Team and school administrators or counselors not on the Foundations Team who deal with discipline issues

---

Task 4: Establish Office Procedures for Dealing With Level 3 Referrals

For the Foundations Team and school administrators or counselors not on the Foundations Team who deal with discipline issues

---

Task 5: Use In-School Suspension Productively

For the Foundations Team and school administrators or counselors not on the Foundations Team who deal with discipline issues

DOCUMENTS*

- Behavior Incident Notification Form (D-03)
- Planning Questions for Dealing With a Severe or Chronic Problem (D-09)
- Expectations posters for main office, principal's office, and principal's hallway (D-15)

* All documents listed are available on the CD. Other documents that are not shown in this presentation are also available on the CD (see Appendix C for a complete list).

INTRODUCTION

This presentation describes procedures that administrators, office staff, and others can use to ensure that teachers and all other staff get the support they need for dealing with misbehavior. If staff members make an effort to refer only truly serious incidents to the administrator and reserve moderate and chronic misbehavior for Level 2 notifications, those notifications must be supported by the entire school team. We also discuss the equally important topic of ensuring that students with severe or chronic behavioral problems get the support they need from the school.

Marcie Polin, principal of an alternative school in the state of Washington, works with some of the toughest kids in the district. She implemented *Foundations* in her school and did a wonderful job with proactive prevention, managing common areas and schoolwide polices, and training staff in classroom management. The school did an especially good job with the topics in Module D about corrective consequences. The students in this alternative school have probably experienced every consequence that the educational system has in its repertoire and are largely immune to them. But Marcie created a framework of support and proactive, positive corrective procedures that really works for her students.

We asked for her insights into effective correction practices for moderate and severe misbehavior. Regarding alternatives to out-of-school suspension, she commented that it takes time and work to implement alternatives, but it pays off. "Time is always a factor, but with skill and practice, appropriate consequences can be assigned in a timely manner," she said. The bottom line is that when students are clear about expectations but also know that they will be dealt with in a fair and respectful manner, behavior problems are reduced."

Marcie also reflected on revisions she made to her in-school suspension program, which incorporates many of the concepts covered in Task 5 of this presentation. She emphasizes instruction rather than punishment or exclusion: "Students actually find in-school suspension more uncomfortable than out-of-school suspension [because they are required to work, not just spend free time away from school]. But even so, the outcome every time is that students report satisfaction with how much work they've accomplished, which of course is required in in-school suspension. Yes, satisfaction, but they're not interested in repeating the process."

Marcie has data that support her observation—in-school suspension recidivism is not significant in her school.

A theme that runs through this module about responding to misbehavior is *as if* treatment of students. All staff should treat students *as if* they are responsible, sensible people and *as if* the incident or misbehavior is just a momentary interruption or mistake. Our friends and colleagues, school administrators B. J. Wise and Kim Marcum, taught us this technique. When speaking to a student sent to the office, they say, "I'm surprised that someone as responsible as you would exhibit behavior like this."

Task 1: Identify Staff and Processes for Dealing With Level 2 Notifications explains the role of the notification reviewer—the person who ensures that the referring staff member gets feedback, that any necessary further actions are taken, and that notifications are recorded in a database.

Task 2: Identify Staff and Processes for Dealing With Level 3 Referrals discusses the importance of identifying designees to handle referrals when the administrator is out of the building and suggests a comprehensive game plan for dealing with referred students.

Task 3: Develop Alternatives to Out-of-School Suspension suggests a menu of corrections for Level 3 infractions (and chronic Level 2 infractions) that you and the administrative designees will use.

Task 4: Establish Office Procedures for Dealing With Level 3 Referrals discusses the roles and responsibilities of office staff when students are sent to the office, including how to interact appropriately with the students.

Task 5: Use In-School Suspension Productively presents ideas learned from *Foundations* schools for implementing instructional in-school suspension.

All these tasks are intended for the administrator, but we recommend that the Foundations Team review them as well. The administrator will be the primary decision maker for the issues we present, and the staff will not be involved in review and adoption processes. But the Foundations Team needs to be involved so they can inform the staff about the decisions made. That communication loop—and ensuring that everyone understands all the policies and procedures—is one of the team's major responsibilities.

TASK 1

Identify staff and processes for dealing with Level 2 notifications

Let's begin with a brief review of Level 2 notifications. Level 2 notifications fall between Level 1 misbehavior (student is corrected in the setting, and the incident requires no paperwork) and Level 3 office referrals (student is removed from the instructional setting, and paperwork is required).

The purposes and advantages of this mid-level consequence include the following:

- Notifications keep students in instructional settings but allow staff to easily get input on whether they handled a particular incident well or should have handled it differently. Staff can also notify appropriate support personnel (counselors, school psychologist, or social workers) that a problem is becoming chronic, thus taking the first step toward elevating the student to Tier 2 support.

- Notifications allow staff to document and inform the administrator and support staff of concerns unrelated to a specific behavior. Level 2 is not just for incidents. If a student's demeanor changes—an outgoing student becomes withdrawn or a high-achieving student's grades drop, for example—staff can complete a notification to alert the administrator and counselor.

- Level 2 notifications enable the staff to collaboratively meet the needs of students who may need an additional level of support *before* the students become highly visible problems.

- Notifications also allow you to create a database of information that over time will become more sensitive to your schoolwide trends and severe incidents. As your office disciplinary referrals decrease, they become less a sensitive measure of school climate and more a reflection of that small percentage of students who have severe emotional or behavioral issues. Level 2 notifications then become a great data source about schoolwide trends and patterns.

This task is about setting up processes to give staff and students the support they need. Part of the process involves paperwork, but that is not the end goal. Staff should not feel they are completing paperwork just to satisfy a bureaucracy; rather, the paperwork is the first step toward gaining needed support, and it is an important contribution to the database that drives the Improvement Cycle.

Below we outline some actions necessary for implementing a system of Level 2 notifications. You (the administrator) and the Foundations Team can discuss these suggestions and determine whether you (and possibly the team) will unilaterally make the decisions or whether some of the actions will be presented to staff for input and proceed through the adoption process of the Improvement Cycle.

Decide on a way to communicate staff concerns about moderate or chronic misbehavior.

In Module D, Presentation 2, Task 3, we discuss the process of developing forms to document Level 2 and Level 3 behavior. Figure 4a on the following pages shows an example of a Behavior Incident Notification Form that staff can use to communicate their concerns about a student to other staff members.

Decide who will review the notifications.

You should identify one dedicated person who will receive Level 2 notifications and decide on further actions. In a small school, this person will probably be the principal. In a larger school with multiple administrators and support staff, notifications might go to the principal, an assistant principal, a counselor, a behavior specialist, a social worker—whoever has expertise with behavior issues and the time each day to respond to notifications. We call this person the *notification reviewer*. You should also identify at least one person who can review notifications when the primary notification reviewer is out of the building.

It's important that all staff know that when they take the time to write a Level 2 notification, a professional-level person will review it and provide feedback—the notification does not just fall into a black hole.

Determine a process for data collection and analysis.

Keep accurate and up-to-date records of all notifications. The notification reviewer or a data entry person in the office needs to enter every notification into a database. The reviewer should be able to easily and quickly check whether an incident is related to past incidents and whether it is the first or the seventh notification for the student.

In the long term, a database of notifications can give you a good picture of which behaviors are improving and which ones still need work. Examine the data for trends and patterns, then identify and evaluate your improvement priorities.

Behavior Incident Notification Form
(Level 2 only)

Student Name: _____   Gender: F / M   Period/Time of Day: _____

Referring Adult: _____   Grade: _____   Date: _____

Location (if classroom, indicate subject): _____

MODERATE (Level 2, paper goes to office)

❑ Chronic misbehavior (e.g., late to class, late or no homework or classwork, disruption)
❑ Not following direction (but eventually complies)
❑ Disrespect to an adult (low-level)
❑ Name calling, put-downs, or mild behavior that might be gender- or race-based
❑ Other _____

Description of problem/situation: _____

_____

_____

Functional hypothesis/contributing factors:

- Lack of: awareness ___   ability ___
- Gain attention from: adults ___   peers ___
- Get desired: items ___   activities ___   power/control ___
- Avoid or escape: activities ___   tasks ___   attention ___
- Avoid or escape: adults ___   peers ___
- Relieve: anxiety ___   stress ___
- Other or function unknown ___

Immediate actions taken by referring adult:

❑ Used a one-liner (e.g., "That is not OK. Keep your hands to yourself.")
❑ Instructional/verbal correction (e.g., for minor disrespect)
❑ Stated that you will follow up ("We'll talk later.")
❑ Off-limits or otherwise restricted activity
❑ Had student stay with supervisor

❑ Problem-solving room
❑ Detention (When: _____)
❑ Parental contact
❑ Had student demonstrate or practice the rule (positive practice)
❑ Restitution
❑ Other _____

Previous actions taken by referring adult for similar behavior (include dates when possible): _____

_____

_____

_____

 This form can be printed from the Module D CD.

Figure 4a (continued)

Action taken by administrator: _____

_____

_____

_____

How did the student disregard the Guidelines for Success? (Check at least one and briefly describe.)

❑ Always try.

_____

_____

❑ Do your best.

_____

_____

❑ Cooperate with others.

_____

_____

❑ Treat everyone with respect.

_____

_____

I understand how my behavior did not comply with [*Kennedy Middle School*]'s Guidelines for Success.

Student signature _____

Develop a protocol of actions for the notification reviewer.

We recommend that you develop a protocol of actions that the notification reviewer should take. Consider these questions.

Who else needs to know about the notification, if anyone?

- Parents should be informed about every notification
- Other school personnel
- Outside agencies

Does someone (notification reviewer, administrator, or another staff member) need to meet with this student as soon as possible, or is the teacher's action sufficient?

Are additional corrective consequences necessary (beyond the teacher's action)?

If the reviewer determines that the teacher's actions were sufficient and appropriate for this stage of the problem, he should provide that feedback to the teacher.

If the reviewer determines that an additional consequence, such as detention or in-school suspension, should be assigned, he should ensure that proper procedures for implementing the consequence are followed. This might include involving other staff members, such as ISS supervisors, and informing the referring staff member, the student, and parents.

Is the behavior chronic or serious enough that we need to design a collaborative intervention process for the student? If so, who will lead that process?

We discuss tiers of support mainly in Module F, but here we introduce a form that the notification reviewer can use for the initial stages of planning Tier 2 or Tier 3 support for students. Form D-09, Planning Questions for Dealing With a Severe or Chronic Problem (Figure 4b on the next page), can be used as is or modified to fit the needs of your school.

> Numbered items below correspond to items on Form D-09.

1. Should other school personnel be involved?

   If the problem is chronic—perhaps this is the fourth or fifth notification—or serious enough that the student needs more support than she can get in the classroom, think about other staff members who can help the student. Consider whether to involve the school counselor, school psychologist, behavior specialist, special education department, school social worker, or someone else.

2. Is the problem beyond the expertise or responsibility of school personnel?

   If the notification indicates a possible medical issue, for example, ask a health professional such as the school nurse to arrange, with the parents' involvement, a

Planning Questions for Dealing With a Severe or Chronic Problem

1. **Should other school personnel be involved?**   ❑ Yes   ❑ No
   If Yes, collaborate with appropriate school personnel such as:

   - School counselor
   - School psychologist
   - Behavior specialist
   - Special education director or consultant
   - Social worker

2. **Is the problem beyond the expertise or responsibility of school personnel?**   ❑ Yes   ❑ No
   If Yes, collaborate with appropriate agencies such as:

   - Physician or public health agencies
   - Police
   - Juvenile justice
   - Mental health
   - Child protective services

3. **Do you have all the necessary (and available) information to design a plan of action for helping the student?**   ❑ Yes   ❑ No
   If No, gather additional information by:

   - Talking with parent(s)
   - Talking with school personnel who know the students
   - Reviewing the student's records
   - Observing the student in problematic settings

4. **Would the student benefit from a Tier 2 support, such as Mentorship, Meaningful Work, or Connections?**   ❑ Yes   ❑ No
   If Yes, read the information about Mentorship, Meaningful Work, and Connections in Module C, Presentation 6, and arrange for the student to participate in one of these (or similar) programs.

5. **Are all of the student's basic human needs being met?**   ❑ Yes   ❑ No
   If No, set up a program to meet a particular need (suggested programs in parentheses are detailed in Module C, Presentation 6):

   - Acknowledgment (Student of the Week, Special Attention for Targeted Students, CARE)
   - Recognition (Positive Reports to Parents, Goal Achieved Book, Golden Tickets)
   - Attention (Falcon Fan Club, Adult-Student Interactions, Homework Room)
   - Belonging (Lunch With the Principal, Adult-Student Interactions, Classwide Goal of the Month)
   - Purpose (Problem-Solving Task Force, Classwide Goal of the Month, Student of the Week)
   - Competence (Honor Roll, Grades, Principal's Award, Homework Room)
   - Nurturing (Special Attention for Targeted Students, Mentorship, Adult-Student Interactions)
   - Stimulation/Change (Lunch With the Principal, CARE, Problem-Solving Task Force)

6. **Would the student benefit from a highly structured reinforcement system?**   ❑ Yes   ❑ No
   If Yes, establish a behavior contract or other reward system to motivate the student to behave more responsibly.

 This form can be printed from the Module D CD.

medical evaluation. If the incident borders on juvenile justice issues and you find out through her records that the student is on probation, determine whether you need to contact her probation officer. You should be able to handle most incidents internally, but this question prompts the notification reviewer to reflect on the possibility of including outside agencies.

3. Do we have all the necessary (and available) information to design a plan of action for helping the student?

This question reminds the notification reviewer about other sources of potentially valuable information: parents and family, other staff members, the student's complete records, and observations of the student in problematic settings.

4. Are all of the student's basic human needs being met?

Module C describes programs such as mentorship, Connections, and Meaningful Work. If the school has these types of Tier 2 programs in place, consider whether one might meet the needs of the student. For example, a student who misbehaves to get attention might benefit from Connections, a program that gives students lots of positive adult attention. If the notification indicates that the student's attendance is poor, a Meaningful Work job can give the student a sense of belonging and motivate him to attend.

5. Would the student benefit from a highly structured reinforcement system?

The student might need the motivation that a behavior contract or other reward system can give.

We discuss the issues that these questions raise in more detail in Module F, but this form can help the notification reviewer begin to formulate a plan for helping the student. If every student who receives a Level 2 notification is given at least this much consideration and thought, no students should fall through the cracks.

Task 1 Action Steps & Evidence of Implementation

Action Steps	Evidence of Implementation
1. Decide on a way to communicate staff concerns about moderate or chronic misbehavior.	Foundations Archive: 3-Level System for Responding to Misbehavior
2. Decide who will review the notifications. This person should be a professional with expertise in behavior issues and the time to respond to notifications daily.	Staff Handbook: 3-Level System for Responding to Misbehavior
3. Determine the process for data collection so that over time these notifications can drive school improvement and help identify students in need of individual behavior improvement plans.	
4. Establish a protocol and a corresponding form so that the notification reviewer asks the key questions.	

TASK 2

Identify staff and processes for dealing with Level 3 referrals

This task is for the school administrator, and it has two major components. First, we discuss why and how to establish designees who can process office referrals and support staff when you are out of the building. Second, we suggest a game plan for handling students who are referred to the office for severe behavior. Readers who are seasoned administrators undoubtedly already have a game plan in place and our suggestions will probably just confirm your procedures, but it's important to ensure that your designees follow your game plan, too. Students should expect consistent consequences and treatment for office referrals no matter who handles them. If necessary, customize our game plan to fit your procedures and distribute it in writing to all designees.

To review, Level 3 infractions are serious misbehaviors that require immediate administrative involvement (office referral) and written documentation. Level 3 encompasses behaviors that are illegal or so severe that the misbehaving student's continued presence in a setting poses a threat to physical safety or to adult authority; that is, the adult could lose control of the situation if the student stays in the setting.

A staff member who observes a Level 3 infraction sends the student to the office or calls for help to remove the student and then completes an incident report form that goes to the administrator (either on paper or through a database such as TRENDS).

Staff should understand that when they remove a student from the setting, they are indicating that the misbehavior was severe—it involved illegal activity, there was real danger of someone getting hurt, or the staff member was at risk of losing control of the situation.

Establish designees to handle Level 3 office referrals.

Implement the following procedures so that Level 3 incidents can be handled effectively when you are out of the building.

Establish a "Who Is Responsible?" list. This lists specific staff members who are authorized to process Level 3 referrals. The building administrator is first on the list, followed by two or three (preferably three) designees who can deal with office referrals when the administrator is out of the building or unavailable (see Figure 4c).

All office personnel should have a copy of the list so they can immediately contact a backup person when the administrator is unavailable.

Figure 4c   Sample "Who Is Responsible?" list

Who Is Responsible?

Please contact the following people when a student has been sent to the office for disciplinary reasons. If the first person is not available, contact the second, and so on.

1. Principal, Ms. Thorne (cell phone: 653-8746 or walkie-talkie)
2. Lead Teacher, Ms. Arizmendi, Room 26 (intercom)
3. Counselor, Mr. Gold (cell phone: 653-9078 or walkie-talkie)
4. Assistant Superintendent, Ms. Tolson (cell phone: 653-7356 or 653-6700 [secretary])

When choosing designees, make sure they will be able to carry out their duties.

If a teacher is one of the designees, his or her students must be mature enough to behave appropriately while the teacher is out of the classroom handling a Level 3 situation.

Counselors and school psychologists are good choices, but often these people work at several different schools and are out of the building frequently. Designees should be available every day.

You might include a district-level person if that person can get to the building quickly. Including someone such as an assistant superintendent also sends a message to staff that Level 3 referrals are for serious misbehavior only.

Ensure that designees know how to process Level 3 referrals. They should be prepared to take the following actions, which are discussed in detail in the next section of this task:

- **Process office referrals immediately.**

- **Make any needed decisions at the time of a referral.** For example:
  - Do the police or other agencies need to be called?
  - Does the student need to be sent home immediately?
  - When can the student be allowed to resume his or her normal schedule?
  - Should a correction be assigned or should the decision be delayed until the administrator is back in the building?
  - Should anyone else—such as parents, referring staff member, other involved students, or witnesses—be included in the meeting with the student?

- **Meet with the administrator** at least twice a year for a "What if this happens?" discussion and to prepare for high-probability events. Think about the referrals and emergencies that occurred during the past 3 or 4 years and talk about how they should be handled.

Other considerations for handling office referrals include the roles and responsibilities of office staff, which we discuss in Task 4, and the range of consequences that are effective and appropriate for severe behavior, which we discuss in Task 3. Administrators and their designees should read through and discuss these tasks so the expectations for staff and students are consistently applied, no matter who is handling office referrals.

Develop a game plan for handling students who are referred to the office for severe behavior.

Our suggested game plan includes the following elements:

- **Preparation:** Actions to take and issues to consider before you meet with a referred student.

- **Meet With the Student:** Plan an effective meeting agenda.

- **Follow-up:** Actions to take after you've met with the student.

Following these suggestions can increase the likelihood that your contact with a referred student will result in improved student behavior and, at the same time, leave the student's dignity intact, the referring staff member feeling supported, and you not overly drained by the whole process.

As you read this task, you may think, "I can't spend this much time on each referral!" However, keep two things in mind. First, suggestions that have taken us several written paragraphs to cover represent decisions that will actually take you only a few seconds to make. Second, if your concern stems from the fact that you are deluged with too many disciplinary referrals, what you really need to do is work with your staff to eliminate referrals for behaviors that they should handle. Remember, the fewer referrals you receive, the more time you will have to deal with them comprehensively and work proactively on preventing problems and helping staff improve their skills.

As principal, you may become involved with an individual student in a variety of ways. The most obvious is when a student is sent to your office with a disciplinary referral because of misbehavior in a classroom or common area. In other cases, you will become involved because a staff member or a parent has expressed concern about a particular student; for example, a teacher came to you about a student who constantly argues. You may also become involved through procedures established by you and your staff to flag certain conditions that indicate a student needs your attention, such as excessive absenteeism, failing grades in two or more classes, or a certain number of notifications. In the latter two circumstances, the student is not waiting in the office to see you, but you will still probably want to meet with the student to discuss the situation.

Regardless of how you become involved with an individual student, the following steps can increase the chances that your involvement will help the student and resolve the problem.

Game Plan, Section 1

Preparation: Actions to take and issues to consider before you meet with the student

STEP 1. Establish procedures for how referred students will get to the office.

All staff should know the procedures for sending students to the office. After the office is notified, you (or a designee) can go to the classroom or other setting and get the student. Or the referring staff member might send the student on his own, carrying a referral slip or hall pass. In some schools, students go to a waiting area, such as an in-school suspension room, until you are ready to see them. This is a good way to ensure students are well supervised and wait in a nonreinforcing environment. (Task 4 has more information about office procedures, such as establishing waiting areas.) The referring staff member will probably need additional time to complete the incident referral form, so you might not get the form until sometime during or after your meeting with the student. Ensure that staff know they should submit the form as soon as possible.

STEP 2. Check your records to see whether the student has been in your office before.

It is important to know whether the student has already been in your office during the current year—for the same behavior or multiple behaviors—because repeat offenders should be handled a little differently from first-time offenders. In either case, you can proceed with the steps described in this section. However, if the student has been referred previously for the same offense during the current school year, review the student's records to verify the corrective consequences you said would be assigned for a repeat offense. During the meeting, let the student know what, if any, consequence (beyond the conference) you are assigning. In addition, if the student has had ongoing behavior problems, follow up on your meeting by considering a more comprehensive intervention plan to help the student.

STEP 3. Ensure that you have adequate and accurate information about the problem or the specific precipitating incident.

When dealing with disciplinary referrals, part of your role is to act as judge. To judge fairly, you need accurate information about the problem or situation that led to the referral. Your first source of information should be the referral form. If you have any unanswered questions or think additional information might be useful, contact the referring staff person before you meet with the student. For more serious offenses (the student seriously injured another student during a fight, for example), you might have to seek out witnesses. In addition, for chronic or pervasive problems (the student constantly argues with the teacher, for example), you may need to talk with other adults who supervise or are in contact with the student to see if the problem extends to other situations and settings.

In general, the more severe the situation, the more time you should spend gathering information before taking action. For example, you would spend more time investigating an allegation that a student stole a purse from the staff room than you would on a playground skirmish involving two second graders. In all cases, however, it is worthwhile to take the time necessary, given the nature of the infraction, to get all the facts.

STEP 4. Identify your goals for your meeting with the student.

You are more likely to have a successful meeting if you identify ahead of time what exactly you hope to accomplish during the meeting. The most obvious goal is to reduce the likelihood that the student will exhibit the same or similar behavior in the future. To accomplish that goal, you should try to:

- Find out what led the student to behave inappropriately.
- Give the student information about why and how to behave more appropriately.

For example, if a student has been aggressive toward others, it may be helpful for her to understand how her acts affect others—that is, for her to develop empathy for the people she is aggressive with. Or you may want to arrange for the student to have anger management sessions with the counselor.

Another major goal should be to make sure that all parties involved in the referral—the student, the referring staff member, and the student's parents—feel supported. This goal means working hard to avoid win/lose situations. Disciplinary referrals often result in adversarial feelings between the referring staff member and the student (and possibly the parents). If the tone of your meeting with the student implies that the referring staff member must "win" and the student must "lose," you risk creating a power struggle between the two and devaluing the student. On the other hand, you are more likely to help a student learn to behave appropriately if you can help him realize that he needs to change his behavior not just because it's what others want, but because it is in his best interest as well.

Finally, strive to help the student repair the obvious and not-so-obvious results of her actions. For example, a student's disrespect toward a staff member can damage her relationship with that staff member. Help her begin to repair the damage done. This step is especially important in cases of defiance—when a student exhibits overt and immediate refusal to follow a reasonable adult direction. In these circumstances, always arrange for the referring staff member and the student to have a conference designed to reestablish their relationship. Consider the following example:

> Jan is walking down the hall wearing a baseball cap. Ms. Garcia, a teaching assistant, is walking in the opposite direction and reminds Jan that hats are not to be worn in the school building. Jan responds, "I am not wearing a hat." Ms. Garcia says, "Jan, you might not be able to see the top of your head, but I can, and the school rule is that all students must take off their hats when they enter the building." Jan begins to walk away, looks over her shoulder, and says, "You can't make me. Why should I listen to you? You're just a stupid teaching assistant." Ms. Garcia states, "Jan, you need to stop right there and think about what you are doing. If you keep walking, I will refer this to the principal as a defiant act." Jan keeps on walking, still wearing the hat. Ms. Garcia fills out a referral form indicating that the student refused to follow a reasonable adult direction.

This behavior reflects a severe problem in the relationship between this student and staff member. However, the adult involved was not necessarily the main cause of the student's defiance—the student may have fought with a parent just before school and took her anger out on the first adult in school who spoke to her. Nonetheless, very few adults are able to experience a scenario similar to the one between Jan and Ms. Garcia without feeling some degree of helplessness, anger, and resentment toward the student.

When dealing with Jan about this referral, the principal understands that if she does not get Jan and Ms. Garcia together to talk about what happened and try to repair some of the damage done to their relationship, Ms. Garcia may harbor some resentment toward Jan. For example, imagine that the principal met with Jan about the incident, had Jan call her parents to explain the situation, and assigned her to lunchtime detention. The principal did not, however, arrange for Jan and Ms. Garcia to meet and did not inform Ms. Garcia of the referral's outcome. Two days later, when Ms. Garcia sees the administrator and Jan talking and laughing together in the halls, she may think that nothing really happened to Jan. While to the administrator and Jan the incident is over, Ms. Garcia may still have it very much on her mind. It is possible that Ms. Garcia's feelings could affect the way she interacts with Jan in the future.

Therefore, in addition to assigning corrective consequences when a student has been defiant, arrange a meeting that includes the referring adult, the student who was defiant, and you. In some cases, the student's parents should attend as well. If the student or parents are known to get emotional or defensive, it might be prudent to have a school counselor—or someone trained in communication skills—facilitate the meeting. Your goal is for the student and the referring adult to talk to each other and to anticipate other situations in which the adult may need to give the student directions. You might even have them role-play some of these situations. *Note:* If emotions are high immediately after an incident, this meeting may be more effective if scheduled for the following day.

Involving the referring adult in this way can mitigate some of the resentment and hurt caused by the student's defiant act. You might ask the referring adult to explain how it feels when a student talks back in such a disrespectful manner. The goal of this conference is to create an atmosphere of mutual respect and cooperation between the student and the referring adult.

STEP 5. Decide whether anyone else should be involved in the meeting.

In addition to mending the relationship with the student, there are other reasons to have the referring staff member participate in your meeting with the student. If you think that the referring staff member could have handled the situation more skillfully, for example, you can model more appropriate ways to interact and problem-solve with students. You may want to assure the referring staff member that you are supportive of her and take her referrals seriously. Or you may want to establish the staff member's authority with the student. For example, if the student has not been taking a playground supervisor seriously, seeing the supervisor and the principal together in the meeting lends support to the authority of the supervisor.

When a student's misbehavior has affected another student (through destruction of property, for example), you may want to see whether the victim is willing to meet with you and the misbehaving student. Be extremely careful not to pressure a victim to participate if he or she does not feel comfortable doing so. In true bullying situations, do not plan to get the student who bullied and the student who was bullied together. The purpose of the meeting is to help the transgressor see the situation through the eyes of the victim—a potentially useful tactic, but not worth further traumatizing the victim.

You might also invite other students and adults who were involved in or witnessed the event so that all parties can tell their version of the situation.

Finally, for severe offenses such as stealing, assaultive behavior, and verbal threats, include the student's parents and possibly outside authorities in the meeting when necessary. In most cases, however, we have found it better to talk to the student before deciding if, when, and how to contact the student's parents. Additional guidelines for making the decision whether to include parents appear in Step 6 of the next section of the game plan, Meet With the Student.

Note: When several students have been referred for one incident (five students trashed a restroom, for example), see the students one at a time. In fact, it is probably best that they wait to see you separately. Keeping the students apart decreases the likelihood that they will engage in too-cool-for-school behavior. In addition, giving them less opportunity to get their stories straight will add an edge of anxiety ("I wonder what the others have told him?") that may help you gather more accurate information.

❧ FOUNDATIONS RECOMMENDATION ☙

To protect yourself from accusations of impropriety, leave your door open or create a context for having another adult as a witness so that you are not alone with any student behind a closed door for a long period of time.

Game Plan, Section 2

Meet with the student: Plan an effective meeting agenda

Keep in mind that your overall objective in meeting with the student is to help the student learn better ways of handling situations in the future. The student's misbehavior provides an opportunity to increase her ability to behave responsibly. Your purpose in meeting with the student is to instruct, not to punish; that is, to help the student master an increased level of personal responsibility and self-control.

STEP 1. Explain to the student why you are meeting.

Tell the student the nature of the referral. If the meeting stems from concern about a chronic problem such as excessive absenteeism, explain that. In addition, make a positive statement that reflects your high expectations for the student. Let him know that you view this problem as a temporary interruption in the success that you know he is capable of. "Your teacher tells me you are one of her most responsible and intelligent students. She also tells me that she can always depend on you to behave responsibly." If you can come up with a specific strength, comment

> 66 The *as if* treatment: All staff should treat students *as if* they are responsible, sensible people and *as if* the incident or misbehavior is just a momentary interruption or mistake. "

on that. If you do not know the student well, use a generic statement such as, "You are such an important and responsible person in this school, I am surprised to see this referral for a behavior such as . . ."

STEP 2. Get information about the incident or problem from the student.

Give the student a chance to tell her side of the story. Ask questions such as:

- What happened?
- Why did you do this?

These open-ended questions provide an opportunity for the student to explain her actions without turning the situation into a snow job where she masks the real issue in a blizzard of disputed facts, blaming others, denial, and so on. Keep in mind that your goal is to figure out why a student has misbehaved so that you can help her learn not to behave that way again.

Note: When a student flatly denies involvement in an incident and you have factual evidence that he is guilty, share the facts and let him know that further denials will be useless. If a student denies involvement and you have no factual knowledge of his guilt, you have three choices:

1. Gather additional information to determine the truth.

2. Give the student the benefit of the doubt and do not assign a corrective consequence.

3. Make a judgment that the student is guilty despite your lack of hard evidence.

The third choice should not be undertaken lightly. Although sometimes you will feel certain, based on his actions, that a student is guilty in spite of his denials, you must proceed with caution.

STEP 3. Clearly state that the particular misbehavior is not allowed in your school and explain why.

Remember that misbehavior represents an instructional opportunity. The student needs to know, with absolute clarity, that the misbehavior will not be tolerated in the school. Also explain why the behavior cannot be allowed to continue. "Cynthia, cheating is not allowed in this or any other school. Sometimes you can work together with others, but other times you have to demonstrate to your teacher and to yourself what you know and what you don't. The only way to do this is to do your own work." With primary-age students, consider saying something like, "Allen, kicking others is not OK."

This is also the time to have students and adults who have been negatively affected by the student's behavior explain how the incident affected them—how it physically or emotionally hurt them or destroyed their trust in the student. The goal here is to try to get the misbehaving student to view his behavior from the other person's perspective.

STEP 4. Give the student information about how to behave more responsibly.

In keeping with the idea that misbehavior should be viewed as an instructional opportunity, use this conference to give the student information about how to behave more appropriately. Among the questions to ask are:

- What are some other ways you could have handled this situation?
- What would have happened if you had handled the situation better?
- What is your plan so the problem will not happen in the future?

Your goal, of course, is to move the student from thinking about the past incident into thinking about how she might handle a similar situation more responsibly in the future. If you find that the student does not have strategies for behaving more responsibly, use this time to teach her or to make arrangements for her to be taught. The ultimate goal is for the student to act in a more responsible manner in the future.

STEP 5. Determine what, if any, corrective consequence (beyond the conference) will be assigned, and inform the student.

In some cases, just being sent to the office and meeting with you serves as an effective corrective consequence. However, if the behavior was severe or the student does not seem at all remorseful, assigning an additional corrective consequence may be necessary to decrease the likelihood that the behavior will occur again. Any additional corrective consequences should, when possible, have some logical association with the misbehavior.

One consequence to seriously consider is an immediate timeout, which will delay the student's return to the setting where the infraction occurred. Giving everyone some time to cool down may be especially critical when the referring staff member is the student's classroom teacher. Classroom misbehavior can be very upsetting to a teacher. If this is the case, give the teacher some time away from the student by keeping the student in the office (or in a timeout room, problem-solving room, or similar setting) for a longer period of time. When a teacher has referred a student for something such as defiance and the student is gone for only 10 or 15 minutes before returning to class, the teacher may think you don't consider the behavior to be as serious as he does.

We discuss consequences in detail in Task 3 of this presentation.

STEP 6. Make a decision about parent contact and inform the student.

In most cases, it's a good idea to let parents know when their children have been referred to the office. If you decide to contact them immediately, you can make the call or have the student do it. In either case, the parents should be told the nature of the referral, what the student says about the situation (Does he admit guilt or deny that the event took place?), and the corrective consequence that will be assigned at school. Implement a school-based consequence, or consider whether the student's parents are willing to support the school's concern and implement a home-based consequence. Regardless of whether the consequence will be school or home based, encourage the parents to talk with the student about the problem. Unfortunately, many students who have behavioral difficulties at school come from dysfunctional family situations. In these cases, the parents may not follow through on consequences, or they may be overly emotional or possibly even physically or mentally abusive.

Be sure to end the call on a positive note. Let the parents know about the traits you value in their child and assure them that this is a learning situation. If the family and the school work together, the student will learn important lessons from the experience.

STEP 7. Tell the student what will happen if the behavior occurs again.

In addition to assigning a corrective consequence for the immediate situation, you may want to specify what the corrective consequences will be if the behavior continues.

When deciding on future corrective consequences, consider the student's history of behavior problems. Also think about whether you will ask staff to refer future situations to you or to handle them without involving you. For example, if a student has been referred for minor classroom disruptions, you might meet with the teacher and student and help them negotiate one or more classroom-based consequences for future incidents rather than have the teacher send the student to your office. However, if you feel that the situation warrants referral to you, try to decide now what corrective consequence you will implement for future incidents. You may use the same consequence you used for the current incident, with or without an additional consequence, or you may assign a completely different consequence.

Inform the student of your decision and end the discussion by telling her that you doubt the consequences will even be necessary because you are sure that she has learned from this experience and will not exhibit this behavior again.

STEP 8. Prepare the student to resume a normal schedule.

If the student will be reentering class, address two major issues before he leaves your office—how to respond to other students' questions and how to interact with the referring teacher.

First, explain to the student that if other students ask what happened in the office, he should reply neutrally—something like, "We talked about the fight, she assigned me after-school detention, and we talked about what might happen if I fight again." Help the student understand that if he brushes the situation off ("Oh, no big deal, I got away with it") or makes it highly adversarial ("The principal is such a _____— I hate her guts"), he is setting himself up to repeat the behavior in front of peers just to save face. In addition, he might be encouraging others to exhibit the same behavior because they think it's "no big deal" or "the principal is the enemy." Tell the student that although you have no control over what he does or says, you hope he will respond neutrally—both for his own sake and for the sake of others in the school.

Second, prepare the student to face the referring staff member. Many students do not have the skill of making amends, so you need to specifically teach them. With the staff, develop a sequence of steps for the student to follow when returning to his daily schedule after an office referral. Plan to model the steps and practice them with the student before sending him back to class. Following is a sample sequence of steps for the student:

- Take a copy of the completed Behavior Incident Referral Form back to the classroom.

- Walk quietly up to the teacher (or staff member who wrote the incident report) and wait until the teacher acknowledges your presence.

- Give the referral form to the teacher, apologize for the incident or at least acknowledge that the behavior was not acceptable, and ask the teacher what to do next.

The teacher should accept the student back into the setting without revisiting the incident. (Ensure that all staff understand this step.)

Keep in mind that although these actions seem to be simple common sense, some students (particularly those with poor social skills) might not know how to implement them. Therefore, always walk a student through the sequence before sending him back to his daily schedule. First explain each of the steps in the sequence, then model for the student how each should look and how each should *not* look. Finally, have the student demonstrate the sequence until he can do it easily and successfully.

When a student is not given sufficient reentry information, he is more likely to saunter into the class, interrupt the teacher, slap the referral form on the desk, and sarcastically say, "I'm back. Aren't you glad to see me?" This in turn may make the teacher even more upset with the student and upset with you because your actions apparently accomplished nothing. Simply put, you are trying to give the student the skill of making amends. Let the student know that whether or not he truly feels bad is up to him, but you expect him to make a sincere effort to get along with the referring staff member.

In some cases, the student will go from meeting with you to a setting with a staff member other than the referring staff member. For example, a middle school student who received a referral from his third-period math teacher may finish meeting with you during his fourth-period science class. Or you may not finish meeting with an elementary student who received a referral from the music specialist until music is over. In these cases, give the student information about reentering the next class and about interacting with the referring staff member at a later time (during lunch, after school, or at the beginning of class the next day). The more specific the information you provide to the student about how to resume contact with the referring staff member, the greater the probability that the staff member will feel you supported him with the referral he made.

STEP 9. End the meeting with a statement of confidence that the student will learn from this situation and not exhibit the behavior in the future.

With this final step, you put closure on the meeting. Communicate that you are confident that the student will learn from her mistake and not exhibit the behavior again. In line with viewing misbehavior as an instructional opportunity, think of this as the lesson summary. Keep it clear, brief, and positive.

Game Plan, Section 3

Follow-up: Actions to take after you've met with the student

STEP 1. Document the incident.

Documenting disciplinary referrals serves a couple of important purposes. First, your records on individual students can help you decide what to do for repeated incidents. They should include what you said would happen if the student engaged in the behavior again and a description of your contacts with the parents. Second, your records should provide enough information for you to answer questions about the incident and your response 1 or 2 years later. For example, let's say a student who has been in your office several times over the past 2 years is arrested for assaulting someone. You go to court because the parents of the victim want you to answer questions about the student's history of assaultive behavior. Your records should allow you to objectively answer the following questions about each of the student's office referrals.

- What was the date and time of the incident?
- What happened?
- Who was involved?
- Were parents contacted?

Module D: Responding to Misbehavior—An Instructional Approach

- What corrective consequence was implemented?
- What corrective consequence did you tell the student would be implemented if the behavior continued?

In most cases, the referral form should provide the documentation you need. Be sure to add any anecdotal notes that may help you recall the critical features of a particular incident and your actions. "Jacob did not sound at all remorseful about hurting Tim's feelings. If any further incidents of hurtful behavior occur, I should talk to the counselor about strategies that might increase Jacob's compassion and empathy."

STEP 2. Follow up with the referring staff member.

Be sure to let the person who made the referral know what action you took regarding that referral. Specifically, tell the person any additional corrective consequences you assigned. If you sent the student back to the setting where the incident occurred, ask whether the student followed through on reentry procedures.

If you want the staff member to handle things differently in the future, give that person clear and direct instructions regarding your expectations. If you think the incident should have been handled as a Level 2—corrected in the classroom or common area with paperwork going to the office—tell the staff member and explain your rationale. Sometimes a referral results as much from a staff member's behavior as from the student's behavior. For example, a playground supervisor who argued with a student may have actually escalated the student's emotional intensity to the point at which the student exhibited defiant behavior. Although you do not want the playground supervisor to feel that she is being punished for the student's misbehavior, it may be advisable for her to get instruction on how to interact with students without arguing. Role-playing can be useful in this context. Let the staff person be the student; you be the staff person and act out different scenarios. Then reverse roles. If a student's behavior is partially a result of problematic staff behavior, your plan should involve trying to get both parties to make a change. However, assure the staff member that you will not tell the student about your efforts with the staff member. Presentation 5, Task 1 provides information about de-escalation strategies for all staff.

STEP 3. Inform the student's classroom/advisory teacher about the meeting if he or she was not present.

When a referral comes from a common area supervisor or from another teacher (the music teacher, for example), the student's classroom teacher (or at the secondary level, the advisory or homeroom teacher) should be informed. The objective is to make the student's classroom or advisory teacher a partner in what is happening with the student in all school settings. Let your staff know that whenever one of their students gets a referral, they will get a copy of the referral form and you expect them to talk briefly with the student about the incident. "Mary, I see that you got a bus referral. Tell me about that. How are you doing now? Are things going better? I know that you can treat the driver with respect—she has a very tough job. You don't have to like her, but you do have to follow her rules."

Share any insights you gained from the student during the meeting and any plans you have made for future interventions.

STEP 4. If appropriate, involve other staff.

Sometimes a referral from one staff member is a sign that all staff (counselor, playground supervisor, and so on) should watch a student more closely or modify how they interact with that student. If a student has been referred for bullying, for example, you may want to ask all staff to keep a close eye on him to ensure that he is not victimizing students in the lunchroom, halls, playground, and so on. Or a referral may prompt you to suspect that a student is starved for adult attention. In that case, you can let other staff who have frequent contact with the student know that he could benefit from some extra positive attention and nurturing.

STEP 5. Make a point to interact positively with the student in the near future.

Try to reestablish a relationship as a positive supporter with the student as quickly as possible after a referral. For example, within a day or two, seek out the opportunity to greet her in the hall (or any other location). Show an interest in what she is doing. If the student is with peers, do not mention the referral itself or her behavior. However, if the student is not with peers and it would not embarrass her, ask how she is doing with managing the behavior that you and she discussed in the office. "Ivette, how are you? Are you playing soccer this season? How is the team doing? Hey, I talked to Ms. Yountz, and she said you did a very nice job of apologizing to her about the problem we worked on in my office. How are you getting along with Ms. Yountz now? Great. If you ever need my help with anything, come and see me."

STEP 6. Follow up with both the referring staff member and the student after about two weeks.

At the time of the referral, make a note on your planning calendar to check with the referring staff member in about two weeks to see how the situation is progressing. If the situation has improved, congratulate the staff member and thank him for helping the student learn to manage an important behavior. You want the staff member to know that the referral and any subsequent actions have provided a very important lesson for the student—one that will help him be successful in future schools and in employment situations. Then, if possible, reinforce the student. For example, the next time you see him, share the positive feedback you received from the staff member.

Also, consider contacting the parents to inform them of the progress the student has made and ask them to congratulate him on learning an important lesson.

If the behavior has not improved, plan to design a comprehensive intervention plan. You might begin by using the form Planning Questions for Dealing With Severe or Chronic Problems that we explained in Task 1. We discuss proactive individual behavior improvement plans in more detail in Module F.

Task 2 Action Steps & Evidence of Implementation

Action Steps	Evidence of Implementation
1. Have the administrator develop a "Who Is Responsible" list of staff members authorized to process Level 3 office referrals. • Include the list in the Foundations Archive. • Ensure that all office staff members have a written copy of the sequence.	Foundations Archive: 3-Level System for Responding to Misbehavior Staff Handbook: 3-Level System for Responding to Misbehavior
2. The administrator should prepare for Level 3 office referrals. • Develop a game plan for dealing with students during the referral process. • Develop a menu of corrections (more about this in Task 3). • Develop a sequence of steps for returning a student to his or her regular schedule. Ensure that designees know the game plan and all procedures for processing office disciplinary referrals. The administrator and designees must handle all aspects of referrals consistently.	
3. Document in writing all relevant staff and administrative procedures for Level 3 infractions. • Include summaries of essential information in the Staff Handbook. • Include detailed descriptions in the Foundations Archive.	

TASK 3

Develop alternatives to out-of-school suspension

You should define a menu of corrections for Level 3 infractions (and chronic Level 2 infractions) that you and the administrative designees will use. We suggest some building-based corrective consequences in this task, and in Task 5 we discuss ways to implement in-school suspension (ISS) as well as some district- and community-based alternatives to out-of-school suspension (OSS). As explained in Presentation 1, OSS probably serves as a reward for most students and is not an effective consequence. It is directly associated with dropping out of school, poor grades, involvement with the juvenile justice system, and other deleterious effects. The overall goal is to keep students in school while ensuring the safety of all students and to use the mildest consequence that reasonably fits the infraction.

For offenses that involve violence, drugs, or weapons, district policy probably mandates OSS. But avoid assigning OSS for less serious, discretionary offenses. Below we suggest a menu of alternatives to OSS for use with Level 3 infractions.

All corrections and responses on the Level 1 and Level 2 menus. See Presentation 3.

Debriefing form. The student completes a debriefing form, such as the Behavior Improvement Form. (See Forms D-10a and D-10b on the Module D CD.)

Problem-solving room. This room should be staffed by a skilled paraprofessional who can talk with the student, have her fill out a debriefing form, and return her to instruction as quickly as possible. This is essentially a very brief visit to in-school suspension.

Detention. You have several possibilities for scheduling detention to fit staff availability and school resources: lunchtime, before school, after school, or Saturday. Some schools that have a consistent early release day hold their detention on that day right after school. We have heard from some schools in Texas, where Friday night football is the big social event of the week, that Friday night detention is very effective. Parents are very supportive, and data show that students do not want to repeat this detention.

Restorative practices. Students make amends or compensate for any damage that results from their actions. Restorative practices can take many forms:

- Apology letter
- Relationship conference: Attempt to restore a damaged relationship by having the student meet with the teacher he was disrespectful to, for

example, or by arranging a conference with peers who are not getting along. Do not use this strategy for bullying or harassment, however. Students who have been bullied or harassed should not be forced to confront the student who bullied or harassed them.

- Repairing damage: Have a student who wrote on a desk wash the desk, for example. Be careful not to imply that maintenance tasks in general are punishment. Instead, the emphasis should be on the valuable job that your custodians do to keep the school clean. If a student damages school property, it is her responsibility to assist with the maintenance of the building.

- Paying for damage: You will probably have to coordinate with the parents when money is involved.

- Community service

- Require the student to devise a restorative plan

Restorative practices are a growing movement in schools and in the juvenile justice system. You might consider providing formal training to some staff on conducting meditations, group circles, and family group conferences. More information is available from the Restorative Practices Foundation (www.restorativepracticesfoundation.org/evidence/) and the International Institute for Restorative Practices (www.iirp.edu/what-is-restorative-practices.php).

Cocurricular activity suspension. The student loses the privilege of participating in sports or clubs for a specified period. Be careful—if a sport or club is the one connection the student has with the school, you might lose the student by using this consequence.

Mini-courses or skill modules. The student completes a course that focuses on the social, emotional, or behavioral skills that he is struggling with. The school counselor or school psychologist can lead the development of these courses.

Short-term skill group. During detention, the counselor conducts group skills training for all students who are present. You might schedule an ongoing social skills group that takes place during the lunch period—students spend 2 or 3 lunch periods with the skill group instead of with their friends in the cafeteria. Some schools conduct recess social skills training. Students who are assigned this consequence go to recess, but instead of free play they participate in a structured social skills group for 2 or 3 days. A counselor or skilled paraprofessional (under the counselor's supervision) teaches social skills using playground games and interactions.

Behavior monitoring. A Tier 2 check-and-connect program can provide students with adult attention and support, structure, and motivation to improve their behavior.

Students carry monitoring cards and have teachers and common area supervisors rate them on specific behaviors throughout the school day. Students are rewarded for improved behavior. We discuss one of these programs, Connections, in detail in Module C, Presentation 5, Task 5.

Behavior contracting (school or home based. Behavior contracting has powerful support in the research literature. The student signs a contract that stipulates consequences for inappropriate behavior as well as incentives for positive behavior.

Parent supervision at school. The student's parent is required to come to school and shadow the student throughout the day. Students find this correction very aversive, but it should be used carefully and sparingly.

In-school suspension. When structured well, ISS can be a very effective alternative to OSS. We discuss ISS in detail in Task 5 of this presentation.

Note: Any of the above consequences can be used as part of or as an initial stage of an individual behavior improvement plan.

Out-of school suspension, expulsion, and filing criminal charges. You will occasionally have to assign OSS, expel a student, or file criminal charges against a student. When you must take these actions, we encourage you to conduct postintervention analyses to understand how you, as a school, can in the future improve and possibly prevent the behavior that led to these actions. A metaphor for the postintervention analysis is the postmortem that hospitals conduct after a patient's death. The purpose is not to point fingers or place blame. The physicians' priority is to determine whether they might have prevented the death by doing something differently or better. And so it should be with your postintervention analysis. Ask yourself, Could we have provided a better quality of care?

In addition to the alternatives to OSS mentioned in this task, there are a few research-based broad strategies that the Center for Civil Rights Remedies (Losen and Martinez, 2013) labels Alternatives That Work. One is modifying your code of conduct to be more constructive than punitive and to allow more alternatives to OSS. This issue would probably be considered by the school board, not individual schools. Another strategy is to implement systemwide positive behavior support to change the underlying attitudes and policies regarding behavior management. *Foundations* is, of course, a great example of positive and proactive behavior support. The Center for Civil Rights Remedies also notes that research supports training for teachers and school leaders in school connectedness, classroom management, cultural sensitivity, and working with students with disabilities. Research has shown that training in strategies for handling students' social and emotional issues resulted in substantial reductions in suspensions and improved school climate. We provide information about understanding emotional escalation in Module D, Presentation 5. The center also notes that evidence is mounting on the positive effects that restorative practices can have on school climate and reducing suspension rates.

Be sure to archive your decisions about Level 3 consequences and discuss them with the designees who will handle office referrals when you are out of the building. And think long term as well—you will not be at the school forever. The practices that you have worked so hard to develop and institute need to be archived in writing so that future administrators and staff have a cultural history of the policies and practices for Level 3 infractions.

Task 3 Action Steps & Evidence of Implementation

Action Steps	Evidence of Implementation
1. Develop a menu of corrections for Level 3 infractions, with as many alternatives to OSS as possible.	Foundations Archive: 3-Level System for Responding to Misbehavior
2. Develop a plan for reducing the number of OSS by addressing your codes of conduct and making recommendations to the school board, if necessary.	

TASK 4

Establish office procedures for dealing with Level 3 referrals

In this task, we suggest procedures that office staff can follow to ensure that students referred to the office are processed efficiently, positively (but without rewarding the student), and consistently. But first, let's briefly consider the roles of administrators and teachers in office referrals.

You, the administrator, should determine *how* referred students get to the office. For example, will you (or a designee) go to the classroom or other setting and escort the student after the office is notified? Will the referring staff member send the student on his own, carrying a referral slip or hall pass? Also decide where in the office students will wait until you can see them. This area must be uninteresting. Too often, referred students sit and wait right in the middle of all the front office's action, so they are entertained and reinforced for getting sent there.

Edythe Jones Hayes Middle School in Lexington, Kentucky, has developed an efficient procedure for referred students. Students go first to the ISS room, where three or four seats are reserved for referred students. When a referred student arrives, the ISS teacher or paraprofessional sends an email to the assistant principal or dean. The students wait in the ISS room until the notified person or their designee arrives to take them to the office, where they are processed. With this procedure, students are properly supervised by skilled adults in a nonreinforcing environment while they wait for an administrator.

Teachers also have responsibilities in the office referral process. The most important is to let the office know immediately when they have referred a student. Teachers should make a quick telephone or walkie-talkie call (or use whatever communication devices your school has) so that the office knows the student is on her way. Ensure that all staff know this expectation and how to contact the office easily and quickly. Teachers must also follow up as soon as possible with the written referral form.

Office staff play important roles in the office referral process. They are often responsible for monitoring students who have been referred for disciplinary reasons. These students can be upset or angry, so office personnel must be skilled in handling these situations. We recommend you provide detailed training to office staff on how to handle office referrals and how to interact with students. The following information can form the basis of this training.

Train office staff on their responsibilities in the referral process.

1. **Monitor the student's arrival at the office.**

   Office staff are responsible for monitoring the student's arrival at the expected time. If the student does not appear within a reasonable period, office staff should notify the administrator or designee. The administrator or designee then decides whether to search for the student, contact the student's parents, or contact the police.

   If the administrator is unavailable when a student has been referred, office staff need to consult the Who Is Responsible? list (see Task 2). Every office staff member should have a copy of the list and know how to contact the people on it.

2. **Ensure that students follow all established procedures while waiting.**

   If the wait will be only a few minutes, the student should sit and do nothing. If the wait will be longer than a few minutes, requiring the student to sit and do nothing is likely to result in additional problem behaviors. For longer wait periods, office staff can have the student complete a Behavior Improvement Form about the incident (younger students might draw a picture) or give the student an age-appropriate book. The Behavior Improvement Form gives the student a chance to tell her side of the story, and the act of writing can divert some of the student's anger. Some schools place the Behavior Improvement Form on a colored clipboard. The clipboard's color alerts other staff members and students to ignore the student—for example, tell staff and students to ignore students with *red* clipboards. When staff and students passing through the office give the referred student attention, they are giving the student power and reinforcing him.

   Figure 4d on the next page shows expectations posters that Keithley Middle School in Tacoma, Washington, developed to clarify how students are supposed to behave in the main office, the principal's office, and the hallway outside the principal's office. These expectations are taught along with all other schoolwide expectations for common areas and schoolwide policies, and the posters are displayed in the corresponding areas. When the expectations are clearly defined and displayed, office staff can easily correct students by simply referring to the poster and saying, "The rule is _____. Please follow the rule."

3. **Arrange an appropriate waiting area.**

   The waiting area should be uninteresting, nonstimulating, and within view of the office staff so they can supervise the student. Office staff should be businesslike and limit their conversations with each other and with the student. When more than one student is waiting, the students should be separated as much as possible. Two or more students together tend to goad one another into creating more trouble and teach each other new techniques in troublemaking.

Expectations posters for the main office, principal's office, and principal's hallway *(D-15); thanks to Keithley Middle School and Franklin Pierce Schools in Tacoma, Washington*

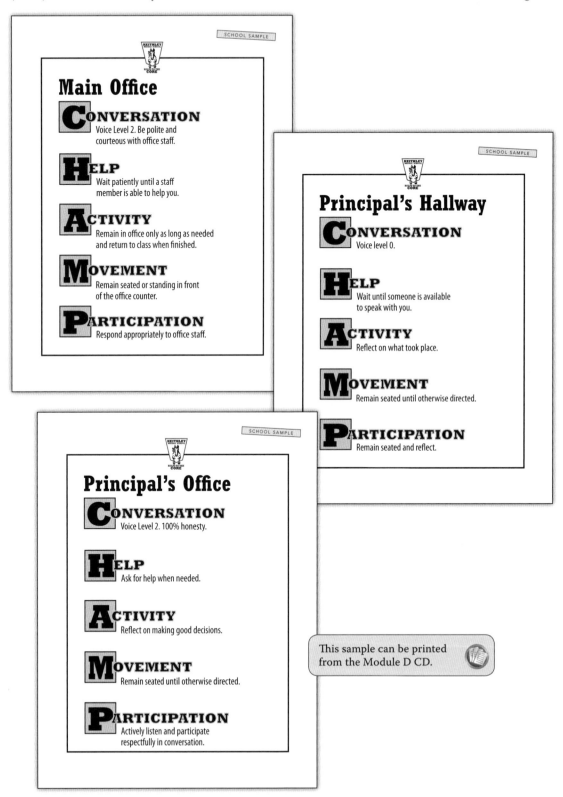

This sample can be printed from the Module D CD.

4. Interact appropriately with students.

Office staff will probably need more training for this skill than for any other procedure we've suggested. They can't be too nice to referred students because the students then find the office environment rewarding. (We've heard of staff giving referred students cookies!) And they can't be harsh or punitive because that might escalate the students' problem behaviors. Here are some ideas for staff about how to appropriately supervise a referred student. Also see the "Example From the Field" on the next page.

- Give the student as little attention as possible. Use a businesslike tone of voice and give clear, brief directions. "Sit in that chair, please."

- Tell students what to do instead of what *not* to do. Say, "Sit down," instead of "Don't just stand there."

- Use empathic responses. Acknowledge the student's feelings and restate his point of view. For example, when a student says, "I hate this school," say something like, "I understand you feel like you hate the school right now." You don't need to agree that the school is terrible or try to convince the student that he doesn't really hate the school.

- Use nonthreatening body language. Keep your arms open instead of folded across your chest, and keep your facial expression neutral.

- Avoid engaging in power struggles or escalating interactions. Questions such as "Wouldn't you like to sit down?" and "How are you supposed to behave in the office?" can invite power struggles. Avoid phrasing directions as questions.

- If the student tries to argue or explain what happened, use a one-liner such as, "I understand." "I understand" can de-escalate emotion and is a great default comment when you don't know what to say. If the student's behavior is verging on inappropriate, say, "That is not OK."

- If the student misbehaves in the office (uses an obscenity, for example), calmly but firmly tell the student to stop and give a clear instruction for what the student should do. "Shanti, you need to quiet down. Please sit in that chair over there and wait for Mrs. Thompson to see you." If the student does not stop, do not repeat the instruction or physically try to make the student stop. Get the administrator immediately.

5. Know when to ask for help.

Staff should know that when a student is out of control, they should immediately turn the situation over to the administrator or a designee.

*E*xample From the Field

I was observing in a high school along with the assistant superintendent of the district. We happened to be in the office when Jason came flying through the door. "I have to call my dad. They're lying! I didn't do it this time, I swear! I did it last time but I didn't do it this time. I gotta call my dad!"

One of the office staff, a young woman, quickly stepped up to the counter. "So, Jason, you think the teachers are not being truthful about the situation. You and Mr. Jones can straighten this out. Please sit down and wait."

"I didn't do it! I have to call my dad right now! I gotta use the phone!"

"Jason, I understand you want to call your dad, and you'll be able to call him as soon as you've seen Mr. Jones. You have to talk with Mr. Jones first."

"I'm gonna use my cell phone. I'll call my dad on my cell phone!"

"Jason, you can only use your cell phone before 8:30 and after 3:30. You can ask Mr. Jones about using the phone. Please just sit down. Mr. Jones will be available in a couple of minutes."

Jason finally sat down.

When we talked with the principal later, the assistant superintendent told him, "We just saw one of your office staff do an excellent job de-escalating and defusing an upset student." The principal was delighted to hear this. The school had been making an effort to train the office staff in how to deal appropriately with students. The principal immediately went to the office staff member and complimented her on her actions with Jason. Imagine how the woman felt to learn that the assistant superintendent had been impressed with how she handled a difficult situation! Because she received immediate positive feedback and the incident ended well, the staff member will always remember the strategies she used:

- She gave the student just enough attention and was businesslike in tone. She didn't gush over him or sympathize, but she wasn't terse, either.

- She didn't engage in a power struggle or escalate the student's emotions. Instead, she used empathic responses—she acknowledged his feelings and restated his point of view. "So, Jason, you think the teachers are not being truthful about the situation. " "Jason, I understand you want to call your dad, and you'll be able to call him as soon as you've seen Mr. Jones." She didn't agree with the student—she just indicated that she heard and understood what he said.

- She responded to the student's demands by stating the cell phone rule. "You can use your cell phone before 8:30 and after 3:30." She didn't tell him he could not use his cell phone.

- She never said "No."

—S.I.

Task 4 Action Steps & Evidence of Implementation

Action Steps	Evidence of Implementation

The team and the administrator should work together on the following actions:
 	
1. Evaluate current office procedures for dealing with referred students.
 	
2. If necessary, modify the current procedures to make the process run more smoothly. Ensure that the following issues are addressed:
 	
   • How will office staff supervise referred students throughout the entire process?
   • What will office staff do if the administrator is unavailable when referred students arrive at the office?
   • Where will referred students wait for the administrator?
   • What should referred students do while waiting for the administrator?
   • How should office personnel interact with referred students?
 	
3. Train all staff on the procedures. (Teachers need to know about their responsibilities for alerting the office; office staff need to know their roles and responsibilities.)
	Foundations Archive: Schoolwide Policies
	
	Staff Handbook: Staff Roles and Responsibilities

TASK 5

Use in-school suspension productively

In this task, we discuss best practices for in-school suspension (ISS) and provide some examples of successful alternative placement programs. (You can find sample ISS procedures [D-16] on the Module D CD.) First, let's review some of the measures schools can take to reduce the need for any kind of ISS program.

Before you devote much time, energy, and effort to building ISS spaces for students, make sure you've done all of the work related to the STOIC framework. If you haven't structured and organized all common areas, developed clear and consistent expectations for behavior in common areas and with schoolwide policies, and created a schoolwide management plan, your efforts on ISS will explode. You'll have too many students in ISS because you didn't do the preventive work up front.

The same is true for classrooms. It's important that teachers have established effective classroom management plans and examined their classroom organization and structure to ensure that they are teaching all of their students how to be successful in every activity and transition.

After common areas, schoolwide policies, and classrooms have been addressed, consider the potential for using ISS and related programs as alternatives to out-of-school suspension (OSS). OSS is not an effective strategy for the vast majority of behavioral infractions, so many schools, especially secondary schools, are now investigating or have set up ISS programs.

What is in-school suspension?

ISS is an in-house program that students may be assigned to for short periods as an alternative to OSS. Unlike OSS, where students miss instruction and potentially have no adult supervision for several days, ISS allows continued instruction, access to academic help, and counseling for students who need it for personal, academic, or behavioral issues.

Research suggests four basic ISS models:

- **Punitive.** The assumption behind a punitive model is that simply putting the student in ISS will automatically reduce the misbehavior.

- **Discussion.** This model assumes that active discussions with the program staff to improve self-esteem, communication skills, and problem-solving skills will help the student develop more appropriate behavior.

- **Academic.** The academic model assumes that most behavior problems arise from academic frustration. If the student can improve her basic academic skills, her behavior will improve.

- **Hybrid.** This model incorporates components from the first three models to form a comprehensive ISS program. The hybrid model is generally accepted as best practice and is the model we recommend.

What are the components of an effective ISS program?

The administrator and staff should develop the ISS program. It can be tempting to just let the person who will run the program develop it, but we strongly discourage that route. Staff, with the leadership of the administrator, should think through their ISS philosophy—policies and procedures, the message they want to give students, the values that ISS staff will emphasize to students—before the first student is assigned to ISS. Develop the program first, then put trained personnel in place to run it.

A good ISS program requires resources, so plan to train personnel and purchase materials and equipment for the ISS space.

Another key ingredient of an effective ISS program is continuous program monitoring. The staff who run the program (ISS teachers, counselors, and social workers, for example) must collect and analyze data on the number of students assigned to ISS, how frequently individual students are assigned, and the impact ISS has on decreasing their misbehavior. They should also examine data about the types of infractions. Are students assigned ISS for minor misbehavior that could be corrected by other means? Are students assigned ISS for very serious misbehavior that requires more serious consequences? We recommend that ISS be assigned only by the administrator or administrator designees so that students are assigned appropriately.

Counseling is an essential ISS component. Students should have the opportunity to work on problem solving with guidance from trained staff. They can debrief the misbehavior: How could I have handled this situation better? How will I handle similar situations in the future?

The evaluation components should be used to measure the effectiveness of the program as a whole as well as its effect on the various groups of students (ninth-grade girls or Hispanic/Latino boys, for example) who are assigned to ISS. The administrator and the ISS staff need to support one another with this work so that the intended effects of the correction—academic support, behavior support, and self-reflection on the incident—take place.

The best practice for ISS is to have students do academic work. This can be tricky because it can take time for teachers to send work to ISS, and sometimes students have nothing to do until the work arrives. We know of one ISS program that provides a library of all textbooks for every subject and every grade, so the ISS teacher can have students work on academics while they wait for specific assignments from teachers.

The last component of an effective ISS program is parent contact. Ensure that parents are notified that their child has been assigned ISS.

What are some common yet ineffective ISS practices?

You should also be aware of some ISS practices to avoid. First, don't set up an ISS program if you don't intend to evaluate its efficacy. It is essential to gather and analyze data. Simply putting students in a room and hoping for the best is not an effective practice.

Try to avoid dividing the role of ISS supervisor among several staff members. You might be tempted to do this if you don't have the financial resources to hire a full-time teacher or paraprofessional. A teacher with a prep period staffs the ISS room for Period 1, another teacher with a free period runs the program in Period 2, someone else comes in for Period 3, and so on. When six or seven different adults are supervising throughout the day, consistency is difficult. If this is your only option, ensure that all staff know the rules and procedures thoroughly. Dividing the role is really not best practice, however, so we recommend you avoid doing so.

Another ineffective practice we see in some schools is filling the ISS program with students who committed minor offenses such as sleeping in class or not completing their work. Teachers should handle these offenses with the corrections for mild and moderate misbehavior we've recommended in *Foundations* (see Module D, Presentation 3).

Some schools also fail to follow up with students who have been in ISS. Did they catch up with their academic work? Are they behaving better in class? Have they used any of the skills they learned in ISS? One ISS supervisor in a *Foundations* middle school visits classrooms whenever he doesn't have any students in ISS. He chats briefly with students who were in his ISS room recently, giving the students some positive noncontingent attention in the context of their regular classroom.

Finally, don't have students sit and do nothing during ISS. You don't want them to fall behind on their schoolwork.

Consider these issues before developing your ISS program.

If you're considering implementing an ISS program, think through these questions. What does your school hope to accomplish through an ISS program?

How will an ISS program affect:

- Student achievement?
- Student discipline?
- School climate and the learning environment?
- Academic achievement of at-risk students and special education students?

Examples of effective programs

SAFE program at Dunbar High School

Paul Laurence Dunbar High School in Lexington, Kentucky, runs an effective ISS program called SAFE: Suspension And Failure Eliminated. SAFE is assigned for a variety of misbehaviors—skipping school, profanity with a teacher, cheating, and cell phone violations, for example. Placement ranges from 1 hour to 5 days.

Dunbar is able to employ a certified teacher and a paraprofessional to be with the ISS students all day (quite a luxury these days!). The ISS schedule begins and ends at the same time as the regular schedule. Lunch is provided inside the ISS classroom, so students don't leave the classroom during the lunch period. Students also require an escort to go to the restroom. While in the ISS classroom, students do their academic work, and peer tutors are available. Some counseling is provided by the ISS teacher, who reviews grades with the students and helps them problem-solve to promote life success. Students are monitored throughout the day, and the ISS teacher can extend the assigned ISS time if students don't follow all the expectations. With this highly structured program, Dunbar High School finds that very few students want to return to SAFE.

Alternatives to ISS at Dunbar High School

Paul Laurence Dunbar High School has taken the bold step of trying to eliminate OSS altogether. To accomplish this goal, Dunbar developed three programs (in addition to SAFE, described above) to respond to increasingly severe misbehavior:

- SAP: Suspension Alternative Placement On-Site Program (up to 5-day placement for repeated infractions)

- SAP: Suspension Alternative Placement Off-Site Program (up to 5-day placement for repeated serious infractions, such as verbal aggression, disrespect, profanity, peer conflicts, and theft)

- TAP: Temporary Alternative Placement (on site, up to 10-day placement for very severe misbehavior and code of conduct violations, such as fighting, drug trafficking, assault, theft, gang activity, harassment, bullying, weapons, and alcohol)

SAP: Suspension Alternative Placement On-Site Program. The students' daily schedule is modified so that they arrive and leave about an hour earlier than other students. Parents are an integral part of this program because they have to provide transportation to and from the school, although the school will help students get bus passes, if necessary. As in SAFE, students do not leave the room during the lunch period, and they are escorted to the restrooms.

During this 5-day period, the dean of students assesses the support each student needs. Together, she and the student:

- Review grades and disciplinary history to problem-solve patterns of behavior that are preventing success in school.
- Set short-term and long-term school and career goals.
- Complete a self-assessment form and sign a behavior contract.

The student participates in a targeted program, such as life skills, conflict resolution, or drug/alcohol education (depending on the offense), and completes academic work. If necessary, outside resources such as mental health providers are called in to work with the student on site.

SAP: Suspension Alternative Placement Off-Site Program. Dunbar worked with the Fayette Urban County Government Division of Youth Services to develop an off-site SAP. The city (Lexington, Kentucky) government pays a full-time special education teacher to work in this program. Parents provide transportation, and the support provided to students is similar to the on-site SAP. According to Betsy Rains, the principal of Dunbar, parents are extremely supportive of this program and so far there have been no problems with parents dropping off and picking up their children. Students may work on credit recovery or bring work from school.

TAP: Temporary Alternative Placement. TAP is for students with serious behavior problems—for example, offenses that, according to the Fayette County code of student conduct, entail a 10-day suspension. This program is highly structured and very strict. It is supervised by a certified teacher and a paraprofessional, and students are assigned for 10 days. The students' daily schedule is modified so that they arrive and leave about an hour earlier than other students. TAP students are not allowed to leave the room except to go to the restroom with an escort. Students are also escorted to and from their mode of transportation, and they are not permitted to participate in extracurricular activities. Support similar to the on-site SAP is provided to students.

If the behavior involved drugs or alcohol, Dunbar staff contacts a mobile drug lab that comes to the school to assess students and connect them with appropriate services. The program might include restitution or community service. Staff might help students with career assessments and learning style inventories, review graduation plans and electives to take based on career interests, and assist with getting part-time jobs or applying to technical schools. Continuous monitoring and coaching is provided based on student needs.

As of this writing, these programs at Dunbar have been active for about six months, and they've had no students receive out-of-school suspension, which is unusual for a large comprehensive high school of 2,200 students. The principal notes several keys to making these programs work. One is personnel. Personnel costs are high thanks to the low teacher-to-student ratio, but because students are not out of school on suspension, the school does not lose state funds. (The school receives funding from the state based on average daily attendance and loses some of that funding when students are suspended). Personnel costs are somewhat balanced by the savings from maintaining average daily attendance.

Secure locations are also needed, and fortunately Dunbar has the luxury of space in the building. The school also received the necessary support from the school board and the superintendent for this unique and unusual program. And probably the biggest key to their success is the community support from the Division of Youth Services to provide the off-site alternative to suspension placement.

Task 5 Action Steps & Evidence of Implementation

Action Steps	Evidence of Implementation
Have a discussion with the Foundations team to determine the following: • What conditions are necessary to effectively implement an ISS program? • What skills do staff need? • Who will develop the program and document program policies and procedures in writing? • How will the program's efficacy be evaluated, and who will evaluate it?	Foundations Process: 3-Level System for Responding to Misbehavior

Preventing the Misbehavior That Leads to Referrals and Suspensions

CONTENTS

INTRODUCTION

Module D guides the entire staff in helping students learn to replace antisocial behaviors—behaviors that can force severe consequences such as office referral—with prosocial behaviors. When a student engages in severe misbehavior, such as calling a teacher an obscene name, the teacher should not hesitate to refer the student to the office nor should administrators avoid implementing severe consequences. We do suggest that school personnel can take many actions to reduce the odds that a student will exhibit severe misbehavior. For example, staff can learn about emotional escalation and how to de-escalate potentially emotional situations, the topics of this presentation.

Imagine a socially unskilled student who also has significant anger issues. Now imagine actions you could take and words you could say that would be within your authority as a school staff member but that would, over time, provoke that student to blow up emotionally and exhibit inappropriate behavior. Given the demands of your complex job, the scores of decisions that you as a professional make every single hour, and the competing demands on your attention, imagine how easy it would be to interact unskillfully with the student and unintentionally and inadvertently contribute to the student's making an unskillful choice about what to do or say.

Decades ago, the psychologist Haim Ginott eloquently summarized the influence that teachers have on their students in his 1972 book *Teacher and Child*:

> *I have come to the frightening conclusion that I am the decisive element in the classroom. It's my personal approach that creates the climate. It's my daily mood that makes the weather. As a teacher, I possess a tremendous power to make a child's life miserable or joyous. I can be a tool of torture or an instrument of inspiration. I can humiliate or humor, hurt or heal. In all situations, it is my response that decides whether a crisis will be escalated or de-escalated and a child humanized or dehumanized. (p. 15)*

We love this quote, but we disagree with one word. The last sentence reads, "In all situations, it is my response that decides whether a crisis will be escalated or de-escalated and a child humanized or dehumanized." The word *decides* implies that if the student's misbehavior escalates, the teacher has caused the escalation. We do not believe that to be true. And though we would never tamper with Ginott's eloquent language, we think the idea would be more accurate if the word *influences* replaced *decides*: "In all situations, it is my response that *influences* whether a crisis will be escalated or de-escalated and a child humanized or dehumanized.

The tasks in this presentation will help all staff members recognize and learn how they can influence student behavior to escalate or de-escalate. The work that you do on preventing the escalation of student misbehavior is part of a broader context—it ties in with the concepts presented in other modules of *Foundations.*

There are three tasks in this presentation:

Task 1: Understand Emotional Escalation explains invitations to anger, the Can't vs. Won't model, and the idea of resistance rather than noncompliance. It also describes the seven phases of acting-out behavior along with strategies for de-escalating behavior at each phase.

Task 2: Use Communications Strategies to Prevent Emotional Escalation covers strategies for helping students maintain their emotional equilibrium and be successful.

Task 3: Teach Students the Expectations for Interacting Appropriately With Adults consists of ten sample lessons you can use to teach students how to interact skillfully with adults. A theme that runs throughout *Foundations* is that if you expect students to behave in a certain way, you need to directly teach students those expectations.

We encourage the Foundations Team to read or view the tasks in this presentation and determine whether the information could benefit the staff. You may decide to use or adapt the tasks for the entire staff. If so, be sure to document those trainings in your Foundations Archive in the Presentations/Communications With Staff section. Archiving is important so you can present the same information to new staff with minimum preparation time and effort, thus ensuring that all staff receive consistent information and training.

TASK 1
Understand emotional escalation

Note: Much of the information in this task has been adapted with permission from Geoff Colvin's *Managing the Cycle of Acting-Out Behavior in the Classroom* (2004) and John Maag's *Powerful Struggles* (2001).

The skills for recognizing and defusing a chain of escalating behavior are needed now more than ever. More and more teachers and schools are challenged with students who can quickly become agitated and accelerate to anger and violence. Students may exhibit challenging behavior for many reasons, including:

- Disabilities (e.g., emotional behavioral disability, other health impairment, or autism spectrum disorder)
- Poor problem-solving skills
- Effects of acute or chronic trauma
- Poverty (can result in more stress-ridden attachments with teachers and other adults)

Many of these students function below grade level despite having sound academic potential. Academic deficits may serve as sources of anger and frustration for these students, and chronic academic failure may cause them to distrust the adults in the school.

Some students exhibit challenging behavior because they are expected to demonstrate social skills for which they have little fluency. Some staff members have difficulty understanding that the social behavior they wish to see in students might not be the behavior that is modeled or taught in the students' homes and neighborhoods. Many principals report that parents of students who have acted out by hitting another child frequently say, "I told him to hit back."

An increasing number of students with behavioral disabilities as well as diagnosed or undiagnosed mental illnesses are taught in general education classrooms. Some of these students frequently draw general education teachers and paraprofessionals into a progression of escalating emotion. Consider the following scenario:

> Mr. Roberts is an eighth-grade math teacher. April is a student.
>
> ***Mr. Roberts:*** *Class, we're going to get into our work groups. Your name and group number are on the board. Once you get into your groups . . .*
>
> ***April (interrupts):*** *Why do I have to work with that group? I HATE those people!*

Module D: Responding to Misbehavior—An Instructional Approach

Mr. Roberts: *April, I chose these groups for a specific reason. I need you to work with your assigned group.*

April: *I want to choose the group I work with, or I'm not working!*

Mr. Roberts: *You will work with the group you are assigned to.*

April: *You are so stupid! You should know that I can't get along with those people!*

Mr. Roberts: *April, you may not speak to me in that tone of voice. I will not tolerate your insolence!*

April: *You aren't my dad. I can talk to you any way I want. Besides, my mom says you're a lousy teacher!*

Mr. Roberts: *I don't care what your mother says. I'd like to see her teach this class! You better get in your group, or you'll be in big trouble.*

April: *You'll be in big trouble when my mom finds out what you just said about her.*

Mr. Roberts: *NO! YOU are already in big trouble. I'm calling security to come and take you to the office!*

April: *You think I'm scared? YOU are the one who better be scared!*

This scenario is an example of an interaction that escalated out of control. The teacher allowed himself to react more and more intensely to the student's emotions, and the student's emotions became heightened with every response from the teacher. Finally, the teacher felt his only option was to remove the student from the situation.

Teachers, as well as paraprofessionals and principals, are often inadvertently trapped in escalating negative social interactions. These interactions are extremely disruptive to the learning environment and damaging to interpersonal relationships. Interactions like the one above can and often do result in the student physically acting out, which further affects the climate of the classroom and school. With some training in strategies to defuse emotional situations, however, teachers can effect more positive outcomes.

Responding to these *invitations to anger* (we discuss this term later in this task) in a skillful manner is often especially frustrating for new and inexperienced teachers and paraprofessionals. Student aggression, tantrums, arguing, and noncompliance have all been cited as reasons that some teachers leave the profession after only a few years.

All staff should understand the importance of learning and using strategies for defusing and de-escalating misbehavior before it becomes severe. When teachers can effectively deal with emotional situations, students can remain in the instructional environment, students *and* staff experience less anger and frustration, and the overall climate of the classroom is more positive.

Most escalating events don't arise out of the blue—they result from a chain of behavioral events. A skillful teacher can circumvent the misbehavior at many points in the chain. We discuss several useful skills in this task:

- Decline the student's invitation to anger.
- Reframe your thinking about noncompliance and resistance.
- Understand the seven-phase model for describing acting-out behavior.

Decline the student's *invitation to anger.*

Most verbal battles begin with an *invitation to anger*, a proposition that school personnel can accept or graciously decline. This notion of the invitation to anger replaces the "that student can really push my buttons" line of thinking. *Button pushing* suggests that the adult has no choice but to respond to the push. *Invitation* suggests that the adult *has a choice* in how he or she responds.

Typical invitations to anger usually result from one or more of the following triggers:

- **Denial** of something the student wants or needs
- **Pressure.** The normal demands of school, such as multitasking and time management, can overwhelm unskilled students.
- **Corrections** (e.g., teacher corrections and debriefings, being required to repeat tasks)
- **Ineffective problem solving.** The student is not skilled at identifying and evaluating problems, negotiating with others, and generating solutions.
- **Errors.** After making errors, the student stops working and avoids new learning.
- **Power or control.** The student wants to display or gain power or control over a situation or person.

What do invitations to anger look and sound like?

- **Questioning and arguing:** "Why do we have to do this stupid assignment?"
- **Noncompliance and defiance:** "I don't have to do anything you tell me—you're not my mom."
- **Threats and intimidation:** "We're calling the superintendent and getting you fired!"
- **Verbal abuse:** "You stupid $#%$er *&%#er!"

Let's look at our example of Mr. Roberts and April again and identify the links in the escalating behavior chain.

Mr. Roberts: Class, we're going to get into our work groups. Your name and group number are on the board. Once you get into your groups . . .

April (interrupts): Why do I have to work with that group? I HATE those people! **Questioning, disrespectful behavior**

Mr. Roberts: April, I chose these groups for a specific reason. I need you to work with your assigned group.

April: I want to choose the group I work with, or I'm not working! **Argumentative, noncompliant behavior**

Mr. Roberts: You will work with the group you are assigned to.

April: You are so stupid! You should know that I can't get along with those people! **Verbal abuse**

Mr. Roberts: April, you may not speak to me in that tone of voice. I will not tolerate your insolence!

April: You aren't my dad. I can talk to you any way I want. Besides, my mom says you're a lousy teacher! **Verbal abuse**

Mr. Roberts: I don't care what your mother says. I'd like to see her teach this class! You better get in your group, or you'll be in big trouble.

April: You'll be in big trouble when my mom finds out what you just said about her. **Verbal threat**

Mr. Roberts: NO! YOU are already in big trouble. I'm calling security to come and take you to the office!

April: You think I'm scared? YOU are the one who better be scared! **Verbal threat**

In this example of an escalating behavior chain, April began with questioning and disrespectful behavior, escalated to arguing and noncompliance, then to verbal abuse of her teacher, and finally to blatant threats. All of her comments could be considered invitations to anger, and Mr. Roberts accepted her invitation about midway through the exchange.

Reframe your thinking about noncompliance and resistance.

Many adults assume that when students respond with anger or aggression, it's because the students *choose* to respond that way. For some students, this might be true, but many respond emotionally because they don't have the emotional control, social skills, or experience to interact with adults appropriately. John Maag, in his book *Powerful Struggles* (2001), elegantly crystallizes this idea into his *Can't vs. Won't* model of resistance.

Can't

The student doesn't have the prerequisite skills to perform the task. For example, the teacher tells the student to "stop annoying others." The student doesn't understand what the word *annoying* means. When the behavior doesn't stop, the teacher interprets the behavior as willful misbehavior. In reality, this student is unaware of how to change her behavior, so she appears resistant.

Won't

The student's beliefs about the situation interfere with his performance of the desired behavior. For example, the student gets into a fight on the playground. As part of the response by the school, the student is required to apologize to the other student. Because this student believes that apologizing will make him look weak, he refuses. The student's belief creates resistance to the direction.

Note on habitual responses: In some cases, the student selects an inappropriate strategy because these behaviors have become automatic (*selecting* is not *deciding*). The interaction between Mr. Roberts and April in the previous task is an example of a student who selects an inappropriate response because it is (at least partially) her habitual behavior. In these cases, the student might need strategies for impulse control to break the habit and perform the desired behavior.

When you keep this model in mind when faced with a resistant student, you'll be more likely to remember and use strategies that can defuse and de-escalate the student's anger. A student who is *unable* to respond appropriately at that moment presents you with a teaching opportunity—and you are a teacher. Perhaps the student's innate behavior isn't the source of the problem. Perhaps your directions and responses contribute to and escalate the student's resistance. Perhaps you can help the student learn that there are other ways of responding to directions, even directions he does not want to follow.

"Whether or not a child complies with an adult directive has as much to do with how the command is framed and delivered as it does with the consequences, or lack of them, that follow the delivery" (Walker, Colvin, & Ramsey, 1995, p. 300).

Let's think about the term *resistance* for a moment. Resistance encompasses noncompliance, refusal to follow directions, and opposition. But while words like *noncompliance* and *opposition* suggest that the problem lies solely with the student, *resistance* focuses on the interaction between adult behaviors and the behaviors of students. You may find it helpful to think of student noncompliance or opposition in terms of resistance.

Understand the seven-phase model for describing acting-out behavior.

Breaking an escalating behavior chain requires understanding the relationship between the ratcheting up of student behavior, the underlying emotional responses, and the role of successive interactions (the back-and-forth exchanges between student and adult).

According to Colvin (2004), emotional escalation generally progresses through five distinct phases, followed by two de-escalation phases. Once you can correlate a student's behavior with a specific phase, you can choose corresponding strategies that are likely to stop the behavior, head off further escalation, and help the student settle down. You can then develop a problem-solving plan so that the problem won't reoccur.

Figure 5a below shows Colvin's model of the phases of acting-out behavior (we sometimes call this model Anger Mountain). Following the figure is a brief description of each phase.

Figure 5a   *Phases of acting-out behavior*

PHASES OF ACTING-OUT BEHAVIOR

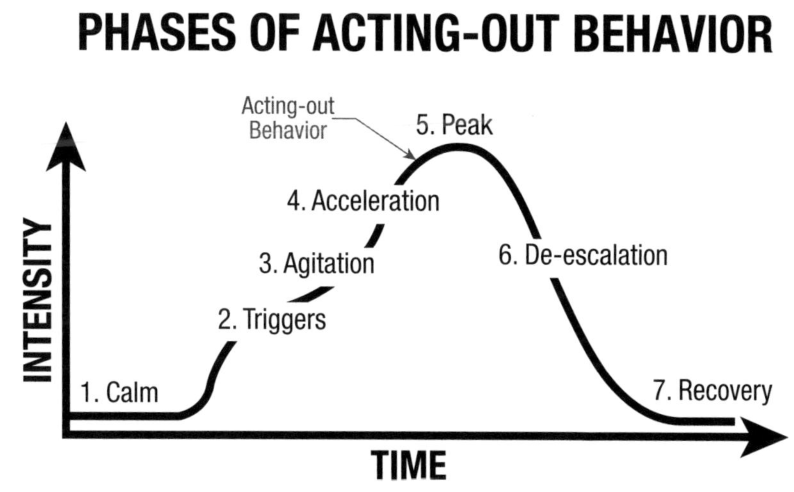

Reproduced with permission from *Managing the Cycle of Acting-Out Behavior in the Classroom* by Geoff Colvin, 2004, Eugene, OR, Behavior Associates

Phase 1: Calm

Students are cooperative and amenable. They are generally on task, follow rules and expectations, respond to praise, initiate appropriate behavior, and respond to goals and success.

Phase 2: Trigger

Triggers are events that set off the progression of acting-out behavior. Anticipate and proactively address sources of triggers (e.g., school events such as conflicts, changes in routine, peer provocations, pressure, ineffective problem solving, difficult work, and correction as well as nonschool triggers such as high-need home or health issues) before escalation begins to snowball.

Phase 3: Agitation

In the Agitation phase, the student is unfocused and distracted. Teachers often describe the student as being on edge. Behaviors such as darting eyes and busy hands might increase, and the student might avoid eye contact, conversation, and group activities. In behavioral terms, an agitated student experiences emotions such as anger, frustration, anxiety, or depression in response to a trigger.

Phase 4: Acceleration

The student's behavior becomes focused and directed, usually toward staff. The student wants to engage the teacher (he or she issues an invitation to anger) and uses arguing, noncompliance, off-task behavior, whining, crying, threats, and other behaviors to do so.

Phase 5: Peak

The student's behavior is out of control and can be so serious that class cannot continue and the safety of the target student and other students is a concern. The student might destroy property, physically attack others, self-abuse, tantrum, or run away.

Phase 6: De-escalation

As the student emerges from out-of-control behavior, he or she is unfocused and distracted, and not particularly cooperative or responsive to adult influences. The student might appear confused and withdrawn, might deny or blame others for the incident, and will probably avoid discussion.

Phase 7: Recovery

The student returns to a relatively normal state, is typically eager for independent busy work, and avoids interacting with others.

What is the relationship between anger and rational thought?

Figure 5b shows the phases of acting-out behavior with some additional information—rational thought is represented by the U-shaped line. It probably doesn't

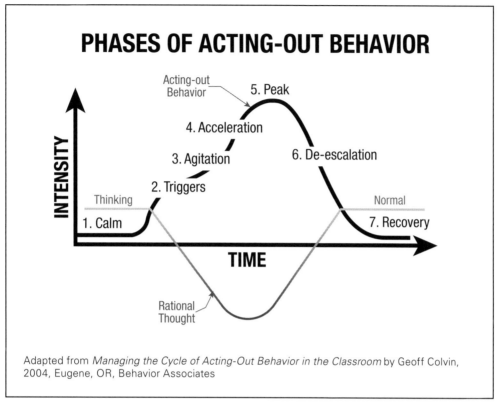

Adapted from *Managing the Cycle of Acting-Out Behavior in the Classroom* by Geoff Colvin, 2004, Eugene, OR, Behavior Associates

surprise you that as a student's emotion escalates, his capacity for rational thought decreases correspondingly. To fully understand this relationship between anger and rational thought, it helps to know a little about how the brain works in response to fear and anger.

The amygdala is a small region in the temporal lobe of the brain. Most research into this structure has centered on the role it plays in fear, but research suggests that it also plays a role in other emotions, such as aggression and anxiety. People who have nonfunctioning amygdalae do not exhibit any fear.

The amygdala receives information directly from the various sensory systems that process the external world. The information you receive when you see, hear, smell, and touch converges in the amygdala. Then the amygdala sends messages to all the systems involved in your emotional reactions. So when you see a snake and you know from experience that it represents potential danger, you might freeze, your blood pressure and heart rate rise, and stress hormones are released, all as a result of the amygdala's output. (See Figure 5c on the next page for a graphic representation of the amygdala's function.

Figure 5c   Graphic representation of the amygdala's function (greatly simplified!)

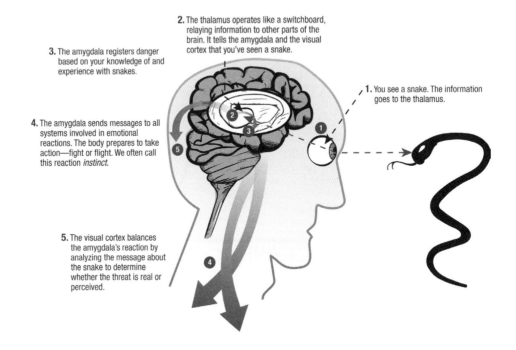

2. The thalamus operates like a switchboard, relaying information to other parts of the brain. It tells the amygdala and the visual cortex that you've seen a snake.

3. The amygdala registers danger based on your knowledge of and experience with snakes.

4. The amygdala sends messages to all systems involved in emotional reactions. The body prepares to take action—fight or flight. We often call this reaction *instinct*.

5. The visual cortex balances the amygdala's reaction by analyzing the message about the snake to determine whether the threat is real or perceived.

1. You see a snake. The information goes to the thalamus.

This response is the same if the sensory input is anger. It might be easier to think of this concept in terms of the body responding to these questions:

- Do I fear this?
- Do I hate this?
- Can this hurt me?

If the answer to any of those questions is yes, the amygdala connects to the response systems that keep our body safe, such as the adrenal system. The fight-or-flight response is activated, and the body is able to mobilize energy rapidly to either deal directly with the danger or run away from it. The visual cortex balances the amygdala's reaction by analyzing the message about the snake to determine whether the threat is real or perceived.

Another area of the brain, the prefrontal cortex, also acts as mediator, taking impulses from the amygdala and deciding whether or not to act on them. Research suggests that the prefrontal cortex is not fully developed in children and teenagers, and if a particular structure of the brain is immature, the functions it governs will show immaturity. That means some students will have poor control over their decisions or emotions, not because they refuse to try to use good judgment, but because their brains are not mature. Adults who encounter student anger must be the ones who are in control of their own emotions, and they must model appropriate behavior for the students.

Break the progression of escalating behavior with strategies to de-escalate at each stage.

We've given you a lot to think about: invitations to anger, the Can't vs. Won't model, the idea of resistance rather than noncompliance, the seven-phase model of acting-out behavior, and the relationship between anger and rational thought. Finally, you've reached the part where we give you strategies!

We said earlier that teachers can choose to accept or decline a student's invitation to anger. Below, for each phase of the acting-out behavior model, we suggest strategies that can *prevent* students from entering the escalating chain of behaviors and help you *respond* to students who are in danger of escalating. Plan to develop behavior support plans for emotionally escalated behavior at each phase.

1: Calm

Signs of Calm	Strategies to Promote Calm Behavior
Students are productively engaged with instruction. Students use appropriate voice levels. Students' activity level is appropriate.	Structure for success. • Be prepared with teaching plans and materials. • Keep classrooms well organized and tidy. • Clarify expectations for behavior in all activities and transitions. • Know and use effective behavior management strategies Provide quality instruction. • Be clear about what students are to learn and explain why the task or behavior will be useful to them. • Relate new tasks to previously learned skills. • Give students a vision of what they eventually will be able to do. • Rally the enthusiasm and energy of students, particularly when asking them to do something difficult or challenging. Provide positive attention. • Give contingent attention—provide positive, descriptive feedback whenever students meet expectations. • Give noncontingent attention—greet students, show an interest in their work, invite them to ask for assistance, and talk with them about their interests.

2: Triggers

Types of Triggers (Unresolved Problems)	Strategies to Anticipate and Address Triggers Before Escalation Begins
Conflicts	Review your expectations.
Changes in routine	Modify the context, if possible (e.g., assign fewer problems or move student away from teasers).
Peer provocation	
Pressure	Cue and precorrect (e.g., give advance notice that you are going to discuss the student's errors and remind student how she is supposed to behave).
Poor problem-solving skills	
Errors during instruction	Rehearse the behavior.
Home situation (health problems, nutrition, home conflicts, or sleep)	Use strong positive reinforcement.
	Prompt appropriate behavior.
	Monitor the behaviors (collect data).
	Provide noncontingent positive interactions (e.g., show caring or concern)

If the above strategies are not effective, consider more formal interventions, such as implementing social skills or problem-solving skills curricula.

3: Agitation

Signs of Agitation (Unfocused/Distracted)	Strategies to Reduce Negative Emotions and Help Student Settle Down and Regain Control
Increases in behavior: • Darting eyes • Busy hands • Moving in and out of groups • Off- and on-task cycle Decreases in behavior: • Staring into space, as if daydreaming • Avoiding conversation (monosyllabic and unwilling to talk) • Contained hands (like sitting on them) • Withdrawal from groups	Accommodate the student's needs early—before the behavior accelerates. Use empathy (more effective when there is a positive relationship with the student). Assist the student to focus (e.g., help him get started on the first part of the assignment). Provide space and some degree of isolation. Provide assurances (e.g., additional time or extra help after class). Permit preferred activities for a short period of time (e.g., jigsaw puzzle).

3: Agitation (continued)

Signs of Agitation (Unfocused/Distracted)	Strategies to Reduce Negative Emotions and Help Student Settle Down and Regain Control
	Use teacher proximity, but back off if student gets more agitated (effective when there is a positive relationship with the student).
	Have the student work on independent activities that mirror the class activities and that require minimal interaction with you or the class.
	Have the student work on passive activities (e.g., watch video or read) or movement activities (e.g., passing out papers).
	Encourage student self-management.
	Consider involving the student in the plan—the student might decide what he needs to do when he feels agitated—e.g., go to a particular place or play a particular game.

*E*xample From the Field

Here's a strategy that can satisfy a student's need to move, leave the class for a few moments, and feel valued and important. It can help some students de-escalate from the agitation phase. Prepare a letter that reads, "Please thank the bearer of this envelope profusely for bringing this important document to you. Tell the student that I would be in big trouble if you did not receive it. Then please give the student a hall pass and send him back to class." Place it in an envelope, seal it, and ask the student to take the important message to the office. Be sure to get the principal's approval to use this strategy, and ask the office staff to play along. Talk about a win-win situation—the staff have fun giving attention to the student, the student feels important, and the teacher has prevented a potential meltdown!   —S.I.

4: Acceleration

Signs of Acceleration (Engagement)	Strategies That Avert Escalation, Maintain Calm, Don't Threaten the Student, and Use Non-confrontational Limit-Setting Procedures
Questioning/arguing Noncompliance/defiance Off-task behavior Provocation of others Partial compliance (complies but also displays inappropriate behavior) Criterion problems (purposely doing less than capable) Rule violation (knowingly breaks rule) Whining/crying (seeks attention) Avoidance and escape Threats/intimidation Verbal abuse (offensive language) Destruction of property	Avoid escalating prompts. • Don't raise your voice or argue. • Avoid cornering the student and moving into her personal space. • Avoid power struggles. • Avoid touching, sudden movements, and body language that communicates anger. • Don't make belittling or sarcastic statements (Don't say, "I appreciate the way everyone is ignoring Tracy.") • Don't hold the door closed when the student is trying to leave. (Say, "You do not have permission to leave," but do not physically intervene.) Do: • Speak privately, quietly, calmly, respectfully, and briefly (less than 15 seconds). • Maintain a level of unemotional detachment. • Be aware of personal space, move slowly and establish eye-level positioning. • Stay with the agenda and don't get sidetracked. • Acknowledge cooperation. • Withdraw from student if the situation escalates and attend to other students. Go to Phase 5 (Peak interventions) if the student escalates. • Advance planning—rehearse with class, establish corrective consequences, and present expectations and consequences as student's decision or choice.

If the above strategies are not effective, move to crisis prevention strategies.

- Establish a bottom-line negative consequence.

  - Present the expected behavior and the bottom-line consequence as a choice or decision that the student has to make. ("You can either sit at your desk or sit in the timeout area. Your choice.")

  - Allow time (a few seconds) for the student to decide. Withdraw from the student and attend to others or engage in another task.

  - Follow up. "What are you going to do?"

- Debrief (only after the student has de-escalated). The student's emotions are probably still high, so you may not conduct a complete debriefing. But consider asking questions like the following:

  - What was your concern or need? (The student can probably more easily answer this question than: Why did you get angry?)

  - What could you have done differently that would have been acceptable and would have met your need?

  - What will you do next time in a similar situation?

5: Peak

Signs of Peak (Out of Control)	Interventions to Ensure the Safety of All Students and Staff
Serious destruction of property • Physical attacks • Self-abuse • Severe tantrums • Running away	Follow through on emergency plans. *Address safety first.* Short-term interventions include: • Isolate the student and remove other students from the setting (room clear). • Contact the parents. • Call the police, if necessary. • Suspend the student (for a brief period). • Physically restrain the student. (Ensure that you know district and state regulations about restraint—restraint must be used judiciously.)

(continued)

5: Peak (continued)

Signs of Peak (Out of Control)	Interventions to Ensure the Safety of All Students and Staff

	It is critical to develop clear processes for managing out-of-control students.
	
	• Provide training for staff members who may use restraint, seclusion, and other intrusive techniques. But remember, there are no safe, effective ways to physically manage children. *Any time restraint is used, there is a high risk of injury.* Restraint should be used only as a last resort.
	• Get help. At least two adults are needed to manage out-of-control students.
	• Document the incident in writing and archive it.
	• Consider conducting a postintervention evaluation to identify ways to de-escalate or prevent the behavior in the future.
	• Obtain parent permission for the use of restraint or seclusion through IEP or 504 processes.
	
	Long-term interventions:
	
	• A student who has reached an emotional peak once will probably do so again. Consider the incident a red flag and modify how you interact with the student with this potential for anger in mind.
	• Plan to intervene earlier in the chain of escalating behavior.
	• Analyze the environment for escalating prompts.
	    ◦ Assess schoolwork—does the student find it frustrating?
	    ◦ Refer for counseling. (Remember, this a long-term process. One or two visits won't fix anything.)
	    ◦ Refer for evaluation.

6: De-escalation

Signs of De-escalation (Confusion, Lack of Focus)	Strategies to Help the Student Process the Incident and Prevent Future Occurrences
Confusion Reconciliation Withdrawal Denial Blaming others Responsiveness to directions Responsiveness to manipulative and mechanical tasks Avoidance of discussion Avoidance of debriefing	Make certain the student has had enough time to calm down. Give the student a simple direction to assess his cooperation. Monitor the student carefully and be prepared to offer an independent activity. The student might want to sleep.

7: Recovery

Signs of Recovery (Eagerness for Work, Reluctance to Interact)	Strategies to Support the Student's Composure, Focus, and Cooperation
Eagerness for something to do Subdued behavior in groups or discussion Defensive behavior	Debrief—use a behavior improvement form. • What did you do? • Why did you do it? • What else could you have done? Restore the environment. Depending on the student's attitude, have the student clean up any minor mess she made in the classroom. If the classroom is very disheveled, the class might pitch in to restore it. Have the student resume her regular schedule as soon as possible. The longer the student is away from her normal routine, the more difficult it is to resume it. Provide a simple reentry task that doesn't require immediate peer interaction, and reinforce the student as soon as she engages in it. Avoid negotiating consequences for serious misbehavior.

(continued)

7: Recovery (continued)

Signs of Recovery (Eagerness for Work, Reluctance to Interact)	Strategies to Support the Student's Composure, Focus, and Cooperation
	Acknowledge the student's problem-solving behaviors. ("Your tantrum lasted only 12 minutes today. Your last tantrum lasted 20 minutes. You are making progress!") Communicate support and high expectations. If necessary, establish a proactive behavior support plan with the assistance of the counselor, school psychologist, or social worker.

What if Mr. Roberts had used one of these strategies with April? The interaction might have been very different—April remains in class, Mr. Roberts doesn't get angry, and both ultimately retain their dignity and self-respect.

Mr. Roberts: Class, we're going to get into our work groups. Your name and group number are on the board. Once you get into your groups . . .

April (interrupts): Why do I have to work with that group! I HATE those people! **Questioning, disrespectful behavior**

Mr. Roberts: April, I chose these groups for a specific reason. I need you to work with your assigned group.

April: I want to choose the group I work with, or I'm not working! **Argumentative, noncompliant behavior**

Mr. Roberts: You will work with the group you are assigned to.

April: You are so stupid! You should know that I can't get along with those people! **Verbal abuse**

Mr. Roberts: April, you're frustrated that you can't choose your group. **Use of empathy at the agitation stage**

April: Yeah!

Mr. Roberts: I want to help you get your work completed and figure out a group that you can work with. Would that help?

April: I guess. **Guiding the student to focus on starting the assignment**

Mr. Roberts: Let me get these groups started, and then we can figure out where you'll be most successful. **Providing some time for the student to calm down**

Over time, Mr. Roberts will work with April to develop the skills she needs to work with others, even when she doesn't like the other students in her group.

TASK 2

Use communication strategies to prevent emotional escalation

This task focuses on simple communication strategies that all staff members should be familiar with. These strategies, when used in a timely manner, can prevent students from climbing Anger Mountain. All adults who work in schools will likely encounter a student who displays angry or aggressive behavior, tantrums, or loses emotional control. Teachers should be committed to avoiding power struggles with students who display angry and aggressive behavior because power struggles trigger escalating behavior events.

Adult responses to students' efforts to gain power and control are sometimes shaped by needs and emotions. Consider the following questions:

- Have you ever felt the need to win a power struggle with a student to prove that you are in control?
- Have you ever felt the need to save face to show other students that you are powerful?
- Have you ever held a grudge against a student because of the student's history of misbehavior?
- Have you ever taken a student's misbehavior personally, resulting in the desire to retaliate against the student?
- Have you ever matched anger and aggression with anger and aggression (often an automatic response)?

Avoid ineffective strategies.

We'll look at some strategies that can have a positive, proactive effect on student anger. But first, let's consider strategies that *don't* work when dealing with resistance to directions or reprimands so you can eliminate them from your repertoire (if you use them).

Don't ask students if they *want to* . . . A question format gives students a choice. In most instances, the adult would not accept "no" from the student. Rhetorical questions may also contribute to resistance and power struggles—for example, "What are you supposed to be doing?" or "Are you supposed to do that?"

Don't give directions from a distance. Research shows that adults frequently give directions from as far as 20 feet away. Give directions when standing 1.5 to 3 feet from the student to increase compliance.

Don't yell. Emotional responses are often a trigger for students to engage in a power struggle, and they find out they have the power to make you angry.

Don't demand eye contact. ("Boy, you better look at me when I'm talking to you!") In some cultures, children are taught to avoid eye contact with adults. Don't assume that all children know that eye contact is expected when interacting with adults.

Don't expect immediate compliance. Give the student several seconds to process the request (walk away while you do this, and continue to listen and scan the area).

Don't give multiple or multistep directions. Example: "Get in your seat, get out your materials, and get started on the warm-up. Oh, and don't forget to write today's date on your paper . . . and your answers need to be in complete sentences." At least one student is going to say, "I don't know what to do," or not complete the task because he missed part of the instructions.

Don't just tell students what *not* to do. Example: A student has his feet in the trashcan, and the teacher says, "Get your feet out of the trashcan." The student may comply initially, but then puts his feet on his backpack. Now the teacher has to tell him to take his feet off his backpack. The initial direction should have told him where he *should* put his feet: "Please put your feet on the floor."

Don't respond emotionally. Some students are looking for opportunities to get into an argument, and you are providing it. Responding emotionally is also not a good model of problem solving. You are solving the problem of misbehavior, so model it well.

Don't beg, plead, or cajole. Appearing desperate can erode the respect that students have for you.

Don't try to convince the student that he needs to follow your directions just because he likes you. Don't say, "Please, just do it for me . . ."

Don't try to make the student feel guilty. Example: "You are the only student that I have to remind every day about bringing materials to class."

Use effective communication strategies.

The following strategies *can* work when dealing with resistance to directions or reprimands. However, note that not all strategies will work in every situation. It is very important to get to know the students who are likely to be resistant so you can plan to use the specific strategies that are most effective for each of them.

Be aware of physical distance. Don't invade the student's personal space (18 to 36 inches), but don't correct from across the room, either. Communication from more than 4 feet away is usually not effective. Students might indicate with their body language that you are too close: clenched fists, hands on hips, movement away from you, or tight facial muscles.

Use effective facial expressions. Establish eye contact, but don't glare or demand that the student look at you. Keep a neutral expression, nod when the student is talking (it indicates you are listening), subtly tilt your head to the side, use soft eyes, and smile only when appropriate.

Be aware of body language. Use a supportive stance—an open body posture with shoulders at 45° to the student, hands at your sides, unclenched fists, and one foot behind the other. This off-center stance gives you a safety margin in case the student lashes out. Do *not* touch the student. Avoid the challenge posture of clenched fists, folded arms, hands behind your back or in pockets, and facial scowl. Keep your hands where students can see them, at your sides or open in front of you.

Use a quiet voice. Use a calm, controlled, soft, slow, and firm voice rather than a loud and emotional voice. Remember, much of your message's meaning comes from your tone, pacing, and volume.

Give time to comply. Allow the student 5 to 10 seconds to comply. Don't expect or demand immediate compliance because some students have difficulty with auditory processing. Shift the attention or focus away from the student.

Use more *start* than *stop* requests. State the desired behavior in positive terms instead of telling students to stop doing something. "Sarah, put your feet on the floor," not "Sarah, get your feet off your backpack!"

Be unemotional. Threatening gestures, ugly faces, guilt-inducing statements, deprecating comments, and sarcasm only increase resistance. Emotional reactions also interfere with building and maintaining a positive relationship. Remember, all students must be treated with respect at all times.

Use alpha commands. These are clear, direct, and specific requests. ("Cal, sit with your assigned group.") Avoid beta commands, which are vague, wordy, and often contain multiple instructions ("Cal, you need to stop playing around—you are wasting time.")

For more information on alpha and beta commands, see:

Walker, H., Ramsey, E., & Gresham, F. M. (2003/2004). Heading off disruptive behavior: How early intervention can reduce defiant behavior—and win back teaching time. *American Educator, 27*(4), 6–15, 18–21, 45–46.

Walker, H., Ramsey, E., & Gresham, F. M. (2003/2004). How disruptive students escalate hostility and disorder—and how teachers can avoid it. *American Educator, 27*(4), 22–27, 47–48.

Reinforce compliance. When the student follows directions, acknowledge it. Positive or nonverbal feedback (a smile or thumbs up, for example) is critical.

Take advantage of behavioral momentum. Follow these steps to generate behavioral momentum.

1. Select a series of behaviors that a student already likes to do—that is, behaviors that the student does on request at least 70% of the time (for example, pass out papers, sharpen some pencils, or erase the board).

2. Ask the student to do several of the behaviors he is likely to do before asking him to do an unlikely behavior ("Please begin working"). Request even one likely behavior before the unlikely behavior if you are pressed for time.

3. Incorporate the technique into your class routine by using games such as Heads Up, Seven Up, Simon Says, and so on. Begin the day with high-probability games or activities, then move on to academic work, problem review, or group work.

Teach students to comply.

In addition to the above strategies, you might teach a replacement behavior to students whose resistance is a result of lack of skills in following directions.

Sure I Will. The Sure I Will program is an excellent tool for teaching or reinforcing students to follow directions. The program involves teaching students a compliance-based behavior as a way to break a behavioral chain that would otherwise result in disobedience. This approach provides students with cues to perform desired behaviors, and it builds momentum for following directions. This program is based on Precision Requests or alpha commands.

- Teach students to respond to a "please" request with "Sure I will" before you make the second request.
- Always acknowledge the "Sure I will" response with a social reward or sometimes (randomly) a small tangible reward.
- Divide the class into teams that compete for the most "Sure I will" responses.
- Insert some variety into the program. Have students vary their responses (for example, "Okey dokey," " Glad you asked," "Sure, anytime," or "No problem").

For more information on the Behavioral Momentum and Sure I Will strategies, see Rhode, G., Jenson, W. R., & Reavis, H. K. (2010). *The Tough Kid book* (2nd ed.; pp. 114–119). Eugene, OR: Pacific Northwest Publishing.

TASK 3

Teach students the expectations for interacting appropriately with adults

One of the most important steps in preventing misbehavior is to teach all students how to interact with adults maturely and respectfully. We've designed a series of lessons that you can use as is or modify to meet the needs of your students.

- Lesson 1: Following Directions, Part 1
- Lesson 2: Following Directions, Part 2
- Lesson 3: Accepting Compliments
- Lesson 4: Accepting "No"
- Lesson 5: Accepting a Correction
- Lesson 6: Analyzing Your Behavior
- Lesson 7: Taking a Break
- Lesson 8: Making an Appointment—Self-Advocacy
- Lesson 9: Dealing With a False Accusation

See Figures 5d–5f on pp. 167–171 for an outline, student worksheet, and sample scripted lesson for Lesson 1: Following Directions, Part 1. Figures 5g–5n on pp. 172–189 show the outlines of all Module D lessons. You can find the outlines, scripted lessons, and worksheets for all the sample lessons on the Module D CD.

These sample lessons have been designed for approximately 20 minutes of instruction and activity at the middle-school level. Depending on your schedule and the age of your students, each lesson might be taught in as little as 15 minutes or as much as 30 minutes. Tailor the lessons for length, grade level, and subject matter. If your school uses a social-emotional curriculum or other schoolwide behavioral lessons, check that the concepts in the sample lessons do not duplicate current teaching efforts.

We also include an example of a comprehensive lesson from Alain Leroy Locke College Preparatory Academy in the Green Dot Public Schools charter school organization in Los Angeles, California. Locke created what they call the Locke Essential Five schoolwide rules.

1. Students are on time to class.
2. Students are prepared for class.
3. Students are in uniform while at school.
4. Students keep personal electronics off and out of sight.
5. Students respond promptly and politely to all adult requests.

The staff had difficulty enforcing the last rule, so they created a very effective lesson to specifically address prompt and polite responses. We are glad they've allowed us to share it with you. See Figure 5o on pp. 190–193. The lesson (adapted from a PowerPoint presentation) is also available on the Module D CD.

Task 3 Action Steps & Evidence of Implementation

Action Steps	Evidence of Implementation
1. Read through the sample lessons and discuss whether and how your school might use them. • Might they supplement your social skills program? • Can you use them as a basis for a social skills program? • Can you use the lessons as is, or must you modify them for the age levels of your students?	Foundations Process: Meeting Minutes
2. If you decide to use the lessons, document all aspects of the training in the Foundations Archive.	Foundations Archive: Lesson Plans for Teaching Expectations for Interacting With Adults

Figure 5d   *How to Interact Appropriately, Lesson 1 Outline*

Following Directions, Part 1

OBJECTIVES

- Students will explain how following directions can help them be successful.
- Students will identify essential steps in following directions appropriately, using the acronym LAPS.

MATERIALS

- Document camera, overhead projector, or interactive whiteboard to display the worksheet and student responses
- Student copies of the Student Worksheet for Lesson 1: Following Directions, Part 1

Introduction

1. Read a scenario about someone who refuses to follow directions in a work environment. Use the example below, or choose a scenario that students can relate to but that also demonstrates that the behavior illustrated in the scenario is immature and somewhat ridiculous. You may wish to tailor the behavior in the scenario to reflect inappropriate responses to directions you frequently see in your school.

   > Imagine it's 20 years from now. You are at your job at a prestigious law firm (or wherever you want to work!). Your boss comes to you and says, "My assistant is out today, and I have a meeting I need to be in right now. I need you to make copies of these papers and then go buy lunch for me." You feel that you are above this kind of task because others usually make copies and run errands.
   >
   > You look at him, roll your eyes, and say, "Ugh, this is stupid." (If possible, say this in your most obnoxious and annoyed tone of voice, roll your eyes, and make an annoyed expression.)

2. In partners, then with the whole group, have students share as many possibilities as they can think of for what might happen if someone did this at work.

3. Explain that students will be learning about the importance of following directions. Tell them that following directions will help them succeed in school and at work.

4. Have students fill in the blanks for Item 1 on the student worksheet with "school" and "work."

Foundations: A Proactive and Positive Behavior Support System

© 2014 Pacific Northwest Publishing

 This lesson can be printed from the Module D CD.

Module D, Presentation 5

Lesson Outline

Page 2 of 2

How to Interact Appropriately
Lesson 1 • Following Directions, Part 1

Lesson Body

1. Introduce the essential steps of following directions: 1) Listen and look,* 2) Acknowledge, 3) Perform the action, and 4) Seek assistance if needed.

   > * Note: If you work with students from cultural backgrounds in which looking at an elder or person of authority is considered disrespectful, teach them to be conscious of when it may or may not be appropriate to look directly at a person. You can teach them to look at the item being discussed or at the ground near the speaker, if needed, and to give other cues to show they are listening, such as nodding their head.

2. Explain **Step 1: Listen and look.*** To show active listening, students can look at the speaker, the item, or written directions. Have students discuss why it might be a problem not to look at the person who is speaking or what the person is talking about. Review Step 1, and have students write "Listen" for Item 2, No. 1 on the worksheet.

   > * See note above on cultural awareness.

3. Explain **Step 2: Acknowledge.** To show that a direction is understood, the listener should nod, say "OK," or give another positive indication of understanding. Review Steps 1 and 2, and have students write "show" to complete Item 2, No. 2.

4. Explain **Step 3: Perform the action** (the most important step). Explain that the action should be done immediately and without argument. Later lessons will explain what to do if you disagree with a direction or feel it is unfair. Review Step 3, and have students write "Perform" to complete Item 2, No. 3.

5. Introduce **Step 4: Seek assistance**, if needed. Explain that later lessons will cover how to appropriately ask questions and clarify understanding. Review Step 4, and have students write "assistance" for Item 2, No. 4.

Conclusion

Review the LAPS acronym and concept. Explain that like doing laps on a track, doing LAPS for following directions will help students grow strong in school and in life.

Possibilities for Follow-Up

- Provide practice opportunities: Give students a variety of directions and have them practice LAPS.
- Give short role-play scenarios and have students act out following LAPS.
- Create video samples of students (or teachers role-playing students) following directions and not following directions. Have students analyze each step of LAPS and identify what the students in the videos are doing correctly or incorrectly.

Foundations: A Proactive and Positive Behavior Support System   © 2014 Pacific Northwest Publishing

 This lesson can be printed from the Module D CD.

Figure 5e   *How to Interact Appropriately, Lesson 1 Worksheet*

Module D, Presentation 5

Student Worksheet

Name _____   Class/Teacher _____   Period ____

Following Directions, Part 1

Item 1

Following directions will help me be successful in _____ and

_____ . Without this skill, I may struggle in many areas of my life.

Item 2

The essential steps of following directions are:

1. _____ and look.
2. Acknowledge (_____ I understand).
3. _____ the action immediately.
4. Seek _____ if needed.

Figure 5f   How to Interact Appropriately, Lesson 1 Scripted Lesson

How to Interact Appropriately
Lesson 1 • Following Directions, Part 1

Following Directions, Part 1

OBJECTIVES

- Students will explain how following directions can help them be successful.
- Students will identify essential steps in following directions appropriately, using the acronym LAPS.

MATERIALS

- Document camera, overhead projector, or interactive whiteboard to display the worksheet and student responses
- Student copies of the Student Worksheet for Lesson 1: Following Directions, Part 1

Introduction

1. Read a scenario about someone who refuses to follow directions in a work environment. Use the example below, or choose a scenario that students can relate to but that also demonstrates that the behavior illustrated in the scenario is immature and somewhat ridiculous. You may wish to tailor the behavior in the scenario to reflect inappropriate responses to directions you frequently see in your school.

   Imagine it's 20 years from now. You are at your job at a prestigious law firm (or wherever you want to work!). Your boss comes to you and says, "My assistant is out today, and I have a meeting I need to be in right now. I need you to make copies of these papers and then go buy lunch for me." You feel that you are above this kind of task because others usually make copies and run errands.

   You look at him, roll your eyes, and say, "Ugh, this is stupid." (If possible, say this in your most obnoxious and annoyed tone of voice, roll your eyes, and make an annoyed expression.)

2. Have students turn to a partner and list off as many possibilities as they can think of for what might happen if someone did this at work. Record some student answers, then share responses with the group.

   Think of consequences that might result from this response. What would happen if you said and did that in front of your boss? Turn to your partner and begin listing possible negative consequences.

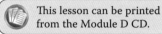
This lesson can be printed from the Module D CD.

How to Interact Appropriately
Lesson 1 • Following Directions, Part 1

Partner One, count on your fingers how many consequences you and your partner come up with. We will share as a whole group after you have had a chance to brainstorm with partners.

(*You might get fired. You might get put on probation. You might get a warning that this kind of behavior is not OK. You might get demoted and lose some of your pay.*)

3. Explain that students will be learning about the importance of following directions so that they can be successful in school and at any job they would like when they are older. They will receive information about what teachers expect in their classes and throughout the school, as well as what to do in a variety of situations when they are given directions or corrections.

   Part of our job at school is to help prepare you for life outside of school. We want to help you achieve the jobs you want and other dreams you may have. As you can see from the story we just discussed, it is really important to learn how to follow directions and respond respectfully to people in positions of authority. If you don't learn this skill, you may struggle in school or at work. Learning to follow directions appropriately will help you stay out of trouble with police and the law, and it will also help you in relationships with family or friends.

   You are probably all experts on how to follow directions because you have been taught this skill for years and years! But we are going to review following directions this week and throughout the year because it is one of the skills that you need to be successful in school and later in life. You will learn the expectations and directions for appropriate behavior in our common areas as well as in your classes. Learning to follow directions will help you to achieve and become whatever you want to be.

4. Have students fill in the blanks for Item 1 on their Lesson 1 worksheets. Demonstrate filling in the blanks with "school" and "work."

   Let's fill in the blanks on our worksheets. Following directions will help me be successful in **school** and **work**. Make sure you have "school" and "work" written in the blanks.

How to Interact
Lesson 1 • Following Di

Lesson Body

1. Introduce the essential steps of following directions:
   - Step 1: Listen and look.*
   - Step 2: Acknowledge.
   - Step 3: Perform the action.
   - Step 4: Seek assistance, if needed.

   * Note: If you work with students from cultural backgrounds in which looking at an elder or pe is considered disrespectful, teach them to be conscious of when it may or may not be approp directly at a person. You can teach them to look at the item being discussed or at the ground if needed, and to give other cues to show they are listening, like nodding their head.

   Many of you are great at following directions. You remember to do cert things so that you look and sound like you are doing what is asked. Wit even knowing it, you are doing the essential steps of following directio

   The essential steps of following directions are:
   1. Listen and look.
   2. Acknowledge.
   3. Perform the action immediately.
   4. Seek assistance, if needed.

   Let's look at each of those steps in more detail.

2. Explain **Step 1: Listen and look.** See the note above about cultural awareness.

   Listening is the first step in being able to follow a direction. In order to follow directions, you need to first hear what the direction is! This means you need to . . . (*listen*).

   To show they are actively listening, students can look at the speaker or what the speaker is talking about.

   You should also be *looking* at the person who is speaking. Or, if they are giving directions about something like an assignment, you could be looking at that assignment. For example, if I am giving you directions about how to complete an item on this worksheet, I might ask you to look at the written directions on your worksheet or at the item itself.

   So you might look at the speaker, the directions, if they are written, or the item the speaker is talking about.

   The first thing you could look at to show you are listening is the . . . (*speaker*). You could also look at the written . . . (*directions*) or at the . . . (*item*) the speaker is talking about.

Figure 5f *(continued)*

Have students turn to a partner and explain why it might be a problem if you are not looking at the person who is speaking or what the person is talking about.

Now, sometimes people look somewhere else, not at the speaker, when they are given a direction. Students sometimes look out the window, at friends, or at a doodle on their paper while the teacher is giving directions. And many times, students are still listening even when they aren't looking! So what is the problem with not looking at the speaker? Turn to your partner and discuss some of the potential problems with looking other places.

(The teacher can't tell if you are paying attention. Your mind might wander away from the direction. You might get distracted. You could miss something that is being demonstrated or shown.)

Call on partners to share one idea with the group, or write down best responses and share them as you acknowledge the partners.

Review Step 1, and have students write "Listen" for Item 2, No. 1.

So, the first step in following directions is to . . . *(listen)* and . . . *(look)*. Write "Listen" in the first blank. You want to show you are listening, so you should look at the speaker or what they are talking about.

Explain **Step 2: Acknowledge.** To show that the direction is understood, the listener should acknowledge the direction by nodding, saying "OK," or giving another positive indication of understanding.

After listening and looking, the next essential step in following directions is to acknowledge the direction—show you understand the direction. There are several ways you can show you understand.

The first way is to simply nod your head. If it is a longer direction, an occasional head nod can show you are still with the person. Most teachers love it when they see their students nod their heads because it means they haven't lost everyone! Your teacher will think, "Oh, what a good student!" Show me a head nod.

Have students nod their heads.

See! I'm thinking I have a lot of great students right now who will be successful because they listen and acknowledge.

At the end of a direction, you can show acknowledgment by saying "OK," "No problem," "I understand," or another positive verbal response.

The reason it is important to acknowledge the direction is that sometimes teachers or bosses will give a direction, and even though someone is looking at and listening to them, they get a blank stare back.

Demonstrate standing for 10 seconds with a blank stare. This will usually get a laugh!

Without a nod or some other acknowledgment, we don't know if you understand or are refusing to follow the direction!

Review Steps 1 and 2, and have students write "show" for Item 2, No. 2.

So, the first step of following directions is to . . . *(listen)* and . . . *(look)*. The next step is to acknowledge the direction. You want to show you understand. Write . . . *(show)* in the blank for Step 2.

4. Explain **Step 3: Perform the action**—the most important step. Explain that the action should be done immediately and without argument. Later lessons will explain how to handle disagreements.

The most important step in following directions is to actually *perform*, or do, the action. After you have listened and acknowledged, follow through immediately and without arguing.

Some of you may wonder what to do if you disagree with the direction or feel that something is not fair. Those are important questions to ask, and we will definitely address them later this week in more detail.

For now, just remember to perform the action immediately and without arguing. Arguing in the moment will lead to lots of negative consequences and usually does not get you the result you want.

Do an informal check of understanding.

Should you follow directions later or immediately? *(immediately)* If you disagree, should you wait, or is it better to argue your point right away? *(wait)*

Just to clarify, sometimes there are directions about things that you cannot complete immediately, like when a teacher assigns homework. Of course your teacher wouldn't expect you to do your homework right away and miss your next class. There are times when a direction has a delayed response, but the key is that you complete the direction immediately during the appropriate time—homework should be completed by the due date, which means you followed the directions to complete it on time.

Review Step 3, and have students write "Perform" for Item 2, No. 3 on their worksheets.

So, Step 3 of following directions is to perform the action immediately and without arguing. Write . . . *(perform)* in the blank for Step 3.

5. Introduce **Step 4: Seek assistance if needed.** Explain that later lessons will go into how to appropriately ask questions and clarify understanding.

When someone gives us a direction, it is very common to have some questions or concerns, or need help. This is an important part of learning. If we never had questions or needed help, we wouldn't have to go to school! Getting help is the way we learn and grow. It is the way we get better at things.

So, Step 4 is to seek assistance if needed, which means to ask for help or ask questions. One of our later lessons will go into detail about what to do if you have questions because there are always appropriate and inappropriate ways to go about getting help.

Review Step 4, and have students write "assistance" for Item 2, No. 4.

So, Step 4 of following directions is to seek assistance if needed. Write . . . *(assistance)* in the blank for Step 4.

Conclusion

- Review the LAPS acronym and concept.

  Notice that the four steps in following directions spell out LAPS if you take the first letter of each step. The L stands for . . . *(look and listen)*, A is . . . *(acknowledge)*, P is . . . *(perform the action)* and S is . . . *(seek assistance)*. Remembering LAPS will help you remember how to follow directions appropriately.

  If you practice doing laps on a track, you will get strong and be successful. If you remember to do your LAPS following directions, you will learn and grow, becoming strong in school and in life.

- Preview the next Following Directions lesson.

  Next time, we'll look more closely into how we respond to directions and corrections. We will practice deciding whether a response is appropriate or inappropriate.

Possibilities for Follow-Up

- Provide practice opportunities: Give students a variety of directions and have them practice LAPS.
- Give short role-play scenarios and have students act out following LAPS.
- Create video samples of students (or teachers role-playing students) following directions and not following directions. Have students analyze each step of LAPS and identify what the students in the video are doing correctly or incorrectly.

Figure 5g   How to Interact Appropriately, Lesson 2 Outline and Worksheet

Module D, Presentation 5

Lesson Outline

Page 1 of 2

How to Interact Appropriately
Lesson 2 • Following Directions, Part 2

Following Directions, Part 2

OBJECTIVES

- Students will identify appropriate and inappropriate responses to directions and corrections.
- Students will evaluate and rate the degree of appropriate vs. inappropriate behavior using multiple examples.

MATERIALS

- Document camera, overhead projector, or interactive whiteboard to display the worksheet and student responses
- Student copies of the Student Worksheet for Lesson 2: Following Directions, Part 2

Introduction

1. Review the previous lesson.

   Have students tell their partners as many of the LAPS essential steps for following directions as they can without looking at their Lesson 1 worksheets. Their partners can help them remember.

   Review as a whole class. Check how much students remember and their confidence level with LAPS. Provide additional review in LAPS using examples, modeling, and role-play if students seem to need extra assistance with these skills.

2. Preview and provide the rationale for the current lesson.

   Provide a rationale for why following directions will help students be successful. Explain that there are appropriate and inappropriate ways to respond to directions and corrections, and this lesson will help them tell the difference.

Foundations: A Proactive and Positive Behavior Support System

© 2014 Pacific Northwest Publishing

 This lesson can be printed from the Module D CD.

Figure 5g (continued)

Lesson Outline

How to Interact Appropriately
Lesson 2 • Following Directions, Part 2

Lesson Body

1. Have students look at the first thermometer diagram on their worksheets. Introduce the concept of a *behavior thermometer.* Have students look at the second thermometer and explain the labels "Appropriate" and "Inappropriate." Explain that, like temperature, there are different degrees of appropriate and inappropriate behavior.

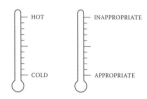

2. Model using the thermometer to rate how well directions were followed. Demonstrate filling in your thermometer to indicate your rating.

3. Model and guide students through Examples 2–6. For example, talk out loud as you demonstrate filling in the thermometer for Example 2 about one third of the way up—explaining that Marianna's behavior was more appropriate than not, but still could have been better.

4. Whenever most students appear to understand the assignment and are ranking behavior with high levels of accuracy, have students work for the remainder of the assigned work time on the examples. Provide additional assistance while circulating to students who appear to be struggling.

Conclusion

Review the LAPS acronym and concept, and assessing the differences between appropriate vs. inappropriate behavior.

Possibil

- Ex
  the
  ha
  the
  wa
  or
  acti

- Pro
  ina

- Hav
  ther

Foundations: A

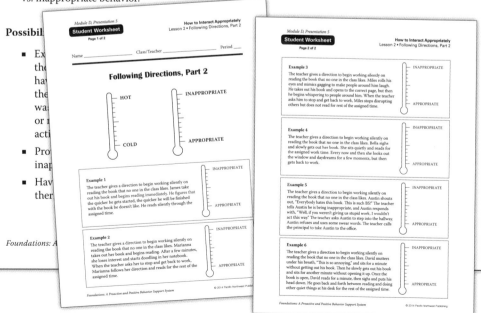

Figure 5h   How to Interact Appropriately, Lesson 3 Outline and Worksheet

Lesson Outline

Page 1 of 2

Accepting Compliments

OBJECTIVES

- Students will explain why it is important to respond appropriately to compliments.
- Students will identify appropriate ways to respond to compliments.

MATERIALS

- Document camera, overhead projector, or interactive whiteboard to display the worksheet and student responses
- Student copies of the Student Worksheet for Lesson 3: Accepting Compliments

Introduction

1. Review why it is important to respond appropriately to directions and features of appropriate versus inappropriate responses to directions (LAPS).

2. Introduce the skill of respectfully accepting a compliment. Provide a rationale:
   - Compliments will occur throughout your life.
   - It is not always comfortable to accept compliments.
   - If you do not receive a compliment in a skillful way, it can prevent other positive interactions in the future.

Lesson Body

1. Model each scenario below. After each, have students fill out their worksheets. (For the first scenario, demonstrate filling out each box as you think aloud. For the second scenario, guide students. For the rest, have students work on their own and then discuss.)

Scenario	Behaviors	What the Complimenter Might Think Is Being Conveyed	Positive or Negative Consequence
1	Looked at the person Smiled Said thank you	Appreciation Pride	Makes the complimenter feel good Strengthens relationship
2	Rolled eyes Sarcastic tone	Disrespect Annoyed	Punishment for disrespect

   - Scenario 1: Look at the person, smile, and say, "Thank you."
   - Scenario 2: Roll your eyes and say, "Thanks," in a sarcastic tone.

Foundations: A Proactive and Positive Behavior Support System   © 2014 Pacific Northwest Publishing

 This lesson can be printed from the Module D CD.

Figure 5h (continued)

- Scenario 3: Ignore the compliment. Don't look up or make eye contact. Continue to work.
- Scenario 4: Shrink down in your seat. Look down at the paper and say, "It was just luck. I'm really bad at this stuff."
- Scenario 5: Laugh, and say, "Oh, good! That was really hard for me, but I'm glad things went OK!"
- Scenario 6: Frown and say, "It's nowhere near as good as anyone else's."
- Scenario 7: Say, "Thank you. I appreciated your help earlier."
- Scenario 8: Keep a flat facial expression, but glance up quickly and give a quick nod. With this example, discuss how the appropriateness of a response can depend on the circumstance. During a silent, independent activity in class, this quick and quiet acknowledgment is probably an acceptable way to accept a compliment. However, this response would likely be considered rude or dismissive during a conversation or if a teacher pulled a student aside after class.

2. For each positive example above, discuss the positive or negative consequences that were listed. Have students add additional positive or negative consequences that may occur when someone accepts a compliment skillfully or unskillfully.

3. Explain and model the steps for accepting a compliment:

   a. Look at the person and listen to what the person is saying. Don't interrupt or ignore the compliment.
   b. Smile and say, "Thank you." Facial expression, body language, and tone all convey a message. Try to convey appreciation for the compliment.
   c. You may wish to follow up by using the compliment to move on to a new topic or provide a compliment to the other person.

4. Have students practice giving and receiving complim[ents] using some of the compliment suggestions if they are[

5. Without naming names, have students discuss thing[s] when accepting a compliment and things they could[

Conclusion

- Have students write on an exit ticket or tell their partn[er] accepting compliments in a skillful way is important.
- Review the steps for accepting a compliment: look at th[e] say "Thank you." If appropriate, follow up with a compl[iment or] move to a new topic.

Foundations: A Proactive and Positive Behavior Support System

Name _____ Class/Teacher _____ Period ____

Accepting Compliments

Scenario	Behaviors	What the Complimenter Might Think Is Being Conveyed	Positive or Negative Consequence
1			
2			
3			
4			
5			
6			
7			
8			

Compliment Suggestion List:
I like your shoes/shirt/pants.
I appreciate how friendly you are.
Your hair looks really nice today.
Thank you for being such a good friend.
You did a great job on the assignment.
You stayed really focused in class.

Foundations: A Proactive and Positive Behavior Support System   © 2014 Pacific Northwest Publishing

Figure 5i How to Interact Appropriately, Lesson 4 Outline (no worksheet for this lesson)

Lesson Outline

Page 1 of 2

How to Interact Appropriately
Lesson 4 • Accepting "No"

Accepting "No"

OBJECTIVES

Students will demonstrate how to accept a "No" response from authority figures in response to a request.

MATERIALS

- Document camera, overhead projector, or interactive whiteboard
- Blank index cards for each partnership or group
- Index card labeled "What NOT To Do" for each partnership or group

Introduction

1. Provide a rationale for the skill of respectfully and appropriately accepting "No."

2. Have students brainstorm examples of when they made a request of a teacher, friend, family member, or employer and the answer was "No."

Lesson Body

1. Explain the steps for accepting "No" in a responsible manner. (Write these for students to see; consider making a poster.)

   Step 1: Stay calm.

   Step 2: Think about the consequences of not following the decision of the person in authority (if/then statement).

   Step 3: Respond by saying "OK," or remain silent. Use respectful body language and other forms of communication.

2. Model what this looks and sounds like using one of the scenarios students brainstormed in Step 2 in the Introduction, with a student playing the role of the adult in authority.

3. Have students brainstorm inappropriate ways to accept or not accept "No" and record them on the What NOT to Do index cards. Then have students share their ideas and discuss potential consequences of inappropriate responses.

 This lesson can be printed from the Module D CD.

Figure 5i (continued)

4. As a group, develop a "looks like/sounds like" T-chart detailing what students should do to respond respectfully at each step of accepting "No." Each student will re-create the T-chart on an index card to use as future reference. For each step, discuss the points below.

> **Step 1: Stay calm.** Elicit from students some strategies for staying calm.
>
> **Step 2: Think about the consequences.** Explain that students should use if/then statements to think through possible consequences before they respond.
>
> **Step 3: Respond by saying "OK," or remain silent.** Elicit from students what respectful body language and other forms of communication look like.

5. Using the scenarios from the student-generated examples and the T-chart, have students role-play the situations. In the role-plays, one student will assume the role of the adult in authority, and the other will play the role of the student.

   Before the role-play starts, remind students of the steps for accepting "No" in a respectful and responsible way.

   Direct students who are watching the scenario to look for each of the accepting "No" steps in the role-play situations.

   After each demonstration, review with the entire class how the actors used the steps in accepting "No."

Conclusion

Review the steps and the T-chart. Ask students to create a memory device to help them remember the steps in accepting "No" (for example, CCQ for Calm—Consequences—Quiet, or Calm Consequences are OK).

Figure 5j   How to Interact Appropriately, Lesson 5 Outline and Worksheet

Accepting a Correction

OBJECTIVES

- Students will determine why it is important to respond appropriately to staff corrections.
- Students will identify and practice appropriate vs. inappropriate responses to staff corrections.

MATERIALS

Student copies (one copy for each pair of students) of the Student Worksheet for Lesson 5: Accepting a Correction

Introduction

1. Introduce the lesson and provide the rationale for why students need to learn the skill of respectfully accepting corrections.

2. Give examples of common corrections students may hear in your school. You may also include brief examples of corrections you often give in the classroom.

Lesson Body

1. Model (or describe) possible student responses to corrections, providing multiple examples of both appropriate and inappropriate responses. After each example, have students show a number from 1–10 on their fingers to indicate whether the response was appropriate or inappropriate (1 = worst possible response, 5 = not bad or good, 10 = best response).

2. Discuss how there are many forms of communication and students should consider all of them when responding to a correction. Actions and words are ways of communicating, but so are tone, voice level, facial expression, and body language!

3. Remind students of the steps in LAPS (see Lesson 1) and explain that LAPS is also a good strategy to remember the steps to follow when accepting a correction: Listen and look, acknowledge, perform the action, and seek assistance, if needed. For the seek assistance step, inform students that a later lesson will help them identify when and how to self-advocate if they disagree with a correction or feel something is unfair.

© 2014 Pacific Northwest Publishing

 This lesson can be printed from the Module D CD.

Figure 5j (continued)

How to Interact Appropriately
Lesson 5 • Accepting a Correction

4. If time permits, break students into pairs and have them role-play and practice only the positive responses for each of the scenarios on their worksheets. They should not actually demonstrate the inappropriate behavior at the start of the scenario. Have them start at the teacher correction. If a student feels uncomfortable role-playing or you have a group that might find this exercise difficult, simply have students write or draw an appropriate response for each scenario.

Conclusion

Exit ticket: Students write down one reason to respond appropriately to a staff correction—either to earn something positive or to avoid something negative. Students write an example of how to appropriately respond to a correction.

Foundations: A Proactive and Positive Behavior Support System

---

Module D, Presentation 5

Student Worksheet

How to Interact Appropriately
Lesson 5 • Accepting a Correction

Name _____ Class/Teacher _____ Period ____

Accepting a Correction

Scenarios for Student Role-Plays:

A student is running in the hall. Teacher says: "Please stop and walk back 10 paces."

Students are clumped at lockers. Teacher says: "Remember to be kind and make room for your peers. Please move to the common area."

A student knocks another student's binder out of his hands (binder checking). Teacher says, "That was unkind. Help this student clean up the papers."

Students are pushing each other in line. Teacher says: "That is unsafe. Please stop and keep your hands to yourself."

A student is swearing. Teacher says: "That language is inappropriate. Please remember to use responsible language for school or the workplace."

A student is wearing a shirt that violates the dress code. Teacher says: "That is not an appropriate shirt for school. Please go to the restroom and turn your shirt inside out or change into your gym shirt."

A student blurts out the answer in class. Teacher says: "Please remember to raise your hand, I'm going to call on someone who was following expectations."

A student is off task—staring out the window instead of completing her assignment. Teacher says: "Julie, you need to pay attention. Please focus."

Students are engaging in horseplay in the cafeteria line. Teacher says: "Please keep your hands to yourself. That will be a 2-minute timeout."

Students are copying each other's homework. Teacher says: "You need to do your own work. I'm going to subtract 20% from each of your final scores on this assignment."

A student is drawing on his desk. Teacher says: "Please keep your and others' space clean. You will need to stay in from recess to wipe this desk and five others."

Foundations: A Proactive and Positive Behavior Support System   © 2014 Pacific Northwest Publishing

Module D, Presentation 5

Lesson Outline

Page 1 of 3

How to Interact Appropriately
Lesson 6 • Analyzing Your Behavior

Analyzing Your Behavior

OBJECTIVES

- Students will explain how the intensity and frequency of behaviors can determine consequences and outcomes.
- Students will explain how they can analyze their own behavior, looking at intensity and frequency of positive and negative behaviors.

MATERIALS

- Document camera, overhead projector, or interactive whiteboard to display the worksheet and student responses
- Student copies of the Student Worksheet for Lesson 6: Analyzing Your Behavior

Introduction

1. Review previous lessons on following directions and appropriate responses to corrections by having students create a T-chart for appropriate vs. inappropriate responses.

2. Introduce this lesson and explain that it will help students self-reflect on how their behavior results in positive or negative consequences.

Lesson Body

1. Tell students that analyzing your behavior involves looking at the intensity and frequency of your positive and negative behaviors.

2. Display the definition for the term *intense* (see below) and have students fill in the missing words on their worksheets. Give examples, and have students provide examples of things that are intense.

   intense \in-'ten(t)s\ means existing in an extreme degree, very strong, or done with a lot of energy, enthusiasm, or effort. (Merriam-Webster)

3. Explain that students may exhibit similar behavior, but it is the intensity of the behavior that causes one student to be noticed more than the other. Provide positive and negative examples and have students determine which person in the examples is more likely to be noticed and rewarded or punished.

Foundations: A Proactive and Positive Behavior Support System

© 2014 Pacific Northwest Publishing

 This lesson can be printed from the Module D CD.

Figure 5k (continued)

Lesson Outline

4. Have students write one example of negative behavior that is too intense and receives correction or punishment, and one positive behavior that is intense and is noticed and rewarded. These can be school, home, or work examples. Have students share their examples with a partner.

5. Explain that students should be self-reflective about their behavior, considering the intensity of behavior and the positive and negative consequences that occur.

6. Display the definition for the term *frequent* (see below) and have students fill in the missing words on their worksheets. Give examples and have students provide examples.

   frequent \\'frē-kwənt\\ means happening often, or regularly. (Merriam-Webster)

7. Explain that two or more students can exhibit the same behavior, but it is how frequently a student demonstrates the behavior that causes that student to be recognized and rewarded or punished more than other students. Provide positive and negative examples.

8. Have students write one example of negative behavior that is too frequent and receives correction or punishment, and one positive behavior that is frequent and is noticed and rewarded. These can be school, home, or work examples. Have students share their examples with a partner.

9. Explain that students should be self-reflective about their behavior, considering the frequency of the behavior.

10. Have students identify and write on their worksheets one positive thing that they do really well or with great intensity and some of the positive consequences that occur as a result. Also have them identify a time when they did something with high intensity that was not good or appropriate and the negative consequences that occurred. Have them repeat for a positive and negative example of frequency. Provide a model for each, thinking aloud as you fill out the worksheet.

Conclusion

Tell students that over the next few weeks, teachers will ask them to self-reflect on various aspects of their behavior. They will use the skills from this lesson to determine whether they can increase the intensity and frequency of positive behaviors or reduce the intensity or frequency of negative behaviors in a variety of situations.

Module D, Presentation 5

Lesson Outline

Page 3 of 3

How to Interact Appropriately
Lesson 6 • Analyzing Your Behavior

Possibilities for Follow-Up

Provide staff with suggestions for how to incorporate Analyzing Your Behavior activities into their content areas so that students have opportunities to practice this skill throughout the next few weeks. For example, have students analyze the frequency and/or intensity of behaviors in a variety of situations.

- In a social studies or civics class, have students analyze the intensity and frequency of behaviors covered in their current lessons: honesty, listening to others' perspectives, tolerance to others, citizenship, etc.

- In PE, have students analyze the intensity and frequency of following rules of the game, good sportsmanship, and putting in their best effort.

- In health, have students analyze the intensity and frequency of healthy vs. unhealthy food and exercise habits, drug and alcohol use, or risk-taking behaviors.

- In music class, have students analyze the intensity and frequency of their practice habits.

Module D, Presentation 5

Student Worksheet

Page 1 of 3

How to Interact Appropriately
Lesson 6 • Analyzing Your Behavior

Name _____ Class/Teacher _____ Period ____

Analyzing Your Behavior

Intense

Intense: existing in an extreme _____, very _____ or done with _____ of energy, enthusiasm, or effort.

Examples of things that are intense:

- _____
- _____
- _____

List one example of a negative behavior that is too intense and leads to correction punishment (at school, home, or work):

_____

List one example of a positive behavior that is intense and leads to recognition rewards (at school, home, or work):

_____

Foundations: A Proactive and Positive Behavior Support System © 2014

Module D, Presentation 5

Student Worksheet

Page 2 of 3

How to Interact Appropriately
Lesson 6 • Analyzing Your Behavior

Frequent

Frequent: happening _____ or _____.

Examples of things that are frequent:

- _____
- _____
- _____
- _____

List one example of a negative behavior that is too frequent and leads to correction or punishment (at school, home, or work):

_____

List one example of a positive behavior that is frequent and leads to recognition and rewards (at school, home, or work):

_____

Foundations: A Proactive and Positive Behavior Support System © 2014 Pacific Northwest Publishing

---

Module D, Presentation 5

Student Worksheet

How to Interact Appropriately
Lesson 6 • Analyzing Your Behavior

really well with intensity (in extreme degree, very strongly, or with lots of ___, or effort) is:

_____

s with intensity, I receive _____

l something with higher intensity that was inappropriate was when:

_____

ces were that I _____

quently very well is: _____

quently, rather than just some of the time, I get the following benefits:

_____

or did frequently that was not appropriate was: _____

s were that I _____

ive Behavior Support System © 2014 Pacific Northwest Publishing

---

 This lesson can be printed from the Module D CD.

Figure 5l *How to Interact Appropriately, Lesson 7 Outline and Worksheet*

Module D, Presentation 5

Lesson Outline

Page 1 of 3

How to Interact Appropriately
Lesson 7 • Taking a Break

Taking a Break

Lesson Consideration

If your staff will teach this or a similar lesson, determine whether all staff members are willing to give students a break if requested. If not all are willing, either do not teach this lesson or include the following activity:

- On the day you teach this lesson, have each student write their class schedule and teachers on a piece of paper they will keep in their notebooks or in a prominent location.

- Throughout the day, each teacher should indicate whether he or she will grant breaks when students request them. Have students record each teacher's decision on their paper.

- Teach students that they may request a break from any of the teachers on their list who said they would grant breaks.

- Teach students other coping strategies for classes in which a break is not appropriate.

OBJECTIVES

- Students will describe how to ask for a break appropriately.
- Students will identify times when they may need to ask for a break and acceptable activities that may help them calm down if and when they need a break.

MATERIALS

- Document camera, overhead projector, or interactive whiteboard to display the worksheet and student responses
- Student copies of the Student Worksheet for Lesson 7: Taking a Break

Introduction

1. Review appropriate responses to directions, corrections, and compliments.

2. Introduce the lesson by explaining that asking for a break can help someone who is upset cool down and thus prevent aggressive acts.

Foundations: A Proactive and Positive Behavior Support System   © 2014 Pacific Northwest Publishing

Presentation 5: Preventing the Misbehavior That Leads to Referrals and Suspensions   **183**

Module D, Presentation 5

Lesson Outline

Page 2 of 3

How to Interact Appropriately
Lesson 7 • Taking a Break

Lesson Body

1. Describe a situation in which a student who typically does not act out aggressively learns about something very upsetting outside of school, then acts out aggressively in school (e.g., divorce at home, dog dies, family member is sick, finds out the family is moving, etc.).

   Have students discuss whether students have a right to be upset about things inside or outside school. But does that right excuse acting out aggressively?

2. Explain that when someone is upset about something, it would be better to ask for a break and find a way to calm down than to explode.

   Breaks can be long or short, depending on the severity of the problem and how upset or angry the student is. When students ask for breaks, they should ask for the smallest amount of time they think they need to calm down so that they don't abuse this privilege. Provide examples.

3. Tell students that there are many activities they can perform during a break to cool off and calm down. Students should pick several strategies that will help them calm down and move forward. Display examples on the student worksheet and have students circle those strategies they think would be helpful when they need a break.

4. Have students, in partners or groups, list times or situations in which a person might need to take a break. Encourage them to consider examples from both in school and out of school.

5. Discuss the steps for asking for a break:

   Step 1: Appropriately gain the teacher's attention (raise your hand, go to the teacher's desk, etc.).

   Step 2: Calmly say or write a note to the teacher:
   I am having a hard time right now. Can I take a break? Is it possible for me to have ____ seconds/minutes to _____?

   Indicate the amount of time you need and the preferred activity that will help you get back on track.

   Step 3: If you feel comfortable doing so, tell the teacher the reason you need a break.

 This lesson can be printed from the Module D CD.

Lesson Outline

How to Interact Appropriately
Lesson 7 • Taking a Break

6. Have students practice asking for a break.

   Demonstrate filling in the Sample Requests section of the student worksheet. Talk aloud as you model brainstorming a minor and a serious problem, determining the time needed for a break, and activities to perform during the break.

   Have students fill in the Sample Requests portion of their worksheets. Circulate and monitor student responses.

   Have students turn to their partner and practice saying the requests. Tell them they do not need to explain what the problem is if they do not feel comfortable. They can just start at, "I am having a hard time right now."

Conclusion

Conclude the lesson and preview the next lesson.

Possibilities for Follow-Up and Extension

- Explain that the more students build trust by following directions, responding appropriately to corrections and compliments, and building positive relationships with their teachers, the more likely a teacher will be to give them a break when needed. This also means that students should not abuse the privilege.

- Some students may need to use a break more than others—they may have more serious and difficult things going on, more trouble with academics, or more concerns at home. But even students who are having many issues need to use breaks carefully.

- If a student uses too many breaks, it is an indication that the student needs additional coping strategies. I will let you take a break...

How to Interact Appropriately
Lesson 7 • Taking a Break

Name _____ Class/Teacher _____ Period _____

Taking a Break

Circle the "cool down" or "take a break" strategies that you think would be most helpful to you. Circle strategies that might be useful for a quick break for a minor problem or for when you are having a major problem and are very upset.

- Put head down.
- Go to quiet corner of the classroom to think positive thoughts.
- Take some deep breaths.
- Read a book.
- Draw.
- Play a silent game (maze, crossword, solitaire).
- Think or write about something happy, calming, or fun.
- Go for a walk.
- Get a drink of water.
- Sit silently in the hallway.
- Go see someone—for example, counselor or administrator.
- Do something physical—run a lap, jump rope, or do jumping jacks.
- Call home for advice or to talk.
- Listen to music on the computer or a class CD or MP3 player.
- Other _____

Sample Requests

1. For each request below, think of a problem that would make you so upset or angry that you would need to ask for a break. Write a minor problem that could be resolved with a quick break, a moderate problem, and a very serious problem that might require a longer break or a more distracting activity to get you back on track.

2. For each problem you list, indicate how long a break you think you would need and the activity that would be most helpful for you to recover and get back on track.

Foundations: A Proactive and Positive Behavior Support System   © 2014 Pacific Northwest Publishing

How to Interact Appropriately
Lesson 7 • Taking a Break

Request 1

Minor problem: _____

_____

I am having a hard time right now. Can I take a break? Is it possible for me to have _____ seconds/minutes to _____?

Request 2

Moderate problem: _____

I am having a hard time right now. Can I take a break? Is it possible for me to have _____ seconds/minutes to _____?

Request 3

Serious problem: _____

I am having a hard time right now. Can I take a break? Is it possible for me to have _____ seconds/minutes to _____?

Foundations: A Proactive and Positive Behavior Support System   © 2014 Pacific Northwest Publishing

Module D, Presentation 5

Lesson Outline

Page 1 of 2

Making an Appointment—Self-Advocacy

OBJECTIVES

- Students will identify when and how to ask for an appointment to discuss an issue with a teacher or common area supervisor.
- Students will identify when and how to ask for an appointment to discuss an issue with an administrator or counselor.

MATERIALS

- Document camera, overhead projector, or interactive whiteboard to display the worksheet and student responses
- Student copies of the Student Worksheet for Lesson 8: Making an Appointment

Introduction

1. Review the previous lesson (Taking a Break).

2. Introduce current lesson and explain that students will learn how and when to make an appointment with someone in authority to get their needs met.

Lesson Body

1. Explain that sometimes it may be necessary to make an appointment to discuss a problem with someone in authority. Give examples and have students mark any situations under No. 1 on their worksheets that they have experienced. Discuss whether they talked about (or wish they could have talked about) the situation with a teacher, supervisor, administrator, or counselor.

2. Explain that at times a student will need to self-advocate—this means standing up for yourself. Some students try to self-advocate but get into trouble because of the way they go about it. For example, students argue or question a correction in the moment rather than waiting for an appropriate time to calmly discuss the issue.

3. Teach students that the key to self-advocacy is to recognize that emotional reactions in the moment do not usually lead to positive outcomes, so they need to wait for an appropriate time to respond. Present the steps for self-advocating:

    Step 1: If necessary, use a calming strategy or ask to take a break.

 This lesson can be printed from the Module D CD.

Figure 5m (continued)

Step 2: Respond appropriately in the moment using LAPS. Do not argue or question.

Step 3: Make an appointment with the person in authority (seek assistance).

Step 4: Before the meeting, reevaluate whether the meeting is necessary.

Step 5: Create a plan for what you want to say.

For **Step 1**, have students list calming strategies they could use in the moment.

For **Step 2**, have students review each letter in LAPS, working with a partner to fill in the blanks.

For **Step 3**, explain that students can ask for an appointment in several ways. As you list options, have students write down those methods they might use.

For **Step 4**, explain that students should self-evaluate how serious the issue is and how necessary it is to speak to the staff member.

For **Step 5**, model creating a plan of what to say.

4. Explain that at times it may be necessary to make an appointment with an administrator or counselor rather than a teacher or common area supervisor:

- You tried making an appointment and discussing the problem with the staff member, but the problem has not been resolved.

- The issue involves harassment, sexual harassment, threats, or violence from a student or staff member.

- You would like to speak with the teacher about so~~...~~ but you are not sure how to approach the difficult~~...~~ to pre-plan your discussion.

Unless it is an emergency or an illegal situation, follow~~...~~ see the administrator or counselor (e.g., fill out a meet~~...~~ or an issue that involves illegal acts, you may tell the o~~...~~ request to wait in the office while they contact the adr~~...~~

Conclusion

Review the steps for making an appointment, emphasizin~~...~~ to remember is to follow the direction or correction in th~~...~~ person in authority, or to continue following the rules wh~~...~~ Then follow up with an appointment with someone in au~~...~~

Foundations: A Proactive and Positive Behavior Support System

Name _____ Class/Teacher _____ Period ____

Making an Appointment—Self-Advocacy

1. Have you ever wished you could talk to someone in authority about:

- A false accusation?
- An unfair consequence or correction?
- A problem with another student (drama, bullying, fighting, etc.)?
- Difficulty with class work?
- Having a hard time with how compliments or corrections are given?
- How to improve your grade?
- Witnessing poor treatment of another student (by students or staff)?
- Having a hard time at home or with personal issues?

2. Steps for Self-Advocacy

Step 1: If necessary, use a calming strategy or ask to take a break:
- _____
- _____

Step 2: Respond appropriately in the moment using LAPS. Do not argue or question.
- L = _____
- A = _____
- P = _____
- S = _____

Step 3: Make an appointment with the person in authority by:
- _____
- _____
- _____

Step 4: Before the meeting, re-evaluate whether the meeting is necessary.

Step 5: Create a plan for what you want to say.

Foundations: A Proactive and Positive Behavior Support System　　　　© 2014 Pacific Northwest Publishing

Module D, Presentation 5

Lesson Outline

Page 1 of 2

How to Interact Appropriately
Lesson 9 • Dealing With a False Accusation

Dealing With a False Accusation

OBJECTIVES

Students will choose a positive strategy to use when they have been falsely accused.

MATERIALS

Document camera, interactive whiteboard, or PowerPoint

Introduction

1. Review the previous lesson—when and how to ask for an appointment.

2. Introduce and provide a rationale for learning the skill of dealing with a false accusation.

   Have student discuss in pairs the meaning of the statement:

   > *Lies have speed, but truth, going slowly, will someday catch up with lies.*
   >
   > —Joel Akande

   Explain that people can be falsely accused at school, at home, and in the workplace. It is important that students learn how to cope with false accusations.

Lesson Body

1. Display the steps for dealing with a false accusation. Ask students to write the steps in their notes. You will discuss each step in more detail after all of them are displayed.

   Step 1: Recognize that you are not guilty of doing what you are accused of (also know that all humans may feel a bit of guilt even when they haven't done anything wrong.)

   Step 2: Judge your situation in relation to the accuser.

   Step 3: Think about why the person may be accusing you.

   Step 4: Discuss ideas for clearing up the situation. Communicate your ideas in a calm manner.

Foundations: A Proactive and Positive Behavior Support System   © 2014 Pacific Northwest Publishing

 This lesson can be printed from the Module D CD.

Figure 5n (continued)

2. Return to Step 1. Tell students that your response to the accusation should be different depending on whether or not you are guilty. If you are guilty, you should take responsibility. If you are not guilty, you should take ownership of Step 1: Recognize that you are not guilty—and then take steps to clear your name.

3. Point to Step 2. Explain that it is important to judge where you stand in relation to the accuser because the strategies for responding will differ depending on the relationship. Consider two questions:

   ▪ Are the two of you in equally powerful positions, or is the accuser in a position of authority over you?

   ▪ Is the accuser in control of his or her emotions or out of control?

   Explain why the student should evaluate whether the accuser is in an equal power position or a position of authority.

   Explain why the student should determine whether the person is in control of his or her emotions.

   Have students discuss ways they can tell if someone is in control or not in control. Make two lists on the board and elicit responses from students to use in both situations.

4. Point to Step 3. Have groups generate and share reasons why someone might be falsely accused.

5. Point to Step 4 and explain how to start a conversation with the accuser while remaining calm.

6. In partners, have students come up with a scenario for being falsely accused. Have them role-play using the strategies to deal with a false accusation.

Conclusion

Review the steps for dealing with a false accusation. Inform students that if this strategy does not resolve the situation and they are still being falsely accused, they should seek assistance from someone in authority. Briefly review the steps for making an appointment with an authority figure.

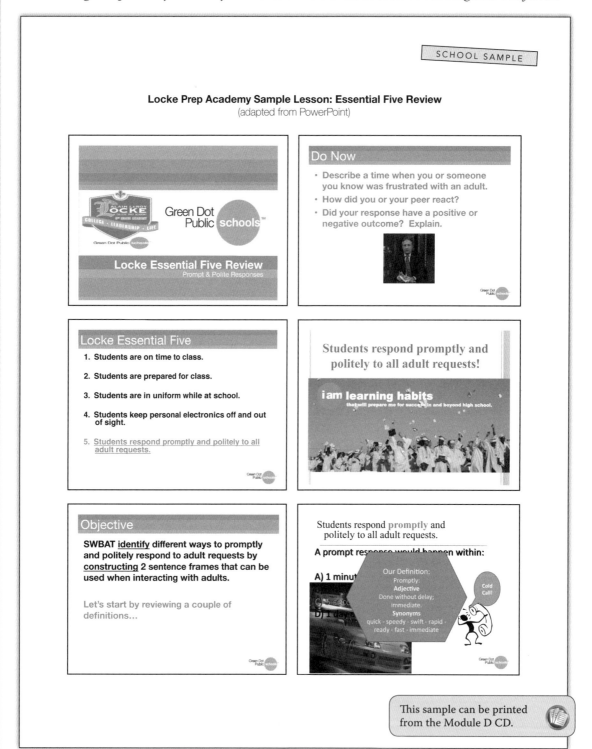

Locke Prep Academy Sample Lesson: Essential Five Review
(adapted from PowerPoint)

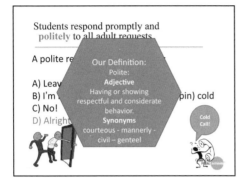

Students respond promptly and **politely** to all adult requests.

A polite re...

Our Definition:
Polite:
Adjective
Having or showing respectful and considerate behavior.
Synonyms
courteous - mannerly - civil – genteel

A) Leav...
B) I'm ... (pin) cold
C) No!
D) Alright...

Cold Call!

Prompt AND Polite

- **The desired response to an adult request should be BOTH** prompt and polite
  - **Choose the appropriate prompt & polite response**
  When asked to take off your non-uniform article of clothing, you…
  A.) Quickly give the adult "the finger."
  B.) Say, "Okay, Miss," but after being asked 3 times.
  C.) Say, "Okay, can I get a loaner?
  D.) Say, "Nope, going to class!"

Why are we learning about prompt & polite responses?

- Effective communication
  - Making eye contact with the adult
  - Using appropriate language and tone
  - Being prompt & polite when responding
- You will be able to use this skill in different settings in your life
- It helps prevent conflict
- It allows you to voice your opinion without negative consequences
- It helps you to develop maturity

Examples & Non-Examples

Examples:
- Making eye contact and saying, "Ok"
- Making eye contact and saying, "Fin"
- Making eye contact and saying, "Yes, Mister/ Miss)
- Making eye contact and saying, "I really don't want to, but I will."

Non-examples:
- Looking away
- Turning your back and starting to talk to your friend(s)
- Cursing or any other inappropriate gestures
- Running away
- Laughing

Do's & Don'ts

Sample Prompt & Polite Sentence Frames

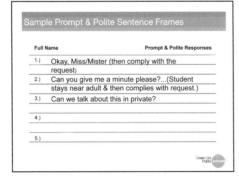

Full Name	Prompt & Polite Responses
1.)	Okay, Miss/Mister (then comply with the request)
2.)	Can you give me a minute please?...(Student stays near adult & then complies with request.)
3.)	Can we talk about this in private?
4.)	
5.)	

If you are DEFIANT or you DIRECT PROFANITY AT AN ADULT, expect the following to happen…

Locke Prep Academy Sample Lesson: Essential Five Review
(adapted from PowerPoint)

Anticipatory Set - Scenarios

• Now let's look at some scenarios

Scenario #1

• As you walk through the front gate, (Mr. Boyes, Mr. Wagner, Mr. Williams, or Ms. Balotro) asks you to check in your white sweatshirt that has a hood. You already have intentions of doing so and you respond by saying…

Scenario #2

• As you are doing your work in class, you forget to turn off your cell phone and it rings in class. The teacher explains the expectations around the electronics policy and asks you to hand over your device. You are upset because you were not on it and respond by saying…

Scenario #3

• You had a long night and were not able to sleep well because you have been demonstrating flu-like symptoms. You came to school in the morning because you did not want to fall behind in your school work. In 3rd period you do not feel well and your head is throbbing, so you place your head on the table. Your teacher then asks you twice to pick your head up and copy the notes. When your teacher asks you a third time, you respond by saying…

Scenario #4

• You are in class and you need to use the restroom after lunch during your advisory class. You ask your teacher to use the restroom, and he responds with a firm, "No, we just returned from lunch." You need to go to restroom, so you ask the teacher again by saying…

Figure 5o (continued)

Locke Prep Academy Sample Lesson: Essential Five Review
(adapted from PowerPoint)

Scenario #5

- In class a student near you makes a remark out loud and the teacher gives you a 5-minute after-school detention because she believes it was you who made the remark. The teacher walks by your table right after this situation and you say to her…

Independent Practice

- Now that we have gone over the definition of prompt and polite, as well as scenarios that may occur in your day-to-day interactions with adults, use this knowledge and record on your worksheet how you would react in the remaining scenarios.
- Be sure to use a one-liner from your index card that demonstrates a prompt and polite response (feel free to add one-liners to your card if the ones you have don't fit the scenarios given).
- We will share some of our responses with the class and judge them to see if they fit our criteria of prompt and polite.

How Would You React?

- The Dean sees you in the quad with your cell phone out. You were reading a text from your mom instructing you to come straight home after school. The Dean reminds you of the electronics policy and requests your phone.
- What is a one-liner that could be used in this scenario?
- How can we prevent this from happening?

How Would You React?

- You are walking into class with your blue and gold sweater on. Your teacher asks you to remove the sweater before entering. You are cold and you really do not want to take off your sweater.

- What is a one-liner that could be used in this scenario?

- How can we prevent this from happening?

BIBLIOGRAPHY

Adams, C. (2011). Recess makes kids smarter. *Instructor, 120*(5), 55–59. Retrieved from http://www.scholastic.com/teachers/article/recess-makes-kids-smarter

Allensworth, E. M., & Easton, J. Q. (2007). *What matters for staying on track and graduating in Chicago public schools: A close look at course grades, failures, and attendance in the freshman year.* Retrieved from http://ccsr.uchicago.edu/sites/default/files/publications/07%20What%20Matters%20Final.pdf

American Lung Association, Epidemiology and Statistics Unit, Research and Health Education Division (2012). *Trends in asthma morbidity and mortality.* Retrieved from http://www.lung.org/finding-cures/our-research/trend-reports/asthma-trend-report.pdf

Applied Survey Research and Attendance Works (2011). *Attendance in early elementary grades: Associations with student characteristics, school readiness and third grade outcomes* (mini-report). Retrieved from http://www.attendanceworks.org/wordpress/wp-content/uploads/2010/04/ASR-Mini-Report-Attendance-Readiness-and-Third-Grade-Outcomes-7-8-11.pdf

Archer, A., & Gleason, M. (1990). *Skills for school success.* North Billerica, MA: Curriculum Associates.

Baker, M. L., Sigmon, N., & Nugent, M. E. (2001). *Truancy reduction: Keeping students in school* (Juvenile Justice Bulletin). Retrieved from U.S. Department of Justice, National Criminal Justice Reference Service website: http://www.ncjrs.gov/pdffiles1/ojjdp/188947.pdf

Balfanz, R., Bridgeland, J. M., Fox, J. H., DePaoli, J. L., Ingram, E. S., Maushard, M. (2014). *Building a grad nation: Progress and challenge in ending the high school dropout epidemic.* Retrieved from http://diplomasnow.org/wp-content/uploads/2014/04/BGN-Report-2014_Full.pdf

Balfanz, R., & Byrnes, V. (2012). *Chronic absenteeism: Summarizing what we know from nationally available data.* Retrieved from Johns Hopkins University Center for Social Organization of Schools website: http://new.every1graduates.org/wp-content/uploads/2012/05/FINALChronicAbsenteeismReport_May16.pdf

Balfanz, R., & Byrnes, V. (2013). *Meeting the challenge of combating chronic absenteeism: Impact of the NYC mayor's interagency task force on chronic absenteeism and school attendance and its implications for other cities.* Retrieved from Johns Hopkins School of Education website: http://new.every1graduates.org/wp-content/uploads/2013/11/NYM-Chronic-Absenteeism-Impact-Report.pdf

Becker, W. C., & Engelmann, S. (1971). *Teaching: A course in applied psychology.* Columbus, OH: Science Research Associates.

Brophy, J. E. (1980). *Teacher praise: A functional analysis.* East Lansing, MI: Institute for Research on Teaching.

Brophy, J. E. (1986). Teacher influences on student achievement. *American Psychologist, 4*(10), 1069–1077.

Brophy, J. (1987). Synthesis of research on strategies for motivating students to learn. *Educational Leadership, 45*(2), 40–48.

Bruner, C., Discher, A., & Chang, H. (2011). *Chronic elementary absenteeism: A problem hidden in plain sight.* Retrieved from http://www.attendanceworks.org/wordpress/wp-content/uploads/2010/04/ChronicAbsence.pdf

Cameron, J., & Pierce, W. D. (1994). Reinforcement, reward, and intrinsic motivation: A meta-analysis. *Review of Educational Research, 64*(3), 363–423.

Chang, H., & Romero, M. (2008). *Present, engaged, and accounted for: The critical importance of addressing chronic absence in the early grades.* New York, NY: National Center for Children in Poverty.

Collins, J. (2001). *Good to great: Why some companies make the leap . . . and others don't.* New York, NY: HarperCollins Publishers.

Colvin, G. (Writer/Producer). (1992). *Managing acting-out behavior: A staff development program* [video]. Longmont, CO: Sopris West.

Colvin, G. (2004). *Managing the cycle of acting-out behavior in the classroom.* Eugene, OR: Behavior Associates.

Cooper, J. O., Heron, T. E., & Heward, W. L. (2007). *Applied behavior analysis* (2nd ed.). Upper Saddle River, NJ: Pearson.

Cotton, K. (1990). *Schoolwide and classroom discipline* (Close-Up #9). Portland, OR: Northwest Regional Educational Laboratory.

Donovan, M. S., & Cross, C. T. (Eds.) (2002). *Minority students in special education and gifted education.* Washington, DC: National Academy Press.

Emmer, E. T., & Evertson, C. M. (2012). *Classroom management for middle and high school teachers* (9th ed.). Upper Saddle River, NJ: Pearson.

Esler, A., Godber, Y., & Christenson, S. (2008). Best practices in supporting school-family partnerships. In A. Thomas & J. Grimes (Eds.), *Best practices in school psychology V* (pp. 917–936). Bethesda, MD: National Association of School Psychologists.

Evertson, C. M., & Emmer, E. T. (2012). *Classroom management for elementary teachers* (9th ed.). Upper Saddle River, NJ: Pearson.

Fabelo, T., Thompson, M. D., Plotkin, M., Carmichael, D., Marchbanks, M. P. III, & Booth, E. A. (2011). *Breaking schools' rules: A statewide study of how school discipline relates to students' success and juvenile justice involvement.* Retrieved from http://csgjusticecenter.org/wp-content/uploads/2012/08/Breaking_Schools_Rules_Report_Final.pdf

Feather, N. T. (1982). Expectancy-value approaches: Present status and future directions. In N. T. Feather (Ed.), *Expectations and actions: Expectancy-value models in psychology.* Hillsdale NJ: Erlbaum.

Furlong, M., Felix, E. D., Sharkey, J. D., & Larson, J. (2005). Preventing school violence: A plan for safe and engaging schools. *Principal Leadership, 6*(1), 11–15. Retrieved from http://www.nasponline.org/resources/principals/Student%20Counseling%20Violence%20Prevention.pdf

Get Schooled and Hart Research (2012). *Skipping to nowhere: Students share their views about missing school.* Retrieved from https://getschooled.com/system/assets/assets/203/original/Hart_Research_report_final.pdf

Glossary of Education Reform for Journalists, Parents, and Community Members. Retrieved from http://edglossary.org/school-culture/

Gottfredson, D. C., Gottfredson, G. D., & Hybl, L. G. (1993). Managing adolescent behavior: A multiyear, multischool study. *American Educational Research Journal, 30*(1), 179–215.

Jensen, E. (2009). *Teaching with poverty in mind: What being poor does to kids' brains and what schools can do about it.* Alexandria, VA: Association for Supervision and Curriculum Development.

Jenson, W., Rhode, G., & Reavis, H. K. (2009). *The Tough Kid tool box.* Eugene, OR: Pacific Northwest Publishing.

Kerr, J., & Nelson, C. (2002). *Strategies for addressing behavior problems in the classroom* (4th ed.). Englewood Cliffs, NJ: Merrill/Prentice Hall.

Kerr, J., Price, M., Kotch, J., Willis, S., Fisher, M., & Silva, S. (2012). Does contact by a family nurse practitioner decrease early school absence? *Journal of School Nursing, 28*, 38–46.

Kim, C. Y., Losen, D. J., and Hewitt, D. T. (2010). *The school-to-prison pipeline: Structuring legal reform.* New York, NY: New York University Press.

Klem, A. M., & Connell, J. P. (2004). Relationships matter: Linking teacher support to student engagement and achievement. *Journal of School Health, 74*(7), 262–273.

Kounin, J. S. (1977). *Discipline and group management in classrooms.* Huntington, NY: Krieger Publishing.

Losen, D. J. (2011). *Discipline policies, successful schools, and racial justice.* Boulder, CO: National Education Policy Center. Retrieved from http://nepc.colorado.edu/publication/discipline-policies

Losen, D. J., & Martinez, T. E. (2013). *Out of school & off track: The overuse of suspension in American middle and high schools.* Retrieved from http://civilrightsproject.ucla.edu/resources/projects/center-for-civil-rights-remedies/school-to-prison-folder/federal-reports/out-of-school-and-off-track-the-overuse-of-suspensions-in-american-middle-and-high-schools/OutofSchool-OffTrack_UCLA_4-8.pdf

Maag, J. (2001). *Powerful struggles: Managing resistance, building rapport.* Longmont, CO: Sopris West.

Marzano, R. J. (2003). *Classroom management that works: Research-based strategies for every teacher.* Alexandria, VA: Association for Supervision and Curriculum Development.

Maslow, A. H. (1962). Some basic propositions of a growth and self-actualization psychology. In A. W. Combs (Ed.), *Perceiving, behaving, becoming: A new focus for education* (pp. 34–49). Washington, D.C: Association for Supervision and Curriculum Development.

McNeely, C. A., Nonnemaker, J. A., & Blum, R. W. (2002). Promoting school connectedness: Evidence from the National Longitudinal Study of Adolescent Health. *Journal of School Health, 72*(4), 138–146.

National Association for Sport and Physical Education (2006). *Recess for elementary school children* (Position Statement). Retrieved from http://www.eric.ed.gov/PDFS/ED541609.pdf

National Center for Education Statistics (2012). *Digest of Education Statistics* (NCES 2014-015). Retrieved from http://nces.ed.gov/programs/digest/d12/ and http://nces.ed.gov/programs/digest/d12/tables/dt12_122.asp

O'Leary, K. D., & O'Leary, S. G. (1977). *Classroom management: The successful use of behavior modification* (2nd ed.). New York, NY: Pergamon Press.

O'Neill, R. E., Horner, R. H., Albin, R. W., Storey, K., & Sprague, J. R. (1996). *Functional assessment and program development for problem behavior: A practical handbook* (2nd ed.). Belmont, CA: Cengage.

Payne, C. (2008). *So much reform, so little change: The persistence of failure in urban schools.* Boston, MA: Harvard Education Press.

Purkey, W. W., & Novak, J. M. (2005). *Inviting school success: A self-concept approach to teaching, learning, and democratic practice in a connected world* (4th ed.). New York, NY: Wadsworth Publishing.

Ready, D. (2010). Socioeconomic disadvantage, school attendance, and early cognitive development: The differential effects of school exposure. *Sociology of Education, 83*(4), 271–289.

Rhode, G. R., Jenson, W. R., & Reavis, H. K. (2010). *The Tough Kid book: Practical classroom management strategies* (2nd ed.). Eugene, OR: Pacific Northwest Publishing.

Sheets, R. H., & Gay, G. (1996). Student perceptions of disciplinary conflicts in ethnically diverse classrooms. *NASSP Bulletin, 80*(580), 84–94.

Skiba, R. J., Horner, R. H., Chung, C.-G., Rausch, M. K., May, S. L., & Tobin, T. (2011). Race is not neutral: A national investigation of African American and Latino disproportionality in school discipline. *School Psychology Review, 40*(1), pp. 85–107.

Skiba, R. J., Michael, R. S., Nardo, A. C., & Peterson, R. L. (2002). The color of discipline: Sources of racial and gender disproportionality in school punishment. *Urban Review, 34*(4), 317–342.

Skiba, R., & Peterson, R. (2003). Teaching the social curriculum: School discipline as instruction. *Preventing School Failure, 47,* 66–73.

Sparks, S. D. (2010). Districts begin looking harder at absenteeism. *Education Week, 30*(6), 1, 12–13.

Spinks, S. (n.d.). Adolescent brains are works in progress. *Frontline.* Retrieved from http://www.pbs.org/wgbh/pages/frontline/shows/teenbrain/work/adolescent.html

Sprague, J. R., & Walker, H. M. (2005). *Safe and healthy schools: Practical prevention strategies.* New York, NY: Guilford Press.

Sprague, J. R., & Walker, H. M. (2010). Building safe and healthy schools to promote school success: Critical issues, current challenges, and promising approaches. In M. R. Shinn, H. M. Walker, & G. Stoner (Eds.), *Interventions for achievement and behavior problems in a three-tier model including RTI* (pp. 225–258). Bethesda, MD: National Association of School Psychologists.

Sprick, R. S. (1995). School-wide discipline and policies: An instructional classroom management approach. In E. Kame'enui & C. B. Darch (Eds.), *Instructional classroom management: A proactive approach to managing behavior* (pp. 234–267). White Plains, NY: Longman Press.

Sprick, R. S. (2009a). *CHAMPS: A proactive and positive approach to classroom management* (2nd ed.). Eugene, OR: Pacific Northwest Publishing.

Sprick, R. S. (2009b). *Stepping in: A substitute's guide to managing classroom behavior.* Eugene, OR: Pacific Northwest Publishing.

Sprick, R. S. (2009c). *Structuring success for substitutes.* Eugene, OR: Pacific Northwest Publishing.

Sprick, R. S. (2012). *Teacher's encyclopedia of behavior management: 100+ problems/500+ plans* (2nd ed.). Eugene, OR: Pacific Northwest Publishing.

Sprick, R. S. (2014). *Discipline in the secondary classroom: A positive approach to behavior management* (3rd ed.). San Francisco: Jossey-Bass.

Sprick, R. S., & Garrison, M. (2000). *ParaPro: Supporting the instructional process.* Eugene, OR: Pacific Northwest Publishing.

Sprick, R. S., & Garrison, M. (2008). *Interventions: Evidence-based behavior strategies for individual students* (2nd ed.). Eugene, OR: Pacific Northwest Publishing.

Sprick, R. S., Howard, L., Wise, B. J., Marcum, K., & Haykin, M. (1998). *Administrator's desk reference of behavior management.* Longmont, CO: Sopris West.

Sprick, R. S., Swartz, L., & Glang, A. (2005). *On the playground: A guide to playground management* [CD program]. Eugene, OR: Pacific Northwest Publishing and Oregon Center for Applied Sciences.

Sprick, R. S., Swartz, L., & Schroeder, S. (2006). *In the driver's seat: A roadmap to managing student behavior on the bus* [CD and DVD program]. Eugene, OR: Pacific Northwest Publishing and Oregon Center for Applied Sciences.

Sugai, G., Horner, R. H., Dunlap, G., Hieneman, M., Lewis, T., Nelson, C. M., & Wilcox, B. (2000). Applying positive behavior support and functional behavioral assessment in schools. *Journal of Positive Behavioral Interventions, 2,* 131–143.

U.S. Department of Education. (2000). *Safeguarding our children: An action guide.* Retrieved from http://www2.ed.gov/admins/lead/safety/actguide/action_guide.pdf

U.S. Department of Health and Human Services, Centers for Disease Control and Prevention (2009). *Fostering school connectedness: Improving student health and academic achievement.* Retrieved from http://www.cdc.gov/healthyyouth/protective/pdf/ connectedness_administrators.pdf

U.S. Department of Health and Human Services, Centers for Disease Control and Prevention. (2012). *Youth violence: Facts at a glance.* Retrieved from http://www.cdc.gov/ violenceprevention/pdf/yv_datasheet_2012-a.pdf

U.S. Department of Health and Human Services, Centers for Disease Control and Prevention. (2013a). *Asthma and schools.* Retrieved from http://www.cdc.gov/healthyyouth/ asthma/index.htm

U.S. Department of Health and Human Services, Centers for Disease Control and Prevention. (2013b). *State and program examples: Healthy youth.* Retrieved from http://www.cdc. gov/chronicdisease/states/examples/pdfs/healthy-youth.pdf

U.S. Department of Justice, Office of Justice Programs, Office of Juvenile Justice and Delinquency Prevention. (2006). *Statistical briefing book.* Retrieved from http://www. ojjdp.gov/ojstatbb/offenders/qa03301.asp

University of Utah, Utah Education Policy Center. (2012). *Research brief: Chronic absenteeism.* Retrieved from Utah Data Alliance website: http://www.utahdataalliance.org/ downloads/ChronicAbsenteeismResearchBrief.pdf

Wald, J., & Losen, D. J. (2003). Defining and redirecting a school-to-prison pipeline. *New Directions for Youth Development, 99,* 9–15. doi:10.1002/yd.51

Walker, H. (1995). *The acting-out child: Coping with classroom disruption.* Longmont, CO: Sopris West.

Walker, H. M., Colvin, G., & Ramsey, E. (1995). *Antisocial behavior in school: Strategies and best practices.* Pacific Grove, CA: Brooks/Cole.

Walker, H., Ramsey, E., & Gresham, F. M. (2003–2004a). Heading off disruptive behavior: How early intervention can reduce defiant behavior—and win back teaching time. *American Educator, Winter,* 6–21, 45–46.

Walker, H., Ramsey, E., & Gresham, F. M. (2003–2004b). How disruptive students escalate hostility and disorder—and how teachers can avoid it. *American Educator, Winter,* 22–27, 47–48.

Walker, H. M., Ramsey, E., & Gresham, F. M. (2004). *Antisocial behavior in school: Evidence-based practices* (2nd ed.). Belmont, CA: Cengage Learning.

Walker, H. M., Severson, H. H., & Feil, E. F. (2014). *Systematic screening for behavior disorders* (2nd ed.). Eugene, OR: Pacific Northwest Publishing.

Walker, H., & Walker, J. (1991). *Coping with noncompliance in the classroom: A positive approach for teachers.* Austin, TX: Pro-Ed.

Wentzel, K. R., & Brophy, J. E. (2013). *Motivating Students to Learn* (4th ed.). New York, NY: Taylor & Francis.

Wise, B. J., Marcum, K., Haykin, M., Sprick, R. S., & Sprick, M. (2011). *Meaningful work: Changing student behavior with school jobs.* Eugene, OR: Pacific Northwest Publishing.

Wright, A. (n.d.). Limbic system: Amgdala. In J. H. Byrne (Ed.). *Neuroscience online.* Retrieved from http://neuroscience.uth.tmc.edu/s4/chapter06.html

APPENDIX A
Foundations Implementation Rubric and Summary

The rubric is a relatively quick way for the Foundations Team to self-reflect on the implementation status of each of the modules. If you are just beginning *Foundations*, you might use this rubric toward the end of your first year of implementation. Thereafter, work through the rubric each year in the spring and consider using it in mid- to late fall to guide your work during the winter.

Each column—Preparing, Getting Started, Moving Along, and In Place—represents a different implementation status. The text in each row describes what that status looks like for each *Foundations* presentation. For each presentation, read the four descriptions from left to right. If the statements in the description are true, check the box. Each description assumes that the activities preceding it in the row have been attained. Stop working through the row when you reach a description that you cannot check off because you haven't implemented those tasks.

Notice that the descriptions for the In Place status include a section about evidence, which suggests where to find objective evidence that the described work is truly in place. If no documentation exists, think about whether the work has really been thoroughly completed. Throughout *Foundations*, we recommend archiving all your work so that policies and procedures are not forgotten or lost when staff changes occur.

When you've worked through every row, summarize your assessment on the Rubric Summary. If any items are rated as less than In Place, or if it has been more than 3 years since you have done so, work through the Implementation Checklist for that module. Of course, if you know that you need to begin work on a module or presentation, you can go directly to the corresponding content.

Print the summary and rubric (Form D-01) from the Module D CD.

For Module B, evaluate (separately) the common areas and schoolwide policies that you have implemented—that is, you've structured them for success and taught students the behavioral expectations. Use the rows labeled Other for your school's common areas and schoolwide policies that do not appear on the rubric by default.

Figure A-1 shows a summary form completed by an imaginary school in the spring of their second year of *Foundations* implementation. They have highlighted the checkboxes to create a horizontal bar graph, giving the evaluation an effective visual component. They've done a great job on most of Module A, the common areas they've prioritized so far (hallways and cafeteria), and Welcoming New Staff, Students, and Families (C7). They need to work a bit more on staff engagement and unity (A5) and most of Module C, which they began in Year 2. Modules D, E, and F are blank because they plan to work on them in future years.

Figure A-1   *Sample Foundations Rubric Summary*

Date _____

Foundations Implementation Rubric and Summary (p. 8 of 8)

	Preparing (1)	Getting Started (2)	Moving Along (3)	In Place (4)
Module A Presentations				
A1. Foundations: A Multi-Tiered System of Behavior Support	X	X	X	X
A2. Team Processes	X	X	X	X
A3. The Improvement Cycle	X	X	X	X
A4. Data-Driven Processes	X	X	X	X
A5. Developing Staff Engagement and Unity	X	X		
Module B Presentations				
Hallways	X	X	X	X
Restrooms				
Cafeteria	X	X	X	X
Playground, Courtyard, or Commons				
Arrival				
Dismissal				
Dress Code				
Other:				
Other:				
Other:				
Other:				
Module C Presentations				
C2. Guidelines for Success	X	X	X	
C3. Ratios of Positive Interactions	X	X		
C4. Improving Attendance	X	X	X	
C5 & C6. School Connectedness and Programs and Strategies for Meeting Needs	X	X		
C7. Welcoming New Staff, Students, and Families	X	X	X	X
Module D Presentations				
D1. Proactive Procedures, Corrective Procedures, and Individual Interventions				
D2. Developing Three Levels of Misbehavior				
D3. Staff Responsibilities for Responding to Misbehavior				
D4. Administrator Responsibilities for Responding to Misbehavior				
D5. Preventing the Misbehavior That Leads to Referrals and Suspensions				
Module E Presentations				
E1. Ensuring a Safe Environment for Students				
E2. Attributes of Safe and Unsafe Schools				
E3. Teaching Conflict Resolution				
E4. Analyzing Bullying Behaviors, Policies, and School Needs				
E5. Schoolwide Bullying Prevention and Intervention				
Module F Presentations				
F2. Supporting Classroom Behavior: The Three-Legged Stool				
F3. Articulating Staff Beliefs and Solidifying Universal Procedures				
F4. Early-Stage Interventions for General Education Classrooms				
F5. Matching the Intensity of Your Resources to the Intensity of Your Needs				
F6. Problem-Solving Processes and Intervention Design				
F7. Sustainability and District Support				

Additional information about the rubric appears in Module F, Presentation 7, Task 1.

Thanks to Carolyn Novelly and Kathleen Bowles of Duval County Public Schools in Florida. We modeled the Foundations Implementation Rubric on a wonderful document they developed called the School Climate/Conditions for Learning Checklist. Thanks also to Pete Davis of Long Beach, California, for sharing samples of rubrics and innovation configuration scales.

Foundations Implementation Rubric and Summary (p. 1 of 8)

Directions: In each row, check off each description that is true for your *Foundations* implementation. Then summarize your assessment on the Rubric Summary form. For Module B, evaluate each common area and schoolwide policy separately, and use the rows labeled Other for common areas and schoolwide policies that do not appear on the rubric by default. *Note:* Each block assumes that the activities in previous blocks in the row have been attained.

Presentation	Preparing (1)	Getting Started (2)	Moving Along (3)	In Place (4)
A1 Foundations: A Multi-Tiered System of Behavior Support	☐ Staff are aware of the *Foundations* approach and basic beliefs, including that *Foundations* is a process for guiding the entire staff in the construction and implementation of a comprehensive approach to behavior support.	☐ *Foundations* multi-tiered system of support (MTSS) processes are coordinated with academic MTSS (RTI) processes, and team organization has been determined (e.g., one MTSS Team with a behavior task force and an academic task force).	☐ Staff have been introduced to the STOIC acronym and understand that student behavior and motivation can be continuously improved by manipulating the STOIC variables: Structure, Teach, Observe, Interact positively, and Correct fluently.	☐ A preliminary plan has been developed for using the *Foundations* modules. For a school just beginning the process, the plan includes working through all the modules sequentially. For a school that has implemented aspects of positive behavior support, the team has self-assessed strengths, weaknesses, and needs using this rubric. **Evidence:** Foundations Implementation Rubric
A2 Team Processes	☐ Foundations Team members have been identified. They directly represent specific faculty and staff groups, and they have assigned roles and responsibilities.	☐ Foundations Team attends trainings, meets at school, and has established and maintains a Foundations Process Notebook and Foundations Archive.	☐ Foundations Team members present regularly to faculty and communicate with the entire staff. They draft proposals and engage staff in the decision-making process regarding school climate, behavior, and discipline.	☐ Foundations Team is known by all staff and is highly involved in all aspects of climate, safety, behavior, motivation, and student connectedness. **Evidence:** Staff members represented by Foundations Team members and presentations to staff are documented in the Foundations Process Notebook.
A3 The Improvement Cycle	☐ Foundations Team is aware of the Improvement Cycle and keeps staff informed of team activities.	☐ Foundations Team involves staff in setting priorities and in implementing improvements.	☐ Foundations Team involves staff in using multiple data sources to establish a hierarchical list of priorities and adopt new policies. Team members seek input from staff regarding their satisfaction with the efficacy of recently adopted policies and procedures.	☐ All staff actively participate in all aspects of the Improvement Cycle, such as setting priorities, developing revisions, adopting new policies and procedures, and implementation. Foundation Team presents to staff at least monthly. **Evidence:** Memos to staff and PowerPoint presentation files are documented in the Foundations Process Notebook.
A4 Data-Driven Processes	☐ Administrators and Foundations Team review discipline data and establish baselines.	☐ Common area observations and student, staff, and parent climate surveys are conducted yearly.	☐ Discipline, climate survey, and common area observation data are reviewed and analyzed regularly.	☐ Based on the data, school policies, procedures, and guidelines are reviewed and modified as needed (maintaining the Improvement Cycle).
A5 Developing Staff Engagement and Unity	☐ Foundations Team regularly communicates with staff through staff meetings, scheduled professional development, memos, and so on.	☐ Foundations Team members understand that they play a key role in staff unity. They periodically assess whether any factions of staff are disengaged and how they can develop greater staff engagement in the *Foundations* process.	☐ A building-based administrator attends most *Foundations* trainings and plays an active role in team meetings and in assisting the team in unifying staff.	☐ For districts with more than five or six schools, a district-based team meets at least once per quarter to keep the *Foundations* continuous improvement processes active in all schools. **Evidence:** Meeting minutes and staff presentations are documented in the Foundations Process Notebook.

If any items are rated as less than In Place or if it has been more than 3 years since you have done so, work through the Module A Implementation Checklist.

School Name _____ Date _____

Foundations Implementation Rubric and Summary (p. 2 of 8)

Common Area	Preparing (1)	Getting Started (2)	Moving Along (3)	In Place (4)
Hallways	☐ Common area observations are conducted and data from multiple sources are collected and analyzed.	☐ Current structures and procedures have been evaluated and protected, modified, or eliminated.	☐ Lesson plans have been developed, taught, practiced, and re-taught, when necessary.	☐ Common area supervisory procedures are communicated to staff and monitored for implementation. **Evidence:** Policies, procedures, and lessons are documented in the Foundations Archive and, as appropriate, in the Staff Handbook.
Restrooms	☐ Common area observations are conducted and data from multiple sources are collected and analyzed.	☐ Current structures and procedures have been evaluated and protected, modified, or eliminated.	☐ Lesson plans have been developed, taught, practiced, and re-taught, when necessary.	☐ Common area supervisory procedures are communicated to staff and monitored for implementation. **Evidence:** Policies, procedures, and lessons are documented in the Foundations Archive and, as appropriate, in the Staff Handbook.
Cafeteria	☐ Common area observations are conducted and data from multiple sources are collected and analyzed.	☐ Current structures and procedures have been evaluated and protected, modified, or eliminated.	☐ Lesson plans have been developed, taught, practiced, and re-taught, when necessary.	☐ Common area supervisory procedures are communicated to staff and monitored for implementation. **Evidence:** Policies, procedures, and lessons are documented in the Foundations Archive and, as appropriate, in the Staff Handbook.
Playground, Courtyard, or Commons	☐ Common area observations are conducted and data from multiple sources are collected and analyzed.	☐ Current structures and procedures have been evaluated and protected, modified, or eliminated.	☐ Lesson plans have been developed, taught, practiced, and re-taught, when necessary.	☐ Common area supervisory procedures are communicated to staff and monitored for implementation. **Evidence:** Policies, procedures, and lessons are documented in the Foundations Archive and, as appropriate, in the Staff Handbook.
Arrival	☐ Common area observations are conducted and data from multiple sources are collected and analyzed.	☐ Current structures and procedures have been evaluated and protected, modified, or eliminated.	☐ Lesson plans have been developed, taught, practiced, and re-taught, when necessary.	☐ Common area supervisory procedures are communicated to staff and monitored for implementation. **Evidence:** Policies, procedures, and lessons are documented in the Foundations Archive and, as appropriate, in the Staff Handbook.
Dismissal	☐ Common area observations are conducted and data from multiple sources are collected and analyzed.	☐ Current structures and procedures have been evaluated and protected, modified, or eliminated.	☐ Lesson plans have been developed, taught, practiced, and re-taught, when necessary.	☐ Common area supervisory procedures are communicated to staff and monitored for implementation. **Evidence:** Policies, procedures, and lessons are documented in the Foundations Archive and, as appropriate, in the Staff Handbook.
Other: _____	☐ Common area observations are conducted and data from multiple sources are collected and analyzed.	☐ Current structures and procedures have been evaluated and protected, modified, or eliminated.	☐ Lesson plans have been developed, taught, practiced, and re-taught, when necessary.	☐ Common area supervisory procedures are communicated to staff and monitored for implementation. **Evidence:** Policies, procedures, and lessons are documented in the Foundations Archive and, as appropriate, in the Staff Handbook.
Other: _____	☐ Common area observations are conducted and data from multiple sources are collected and analyzed.	☐ Current structures and procedures have been evaluated and protected, modified, or eliminated.	☐ Lesson plans have been developed, taught, practiced, and re-taught, when necessary.	☐ Common area supervisory procedures are communicated to staff and monitored for implementation. **Evidence:** Policies, procedures, and lessons are documented in the Foundations Archive and, as appropriate, in the Staff Handbook.

If any items are rated as less than In Place or if it has been more than 3 years since you have done so, work through the Module B Implementation Checklist.

Foundations Implementation Rubric and Summary (p. 3 of 8)

Schoolwide Policy	Preparing (1)	Getting Started (2)	Moving Along (3)	In Place (4)
Dress Code	☐ Foundations Team has discussed the clarity and consistency of the current schoolwide policy.	☐ Data from multiple sources about the efficacy of the policy have been gathered and analyzed.	☐ The policy has been analyzed for clarity, efficacy, and consistency of enforcement.	☐ Schoolwide policies, lessons, and procedures have been written and are reviewed as needed with staff, students, and parents. **Evidence:** Policies, lessons, and procedures are documented in the Foundations Archive and, as appropriate, in the Staff Handbook.
Other: _____	☐ Foundations Team has discussed the clarity and consistency of the current schoolwide policy.	☐ Data from multiple sources about the efficacy of the policy have been gathered and analyzed.	☐ The policy has been analyzed for clarity, efficacy, and consistency of enforcement.	☐ Schoolwide policies, lessons, and procedures have been written and are reviewed as needed with staff, students, and parents. **Evidence:** Policies, lessons, and procedures are documented in the Foundations Archive and, as appropriate, in the Staff Handbook.
Other: _____	☐ Foundations Team has discussed the clarity and consistency of the current schoolwide policy.	☐ Data from multiple sources about the efficacy of the policy have been gathered and analyzed.	☐ The policy has been analyzed for clarity, efficacy, and consistency of enforcement.	☐ Schoolwide policies, lessons, and procedures have been written and are reviewed as needed with staff, students, and parents. **Evidence:** Policies, lessons, and procedures are documented in the Foundations Archive and, as appropriate, in the Staff Handbook.
Other: _____	☐ Foundations Team has discussed the clarity and consistency of the current schoolwide policy.	☐ Data from multiple sources about the efficacy of the policy have been gathered and analyzed.	☐ The policy has been analyzed for clarity, efficacy, and consistency of enforcement.	☐ Schoolwide policies, lessons, and procedures have been written and are reviewed as needed with staff, students, and parents. **Evidence:** Policies, lessons, and procedures are documented in the Foundations Archive and, as appropriate, in the Staff Handbook.
Other: _____	☐ Foundations Team has discussed the clarity and consistency of the current schoolwide policy.	☐ Data from multiple sources about the efficacy of the policy have been gathered and analyzed.	☐ The policy has been analyzed for clarity, efficacy, and consistency of enforcement.	☐ Schoolwide policies, lessons, and procedures have been written and are reviewed as needed with staff, students, and parents. **Evidence:** Policies, lessons, and procedures are documented in the Foundations Archive and, as appropriate, in the Staff Handbook.
Other: _____	☐ Foundations Team has discussed the clarity and consistency of the current schoolwide policy.	☐ Data from multiple sources about the efficacy of the policy have been gathered and analyzed.	☐ The policy has been analyzed for clarity, efficacy, and consistency of enforcement.	☐ Schoolwide policies, lessons, and procedures have been written and are reviewed as needed with staff, students, and parents. **Evidence:** Policies, lessons, and procedures are documented in the Foundations Archive and, as appropriate, in the Staff Handbook.
Other: _____	☐ Foundations Team has discussed the clarity and consistency of the current schoolwide policy.	☐ Data from multiple sources about the efficacy of the policy have been gathered and analyzed.	☐ The policy has been analyzed for clarity, efficacy, and consistency of enforcement.	☐ Schoolwide policies, lessons, and procedures have been written and are reviewed as needed with staff, students, and parents. **Evidence:** Policies, lessons, and procedures are documented in the Foundations Archive and, as appropriate, in the Staff Handbook.
Other: _____	☐ Foundations Team has discussed the clarity and consistency of the current schoolwide policy.	☐ Data from multiple sources about the efficacy of the policy have been gathered and analyzed.	☐ The policy has been analyzed for clarity, efficacy, and consistency of enforcement.	☐ Schoolwide policies, lessons, and procedures have been written and are reviewed as needed with staff, students, and parents. **Evidence:** Policies, lessons, and procedures are documented in the Foundations Archive and, as appropriate, in the Staff Handbook.

If any items are rated as less than In Place or if it has been more than 3 years since you have done so, work through the Module B Implementation Checklist.

Foundations Implementation Rubric and Summary (p. 4 of 8)

Module C

Presentation	Preparing (1)	Getting Started (2)	Moving Along (3)	In Place (4)
C2 Guidelines for Success (GFS)	☐ All staff understand what Guidelines for Success (GFS) are and why they are important.	☐ Foundations Team has drafted proposals and engaged all stakeholders in the decision-making process of developing GFS.	☐ GFS have been finalized and posted and are reviewed regularly.	☐ GFS are embedded into the culture and are part of the common language of the school. **Evidence:** Procedures for teaching and motivating students about GFS are documented in the Foundations Archive, Staff Handbook, and Student and Parent Handbook.
C3 Ratios of Positive Interactions	☐ Staff have been taught the concept of 3:1 ratios of positive interactions and the importance of creating a positive climate and improving student behavior.	☐ Staff have been taught how to monitor ratios of positive interactions and are encouraged to evaluate their interactions with students.	☐ Administrator plans for teachers to observe and calculate other teachers' classroom ratios of interactions; the teachers involved meet to discuss outcomes.	☐ Observation data show that most staff at most times strive to interact with students at least three times more often than when students are behaving responsibly than when they are misbehaving. **Evidence:** Procedures for teaching and motivating staff are documented in the Foundations Archive and Staff Handbook.
C4 Improving Attendance	☐ Average daily attendance is monitored to view long-term trends and patterns. Faculty and staff have been made aware of the importance of encouraging regular attendance by all students.	☐ All students with chronic absenteeism (absent 10% or more of school days) are identified at least quarterly; Foundations Team determines whether universal intervention is warranted.	☐ Each student with chronic absenteeism is identified and assigned one school-based support person who monitors whether additional support is needed. Foundations Team has analyzed attendance data and analyzed policies for clarity and efficacy.	☐ Every student with chronic absenteeism that has been resistant to universal and Tier 2 supports becomes the focus of a multidisciplinary team effort. **Evidence:** Data on average daily attendance and chronic absenteeism as well as efforts to improve attendance (e.g., parent newsletters) are documented in the Foundations Process Notebook.
C5 & C6 School Connectedness and Programs and Strategies for Meeting Needs	☐ Foundations Team has analyzed the degree to which current programs and practices meet the needs of all students (outstanding, average, and at risk).	☐ Foundations Team has developed proposals for programs and practices that might help meet unmet needs of students (e.g., the average student's need for purpose and belonging).	☐ Faculty and staff have implemented programs and practices designed to meet basic needs of all students (e.g. Mentorship, Student of the Week, Meaningful Work).	☐ Programs to meet students' basic needs are in place and analyzed at least once per year to determine their effectiveness and assess whether the needs of any student groups are not being met. **Evidence:** Analysis is documented in the Foundations Process Notebook, and programs and practices for meeting needs are documented in the Foundations Archive.
C7 Welcoming New Staff, Students, and Families	☐ Foundations Team has reviewed the welcoming aspects of the school, such as signage, website, and phone and front office procedures, and has suggested improvements.	☐ Foundations Team has analyzed and suggested improvements for welcoming and orienting new students and families at the beginning of the school year. (New students include those in a new grade-level cohort [e.g., ninth graders in high school] and students who are not part of that cohort.)	☐ Foundations Team has analyzed procedures and suggested improvements for welcoming new students and families who arrive during the school year. Improvements might include written information about rules, procedures, GFS, and so on.	☐ Foundations Team has analyzed procedures and suggested improvements for welcoming new staff members, both professional and nonprofessional, at the beginning of the year. New staff members are oriented to essential procedures and the culture and climate defined by the school's behavior support procedures. **Evidence:** All policies and procedures for welcoming and orienting staff, students, and families are documented in the Foundations Archive.

If any items are rated as less than In Place or if it has been more than 3 years since you have done so, work through the Module C Implementation Checklist.

Foundations Implementation Rubric and Summary (p. 5 of 8)

Presentation	Preparing (1)	Getting Started (2)	Moving Along (3)	In Place (4)
D1 Proactive Procedures, Corrective Procedures, and Individual Interventions	☐ Foundations Team is aware of data and staff opinions about consistency in correcting misbehavior, including clarity of staff roles in discipline compared with administrative roles.	☐ Staff understand the potential limitations of office referral as a corrective procedure and avoid using it whenever possible.	☐ Staff have been made aware of the limited benefits and potential drawbacks (including disparate impact) of out-of-school suspension (OSS) as a corrective consequence.	☐ Staff avoid pressuring administrators to use OSS. Staff perceptions of consistency and administrative support for disciplinary actions are documented in staff survey results. **Evidence:** Discussions on these topics are documented in the Foundations Process Notebook.
D2 Developing Three Levels of Misbehavior	☐ Staff are aware of the concept of three levels of misbehavior: Level 1 (mild), Level 2 (moderate), and Level 3 (severe) misbehavior.	☐ Annually, staff discuss and agree on what behavior *must* be sent to the administrator, what can be sent to the administrator, and what should be handled in the setting in which the infraction occurred (3-level system for responding to misbehavior).	☐ A referral form that reflects the agreed-upon definition of Level 3 misbehavior has been developed. A notification form that reflects the agreed-upon definition of Level 2 misbehavior has been developed. (Alternatively, both Level 2 and Level 3 may be on one form.) Accurate data are kept and analyzed quarterly for all Level 2 and Level 3 misbehaviors and consequences.	☐ Data are collected on the implementation of the 3-level system for responding to misbehavior and on staff and administrator satisfaction with the system. **Evidence:** All aspects of the policy are documented in the Foundations Archive and Staff Handbook.
D3 Staff Responsibilities for Responding to Misbehavior	☐ Staff have generated and administrators have approved a menu of corrective consequences for use in common areas.	☐ Staff have generated and administrators have approved a menu of corrective consequences for use in classrooms.	☐ Staff have been trained in how to use Level 2 notifications as a process for moving toward collaborative planning for severe or chronic behavior problems.	☐ Staff have been trained in writing objective and appropriate office referrals for Level 3 misbehavior. **Evidence:** Menus and procedures are documented in the Foundations Archive and Staff Handbook.
D4 Administrator Responsibilities for Responding to Misbehavior	☐ Procedures have been developed for responding to Level 2 notifications to ensure that the reporting staff member receives timely feedback and that administrators and support staff take appropriate actions.	☐ Office procedures for dealing with students sent to the office have been analyzed and streamlined. Students do not get too much attention from office staff or staff members who visit the office.	☐ Administrators are familiar with the game plan for dealing with Level 3 incidents. The game plan includes a menu of alternative consequences to out-of-school suspension.	☐ If the school has an ISS program, that program has been analyzed and revised as needed to ensure that it is highly structured and includes an instructional component. **Evidence:** All procedures for Level 2 and Level 3 infractions are documented in the Foundations Archive.
D5 Preventing the Misbehavior That Leads to Referrals and Suspensions	☐ Foundations Team has examined data on Level 2 and Level 3 infractions to determine what misbehaviors get students into trouble.	☐ Foundations Team has reviewed the lessons in Module D (how to interact appropriately with adults) and discussed whether they might reduce misbehaviors that get students into trouble.	☐ To avoid duplication, the Foundations Team has compared the Module D lessons with other social skills or social-emotional curricula currently in use. Staff have agreed on a plan for when and how to teach expected behaviors to all students.	☐ Foundations Team has discussed whether re-teaching the Module D lessons (or similar) in ISS or detention settings would be beneficial; if so, the team has planned when and how to re-teach. **Evidence:** Lesson plans and teaching logistics and schedule are documented in the Foundations Archive.

If any items are rated as less than In Place or if it has been more than 3 years since you have done so, work through the Module D Implementation Checklist.

Foundations Implementation Rubric and Summary (p. 6 of 8)

Presentation	Preparing (1)	Getting Started (2)	Moving Along (3)	In Place (4)
E1 Ensuring a Safe Environment for Students	Team members are aware of their responsibilities for overseeing school safety efforts. The team coordinates with other teams or task forces that may be doing similar work and avoids duplicating other efforts.	Foundations Team has viewed or read Module E and has compared that content with the school's current efforts toward safety, managing conflict, and bullying prevention. The team has developed a proposal for closing any gaps in the current efforts.	Foundations Team has made staff aware of the importance of a comprehensive view of safety that includes preparing for outside attackers as well as the more common occurrences of playground injuries, student fights, bullying, and so on.	Foundations Team has assessed problems with safety, conflict, and bullying within the last 3 years. If problems exist, a plan for using or adapting information from this module and integrating them with current curriculum or procedures has been completed. **Evidence:** Data analyses are documented in the Foundations Process Notebook, and final policies and procedures are documented in the Foundations Archive.
E2 Attributes of Safe and Unsafe Schools	Team members and other staff directly involved with safety concerns have viewed or read Presentation 2 and have completed (individually) the form Understanding the Attributes of Safe and Unsafe Schools.	Foundations Team has compiled individual responses to Understanding Attributes of Safe and Unsafe Schools and correlated those data with safety assessments completed in the last 3 years. Information about strengths and concerns has been shared with staff, and priorities have been set.	Foundations Team and other staff involved with safety concerns have completed the form Assessing Emergency Preparedness, evaluated current plans for natural disasters and man-made emergencies, revised any weak procedures, including training on policies regarding seclusion and restraint.	Foundations Team has completed the form Lessons to Increase Safety and Belonging, reviewed the Module E sample lessons, and evaluated whether current problems and policies address all features of the sample lessons. If there are gaps, a plan to teach some or all of the *Foundations* lessons is established. **Evidence:** Lesson plans and procedures are documented in the Foundations Archive.
E3 Teaching Conflict Resolution	Foundations Team has assessed whether the school has a conflict resolution strategy that students and staff use when necessary. If so, document the effective procedures in the Foundations Archive (and skip the rest of this row).	Foundations Team has reviewed the concepts and lessons in the Stop-Think-Plan (STP) approach and has prepared an implementation plan for staff.	With staff input, lessons have been revised, an implementation plan has been established, and a process is in place for training all staff in how to encourage students to use the conflict-resolution strategy.	Foundations Team has established a process for evaluating the effectiveness of STP by analyzing multiple data sources. The policy and lessons are revised and staff are retrained when necessary, and successes are celebrated. **Evidence:** Data analyses are documented in the Foundations Process Notebook, and lessons and teaching procedures are documented in the Foundations Archive.
E4 Analyzing Bullying Behavior, Policies, and School Needs	Foundations Team is aware of the content of this presentation and can compare it with current policies and procedures related to bullying.	Foundations Team has completed the form School-Based Analysis of Bullying Data and has identified whether new or revised procedures need to be implemented to enhance the current use of data related to bullying.	Foundations Team has completed the form School-Based Analysis of Bullying Policies and has identified whether new or revised policies need to be implemented to enhance current policies related to bullying.	Quarterly, the Foundations Team reviews data related to bullying. Annually, the team uses those data to answer each of the questions in the form STOIC Analysis for Universal Prevention of Bullying (or an equivalent process), and improvement priorities are established. **Evidence:** Data analyses are documented in the Foundations Process Notebook.
E5 Schoolwide Bullying Prevention and Intervention	Foundations Team has completed the form Staff Training in Preventing and Responding to Bullying and has developed and implemented a plan to fill in any identified gaps in current practices.	Foundations Team has completed the form Student Training in Preventing and Responding to Bullying. As part of a previously adopted bullying curriculum or through the *Foundations* lessons, students are taught about bullying prevention.	Foundations Team has completed the form Family Training in Preventing and Responding to Bullying and has developed an implementation plan to fill in any identified gaps in current practices.	Foundations Team has completed the form Active Engagement for the Prevention of Bullying and has developed an implementation plan to fill in any gaps in current practices. Bullying issues are a regular part of the team's work and are integrated into staff development efforts. **Evidence:** Ongoing discussions are documented in the Foundations Process Notebook. Established programs to enhance student engagement are documented in the Foundations Archive.

If any items are rated as less than In Place or if it has been more than 3 years since you have done so, work through the Module E Implementation Checklist.

Foundations Implementation Rubric and Summary (p. 7 of 8)

Presentation	Preparing (1)	Getting Started (2)	Moving Along (3)	In Place (4)
F2 Supporting Classroom Behavior: The Three-Legged Stool	☐ A research-based model for classroom management has been adopted at the building or district level. All teachers have access to training, and teachers new to the building or district receive the same training.	☐ School and district personnel are identified as resources for teachers who would like observations, feedback, and coaching. An effort is made to actively market the benefits of coaching support.	☐ The administrator has communicated clear outcomes and goals of effective classroom management: • 90% engagement • 95% respectful interactions • 95% of behavior matches posted expectations	☐ The model creates a common language among teachers, support staff, coaches, and administrators for problem solving and intervention. Data are collected and analyzed to evaluate classroom management efforts. **Evidence:** Information on the model, administrative walk-through visits, and coaching supports is included in the Foundations Archive and Staff Handbook.
F3 Articulating Staff Beliefs and Solidifying Universal Procedures	☐ Foundations Team has reviewed sample staff beliefs about behavior management.	☐ In faculty and staff meetings, faculty and staff have examined and discussed sample staff beliefs about behavior management.	☐ All staff have developed and adopted a set of written staff beliefs regarding discipline and behavior, and ensured that it aligned with the school's mission statement.	☐ To solidify the culture of the school and to guide the ongoing development of school policies and procedures, staff beliefs are reviewed, discussed, and revised as needed at least annually. **Evidence:** Staff beliefs and the review process are documented in the Foundations Archive and Staff Handbook.
F4 Early-Stage Interventions for General Education Classrooms	☐ Foundations Team and support staff (counselor, school psychologist, and so on) understand the concept of early-stage intervention.	☐ Foundations Team, support staff, and principal (or district administrators) agree on the interventions that should be included in the early-stage protocol.	☐ All teachers and support staff have been trained on the interventions in the school or district early-stage protocol, including how and why to keep records of each intervention.	☐ Data Collection and Debriefing (or an equivalent) is adopted as a required intervention for most chronic behavioral problems. Data must be charted before assistance is requested from support staff or problem-solving teams. **Evidence:** Expectations about when and how to get assistance are included in the Foundations Archive and Staff Handbook.
F5 Matching the Intensity of Your Resources to the Intensity of Your Needs	☐ Foundations Team and support staff (counselor, psychologist, and so on) have identified a set of red-flag criteria and (if possible) have conducted universal screening to identify students who may need individual behavior support.	☐ Foundations Team, support staff, and principal (or district administrators) agree on who can serve as advocates for students who need additional support.	☐ The advocates meet regularly to discuss progress and case studies to ensure that each student's needs are being met. Patterns of need are communicated to the Foundations Team so prevention efforts can be implemented.	☐ All support staff and problem-solving teams have written brief job descriptions that outline the services they can provide. The documents are shared with staff to inform them about available resources. **Evidence:** Suggestions for accessing these services are in the Foundations Archive and Staff Handbook.
F6 Problem-Solving Processes and Intervention Design	☐ Foundations Team understands that it will not conduct staffings (team-based problem solving) on individual students, but the team should examine current processes for supporting students and staff.	☐ Foundations Team and support staff (counselor, school psychologist, and so on) have discussed the range of problem-solving support (individuals and teams) currently available to students and staff.	☐ Foundations Team and support staff have discussed the problem-solving processes suggested in *Foundations* (e.g., the 25-Minute Planning Process), and have determined whether the processes would strengthen current practices.	☐ A flowchart or description of how the school meets the needs of students and staff has been created. It clarifies how the intensity of student needs matches the intensity of both problem-solving processes and intervention design and implementation. **Evidence:** This information is documented in the Foundations Archive and summarized in the Staff Handbook.
F7 Sustainability and District Support	☐ Foundations Team archives data, in-process work, and all completed policies and procedures, and builds on this work each year.	☐ Foundations Team orients new staff and re-energizes returning staff about all policies and procedures, and emphasizes unity and consistency.	☐ Foundations Team uses the rubric annually and the Implementation Checklists as individual modules near completion and every 3 years thereafter. The team uses this information to guide staff in setting improvement priorities.	☐ In larger districts (more than four schools), a district-based team works on sustainability. The team reminds schools about important milestones (e.g., surveys, year-end tasks, etc.) and ongoing staff development opportunities on behavior support. **Evidence:** This information can be found in district communications (e.g., emails) to schools and agenda items for principals' meetings.

If any items are rated as less than In Place or if it has been more than 3 years since you have done so, work through the Module F Implementation Checklist.

Foundations Implementation Rubric and Summary (p. 8 of 8)

	Preparing (1)	Getting Started (2)	Moving Along (3)	In Place (4)
Module A Presentations				
A1. Foundations: A Multi-Tiered System of Behavior Support				
A2. Team Processes				
A3. The Improvement Cycle				
A4. Data-Driven Processes				
A5. Developing Staff Engagement and Unity				
Module B Presentations				
Hallways				
Restrooms				
Cafeteria				
Playground, Courtyard, or Commons				
Arrival				
Dismissal				
Dress Code				
Other:				
Other:				
Other:				
Other:				
Module C Presentations				
C2. Guidelines for Success				
C3. Ratios of Positive Interactions				
C4. Improving Attendance				
C5 & C6. School Connectedness and Programs and Strategies for Meeting Needs				
C7. Welcoming New Staff, Students, and Families				
Module D Presentations				
D1. Proactive Procedures, Corrective Procedures, and Individual Interventions				
D2. Developing Three Levels of Misbehavior				
D3. Staff Responsibilities for Responding to Misbehavior				
D4. Administrator Responsibilities for Responding to Misbehavior				
D5. Preventing the Misbehavior That Leads to Referrals and Suspensions				
Module E Presentations				
E1. Ensuring a Safe Environment for Students				
E2. Attributes of Safe and Unsafe Schools				
E3. Teaching Conflict Resolution				
E4. Analyzing Bullying Behaviors, Policies, and School Needs				
E5. Schoolwide Bullying Prevention and Intervention				
Module F Presentations				
F2. Supporting Classroom Behavior: The Three-Legged Stool				
F3. Articulating Staff Beliefs and Solidifying Universal Procedures				
F4. Early-Stage Interventions for General Education Classrooms				
F5. Matching the Intensity of Your Resources to the Intensity of Your Needs				
F6. Problem-Solving Processes and Intervention Design				
F7. Sustainability and District Support				

APPENDIX B
Module D Implementation Checklist

The Implementation Checklist is a detailed checklist of the processes and objectives in each *Foundations* module. The Module D checklist (Form D-02) appears in this appendix and can be printed from the Module D CD.

As you near completion on the module, use the Implementation Checklist to ensure that you have fully implemented all recommendations. If you've decided not to follow some recommendations—you've adapted the procedures for your school—indicate the reason on the checklist. If data show problems later, this record of what you implemented and what you chose not to implement could be helpful in deciding what to do to address the problem.

In addition to using the checklists as needed, plan to work through all *Foundations* checklists every 3 years or so. See the sample schedule below. Additional information about Implementation Checklists appears in Module F, Presentation 7, Task 1.

Sample Long-Term Schedule: Improvement Priorities, Data Review & Monitoring

Year 1	Work on:
	• Modules A and B (continuous improvement process, common areas and schoolwide policies)
	• Cafeteria
	• Guidelines for Success
	In late spring, work through the Foundations Implementation Rubric for Modules A, B (cafeteria), and C2 (Guidelines for Success).
	Use the Modules A and B Implementation Checklists to assess status as you near completion of those modules.
Year 2	Work on:
	• Module C (inviting climate)
	• Hallways
	In the fall, evaluate cafeteria data.
	In late spring, work through the Foundations Implementation Rubric for Modules A, B (cafeteria and hallways), and C.
	Use the Module C Implementation Checklist to assess status as you near completion of Module C.

Year 3	Work on:
	• Module D (responding to misbehavior)
	• Playground
	In the fall, evaluate hallway data.
	In late spring, work through the Foundations Implementation Rubric for Modules A, B (cafeteria, hallways, and playground), C, and D.
	Use the Module D Implementation Checklist to assess status as you near completion of Module D.
Year 4	Work on:
	• Module E (safety, conflict, bullying prevention)
	• Arrival and dismissal
	In the fall, evaluate playground data.
	In late spring, work through the Foundations Implementation Rubric for Modules A, B (cafeteria, hallways, arrival and dismissal), C, D, and E.
	Use the Module E Implementation Checklist to assess status as you near completion of Module E.
	Monitor Year 1 priorities:
	• Module A Implementation Checklist
	• Module B Implementation Checklist for cafeteria
	• Module C Implementation Checklist for Guidelines for Success (C2 only)
Year 5	Work on:
	• Module F (classroom management and sustaining *Foundations*)
	• Assemblies
	• Guest teachers
	In the fall, evaluate arrival and dismissal data.
	In late spring, work through the Foundations Implementation Rubric for Modules A, B (playground, arrival and dismissal, assemblies, guest teachers), C, D, E, and F.
	Use the Module F Implementation Checklist to assess status as you near completion of Module F.
	Monitor Year 2 priorities:
	• Module B Implementation Checklist for hallways
	• Module C Implementation Checklist

Year 6	In the fall, evaluate assemblies and guest teacher data.
	Work through the Foundations Implementation Rubric for all modules.
	Monitor Year 3 priorities:
	• Module B Implementation Checklist for playground
	• Module D Implementation Checklist
Year 7	In the fall, work through the Foundations Implementation Rubric for all modules and all common areas and schoolwide policies.
	Monitor Year 4 priorities:
	• Module A Implementation Checklist
	• Module B Implementation Checklist for arrival, dismissal, and cafeteria
	• Module C Implementation Checklist for Guidelines for Success (C2 only)
	• Module E Implementation Checklist
Year 8	In the fall, work through the Foundations Implementation Rubric for all modules and all common areas and schoolwide policies.
	Monitor Year 5 priorities:
	• Module B Implementation Checklist for assemblies, guest teachers, and hallways
	• Module B Implementation Checklist for hallways
	• Module C Implementation Checklist
	• Module F Implementation Checklist
Year 9	In the fall, work through the Foundations Implementation Rubric for all modules and all common areas and schoolwide policies.
	Monitor Year 6 priorities:
	• Module B Implementation Checklist for playground
	• Module D Implementation Checklist

Implementation Actions	Completed Y/N	Evidence of Implementation	Evidence Y/N
Presentation 1: The Relationship Between Proactive Procedures, Corrective Procedures, and Individual Student Behavior Improvement Plans	✓		✓
1. Data are collected (e.g., from staff surveys) and staff have discussed concepts relating to consistency in correcting student misbehavior.	☐	Foundations Process: Presentations/ Communications With Staff	☐
2. Staff have discussed and identified their perceptions of their roles in correcting misbehavior in relation to the principal's (or assistant principal's) role.	☐	Foundations Process: Presentations/ Communications With Staff	☐
3. Staff understand the potential limitations of office referrals. At the elementary level, staff understand the potential inconsistencies of a progressive discipline system (in which students must be removed from class after the third or fourth infraction) and modify the system so it is fair and consistent.	☐	Foundations Process: Presentations/ Communications With Staff	☐
4. Staff are aware of the limited benefits of and potential drawbacks to out-of-school suspension (OSS) as a corrective consequence.	☐	Foundations Process: Presentations/ Communications With Staff	☐
5. Staff are aware of and can have honest discussions about national data on the disparate impact of OSS on minority students and students with disabilities.	☐	Foundations Process: Presentations/ Communications With Staff	☐
6. Staff avoid pressuring administrators to use OSS.	☐	Interview with administrator	☐
Presentation 2: Developing Three Levels of Misbehavior			
1. The Foundations Team has communicated to staff the *Foundations* concept of three levels of misbehavior: Level 1 (mild), Level 2 (moderate), and Level 3 (severe). Staff understand that the levels are defined more by the staff member's response to the misbehavior than by the misbehavior itself.	☐	Foundations Process: Presentations/ Communications With Staff	☐
2. The Foundations Team has solicited information from the administrator about the types of misbehaviors that currently result in office referrals.	☐	Foundations Process: 3-Level System for Responding to Misbehavior	☐
3. Administrators have defined the specific behaviors that *must* be considered Level 3 (e.g., weapons).	☐	Foundations Archive: 3-Level System for Responding to Misbehavior	☐

(continued)

Implementation Actions	Completed Y/N	Evidence of Implementation	Evidence Y/N
Presentation 2 (*continued*)	✓		✓
4. Staff have reached consensus on the types of behaviors that *must* be referred to the office as Level 3 and those that *may* be referred.	☐	Foundations Archive and Staff Handbook: 3-Level System for Responding to Misbehavior	☐
5. Staff understand that Level 2 notifications provide a way to get support for the staff member and to keep administrators and support staff informed about students with severe or chronic behaviors who may need additional support.	☐	Foundations Process: Presentations/ Communications With Staff	☐
6. A referral form or forms and a data system have been developed to facilitate efficient and clear communication and data collection.	☐	Foundations Process: Presentations/ Communications With Staff	☐
Presentation 3: Staff Responsibilities for Responding to Misbehavior			
1. Staff have reached consensus on menus of corrective actions for Level 1 mild misbehaviors for both classrooms and common areas.	☐	Foundations Archive and Staff Handbook: 3-Level System for Responding to Misbehavior	☐
2. Staff have reached consensus on staff procedures for Level 2 moderate misbehaviors for both classrooms and common areas.	☐	Foundations Archive and Staff Handbook: 3-Level System for Responding to Misbehavior	☐
3. Administrators have developed procedures for responding to Level 2 moderate notifications that support the staff member who wrote the notification.	☐	Foundations Archive: 3-Level System for Responding to Misbehavior	☐
4. Staff have reached consensus on a menu of corrective actions for Level 2 moderate misbehavior that includes all Level 1 corrections and all schoolwide consequences that do not require administrator involvement.	☐	Foundations Archive and Staff Handbook: 3-Level System for Responding to Misbehavior	☐
5. Staff have reached consensus on Level 2 notification procedures, such as whether to contact parents and whether to have students sign the form.	☐	Foundations Archive and Staff Handbook: 3-Level System for Responding to Misbehavior	☐
6. Staff have been given information about writing effective referrals, with an emphasis on correct grammar and spelling and on use of objective descriptions rather than labels or emotional language.	☐	Foundations Process: Presentations/ Communications With Staff	☐

Implementation Actions	Completed Y/N	Evidence of Implementation	Evidence Y/N
Presentation 4: Administrator Responsibilities for Responding to Misbehavior	✓		✓
1. Decisions have been made about who will process Level 2 notifications.	☐	Foundations Archive: 3-Level System for Responding to Misbehavior	☐
2. Staff, administrator, and support-staff procedures have been coordinated to ensure that students who receive notifications get the support they need to be successful.	☐	Foundations Archive: 3-Level System for Responding to Misbehavior	☐
3. Data collection procedures for Level 2 notifications have been developed so trends and patterns of notifications can drive school improvement.	☐	Foundations Archive: 3-Level System for Responding to Misbehavior	☐
4. Administrators have developed detailed procedures for managing Level 3 office referrals, including the following: • "Who Is Responsible" list • Game plan for dealing with referred students • Menu of corrective consequences that includes alternatives to out-of-school suspension • Sequence of steps for returning students to their regular schedules	☐	Interview with administrator Foundations Archive: 3-Level System for Responding to Misbehavior	☐
5. Current office procedures have been analyzed and streamlined, if needed, to address the following questions: • How will office staff supervise referred students throughout the entire process? • What will office staff do if the administrator is unavailable when referred students arrive at the office? • Where will referred students wait for the administrator? • What should referred students do while waiting for the administrator? • How should office personnel interact with referred students?	☐	Foundations Archive: Common Area Policies and Procedures Staff Handbook: Staff Roles and Responsibilities	☐

(continued)

Module D Implementation Checklist

Implementation Actions	Completed Y/N	Evidence of Implementation	Evidence Y/N
Presentation 4 (*continued*)	✓		✓
6. If the school has an in-school-suspension process, that process has been analyzed and streamlined, if needed, to address the following questions: • What conditions are necessary to effectively implement an ISS program? • What skills do staff need? • Who will develop the program and document the program policies and procedures in writing? • How will the program's efficacy be evaluated, and who will evaluate it?	☐	Foundations Archive: 3-Level System for Responding to Misbehavior	☐
Presentation 5: Preventing the Misbehavior That Leads to Referrals and Suspensions			
1. The Foundations Team has analyzed whether students would benefit from lessons on how to interact appropriately with adults. Would these skills reduce the behaviors that lead to referrals and suspensions (e.g., refusal to follow reasonable directions from staff)?	☐	Foundations Process: Meeting Minutes, Presentations/ Communications With Staff	☐
2. The Foundations Team has reviewed the sample lessons in *Foundations* and has compared them with student skill deficits and social skills or social-emotional curricula currently in use to determine whether the lessons might benefit some or all students.	☐	Foundations Process: Meeting Minutes Foundations Archive: Lesson Plans for Teaching Expectations for Interacting With Adults	☐
3. If appropriate, a process has been established for finalizing lesson content, and a timeline has been set for lesson delivery.	☐	Foundations Archive: Lesson Plans for Teaching Expectations for Interacting With Adults	☐

APPENDIX C
Guide to Module D
Reproducible Forms and Samples

The CD provided with this book contains many materials to help you implement *Foundations*. A thumbnail of the first page of each form, figure, or sample on the CD appears in this appendix. Most forms can be completed electronically. See the "Using the CD" file for more information about using fillable forms. Unless otherwise noted, all files are in PDF format.

Folders included on the CD are:

- Forms (D-01 through D-10)
  - Fillable Forms
  - Print Forms
- Samples (D-11 through D-17)
- Lessons for How to Interact Appropriately
  - Lesson 1
  - Lesson 2
  - Lesson 3
  - Lesson 4
  - Lesson 5
  - Lesson 6
  - Lesson 7
  - Lesson 8
  - Lesson 9
- PowerPoint Presentations (D1 through D5)
  - D1 Introduction.pptx
  - D2 3 Levels of Misbehavior.pptx
  - D3 Staff Response.pptx
  - D4 Admin Response.pptx
  - D5 Prevention.pptx

Forms
(D-01 to D-10)

D-01 *Foundations Implementation Rubric and Summary (8 pages)*

D-02 *Module D Implementation Checklist (4 pages)*

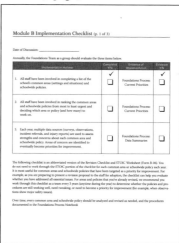

Form D-03 *Behavior Incident Notification Form (2 pages; Word format)*

Form D-04 *Behavior Incident Referral Form (2 pages; Word format)*

D-05 *TRENDS Referral Forms (2 pages)*

D-06 *Behavior Counting Form*

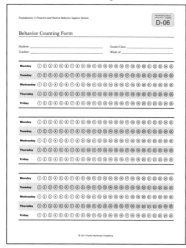

D-07 *Corrective Procedures for Mild and Moderate Classroom Behavior (4 pages)*

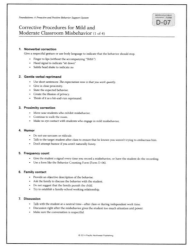

D-08 *Family Contact for Early-Stage Problems*

D-09 *Planning Questions for Dealing With Severe or Chronic Problems*

D-10a *Behavior Improvement Form, Version 1*

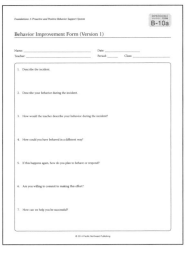

D-10b *Behavior Improvement Form, Version 2*

Samples
(D-11 to D-17)

D-11 *Sample 3-Level System for Responding to Misbehavior (4 pages)*

D-12 *Sample Three Levels of Behavior Definitions (4 pages)*

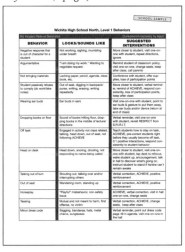

D-13 *Sample Staff Handbook Entry on Correcting Misbehavior (4 pages)*

D-14 *Sample Foundations Archive Entry on Correcting Misbehavior (7 pages)*

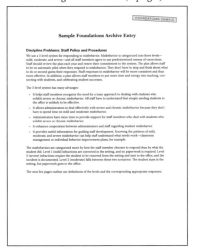

D-15 *Main Office, Principal's Office, and Principal's Hallway Expectations Posters (3 pages)*

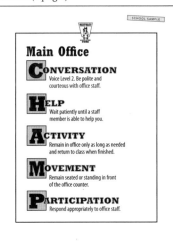

D-16 *Sample In-School Suspension Procedures (11 pages)*

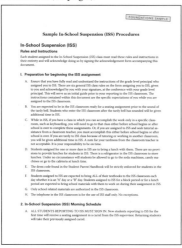

D-17 *Locke Essential Five Review (adapted from PowerPoint; 4 pages)*

Lessons

How to Interact Appropriately, Lessons 1–9

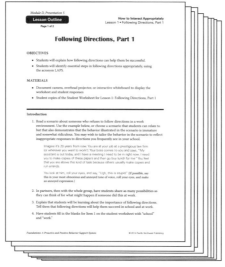

PowerPoint Presentations

(D1 to D5)